Let the Games Begin!

Engaging Students with Field-Tested Interactive Information Literacy Instruction

D1270371

Edited by Theresa R. McDevitt

Neal-Schuman Publishers, Inc.

New York   London

Published by Neal-Schuman Publishers, Inc.
100 William St., Suite 2004
New York, NY 10038

The paper used in this publication meets the minimum requirements of American National Standard for Information Sciences—Permanence of Paper for Printed Library Materials, ANSI Z39.48-1992.

Library of Congress Cataloging-in-Publication Data

Let the games begin! : engaging students with field-tested interactive information literacy instruction / edited by Theresa R. McDevitt.
    p. cm.
  Includes bibliographical references and index.
  ISBN 978-1-55570-739-2 (alk. paper)
  1. Information literacy—Study and teaching (Higher) 2. Educational games. 3. Active learning. I. McDevitt, Theresa R.

ZA3075.L48 2011
028.7071—dc23
                                                       2011017245

Contents

Figures

Foreword

No one would argue that information literacy instruction should not be designed to be effective; unfortunately, however, at times some have looked askance at efforts to ensure that instruction is engaging and, dare it be said, entertaining. We are fortunate to have today's research in cognitive and educational psychology to assure us that engaged learning is also effective learning. Indeed, engaged learning is even more effective learning!

My favorite definition of active learning is a simple one. Drawing on Chickering and Gamson's (1987) "Seven Principles for Good Practice in Undergraduate Education," Bonwell and Eison (1991) propose that "strategies promoting active learning be defined as instructional activities involving students in doing things and thinking about what they are doing." This is such a straightforward description of a powerful pedagogical practice—students doing things and thinking about what they are doing. And with games, that is exactly what is enabled in the information literacy classroom—students do things and think about what they are doing.

Games also assist information literacy instructors with issues related to student motivation. In *Motivating Students in Information Literacy Classes*, Xu and Jacobson (2004) detailed the application of the ARCS (Attention, Relevance, Confidence, Satisfaction) model of motivational design to information literacy instruction. Games can be a high-impact strategy for gaining attention, particularly if students have stereotyped perceptions of libraries and librarians, but they can also be a component of the design for relevance, confidence, and satisfaction.

This book, *Let the Games Begin! Engaging Students with Field-Tested Interactive Information Literacy Instruction*, is a practical handbook for the busy information literacy educator to call upon for inspiration, innovation, and insight. Because the games have been tested in practice, the information literacy librarian can draw upon the examples in this book with confidence. This book continues in the proud tradition of resource books containing techniques grounded in practice and theory, such as *Classroom Assessment Techniques: A Handbook for College Teachers* (Angelo and Cross, 1993) and *Designs for Active Learning: A Sourcebook of Classroom Strategies for Information Education* (Gradowski, Snavely, and Dempsey, 1998). Though designed for use in information literacy instruction sessions, many of the games can also be used in staff training programs, particularly those designed for undergraduate student library assistants, with minor adaptations.

Game on!

Lisa Janicke Hinchliffe
Coordinator for Information
Literacy Services and Instruction
Associate Professor of Library Administration
University of Illinois at Urbana-Champaign

References

Angelo, Thomas, and K. Patricia Cross. 1993. *Classroom Assessment Techniques*. 2nd ed. San Francisco: Jossey-Bass.

Bonwell, Charles C., and James A. Eison. 1991. "Active Learning: Creating Excitement in the Classroom." *ERIC Digest*, September. ED340272. http://www.ntlf.com/html/lib/bib/91-9dig.htm.

Chickering, Arthur W., and Zelda F. Gamson. 1987. "Seven Principles for Good Practice in Undergraduate Education." *AAHE Bulletin* 39 (March): 3–7.

Gradowski, Gail, Loanne Snavely, and Paula Dempsey, eds. 1998. *Designs for Active Learning: A Sourcebook of Classroom Strategies for Information Education*. Chicago: Association of College and Research Libraries.

Xu, Lijuan, and Trudi E. Jacobson. 2004. *Motivating Students in Information Literacy Classes*. New York: Neal-Schuman.

Preface

On campuses across the globe, instructors in disciplines from the natural sciences to the fine arts are increasingly turning to active learning techniques. As they do so, they discover that active learning activities, like the games in this book, have the power to enhance teaching, because the focus moves from the instructor to the students and to the material being introduced (where it belongs). As teachers are transformed from lecturers to facilitators, the students become the center of activity, working independently or in groups to master the material for themselves.

Teachers who transform their instruction in this way quickly discover what active learning proponents have been preaching for decades: using games and other active learning techniques in instruction is engaging and energizing for both students and faculty. Whether they're played in person or virtually, research suggests that games have the power to engage learners, provide opportunities for practice, motivate participants, and otherwise enhance learning. That both the professor and students are energized and have fun while playing them is an added bonus.

As the librarians and professors of subject disciplines who have contributed to *Let the Games Begin! Engaging Students with Field-Tested Interactive Information Literacy Instruction* will attest, those instructors who use games to teach information literacy get good results. Whether playing *Information Literacy Jeopardy!*, using *Library Mystery Orientations* to orient students, or working with alternate reality games that center on the library, they are discovering the positive power of games to improve instruction! If you want to join the growing community of information literacy gamers, this book is for you!

Purpose

Let the Games Begin! offers 60 ready-to-be-played games contributed by librarians and professors in subject disciplines. The goals of this book are to help other librarians and instructors:

- liven up the classroom experience,
- provide practice in information literacy skills and concepts,
- increase classroom discussion,
- engage and energize both student and instructor,
- increase student motivation, and
- put the fun back into learning.

The games are not intended to replace traditional instruction totally. Instead, one short game (or more) can be added to liven up traditional learning techniques. For example, some of the games are 10- to 15-minute activities that can be used as icebreakers in anything from a single-shot orientation session to a semester-long class. Others can be used at the end of a class to provide an opportunity for skill practice or as a way to demonstrate student mastery of concepts or processes. Some games are longer and take up an entire class period. These might be used individually or in a sequence where one builds upon another. Some of the digital games can be used after a class period to provide instruction and/or test mastery. Others can be played independently to provide instruction, offer practice, and even provide successful finishers with a certificate of completion that can be turned in to the instructor.

Content

The games included in *Let the Games Begin!* are proven winners. They have all been used successfully in college and university instruction by the librarians and English, history, business, and communications professors from across the nation who contributed them.

So what are games? In *The Study of Games*, Avedon and Sutton-Smith (1971: 2) note that one common definition of a game is "a form of play, amusement, recreation, sport, or frolic involving specific rules, sometimes utilizing a set of equipment, sometimes requiring skill, knowledge, and endurance." In *Fundamentals of Game Development*, Chandler and Chandler (2010: 1) define a game as "a play activity defined by interactive challenges, discernable rules, and attainable goals." For the purpose of this book, a game is an engaging and enjoyable activity that challenges its players, addresses at least one of the ACRL (2000) *Information Literacy Competency Standards for Higher Education*, and is designed around specific learning objectives.

Organization

Let the Games Begin! starts with "'Everybody Wins': Energizing Information Literacy Instruction with Educational Games," a short literature review documenting the effectiveness of games and the benefits of incorporating games into instruction and how libraries are using games in instruction. This is followed by 60 games divided into 11 topical parts.

Each game includes the following 12 elements:

1. Title and Author
2. Introduction
3. Objectives
4. Information Literacy Competency Standards Addressed
5. Game Background
6. Audience
7. Time Required
8. Materials and Equipment
9. Preparation
10. Playing the Game
11. Evaluation
12. Tips for Introducing Subject Faculty to the Game

Types of Games

Part I, "Icebreakers: Engaging Games for Beginning Information Literacy Sessions," is made up of games that can be used as icebreakers—from a classic *Jeopardy!* game to others that use online jigsaw puzzles and Tinkertoys to begin sessions. Part II, "Games to Energize and Engage in One-Shot Library Orientation Sessions," includes games to use in one-shot library instruction sessions, from a library mystery orientation or a game in which students discover library places and services on their own and report back to the *Information Literacy Game* and *Nightmare on Vine Street* digital games that students can play by themselves or with others.

Part III, "Organization of Information Sources Games," includes contests that deal with the organization of information sources, addressing topics from call numbers to the theory behind library classification systems. Part IV, "Research Races and Processes Games," offers challenges in which students race to see who can find facts most quickly on their cell phones, participate in a *Research Relay*, or be named the *Biggest Researcher*. Part V, "Online Search Techniques Games," is next. It includes games in which students play cards or demonstrate their understanding of Boolean search operators and find the "Just Right" terms for their searches. In Part VI, "Evaluating the Quality and Authority of Information Resources Games," students address quality issues of sources in a variety of ways, from a *Trivial Pursuit*–like game to one that mirrors *Truth or Consequences*.

Games in Part VII, "Bibliographic Citation Games," address the important topic of appropriate documentation of resources; games include the *MLA Obstacle Course* and *Citation Races*. In Part VIII, "Plagiarism Awareness and Prevention Games," games address the difficult and sometimes intimidating issue of plagiarism awareness and avoidance with games from *Plagiarism Busters* to the award-winning digital games *Goblin Threat* and *A Planet in Peril: Plagiarism* and clicker games such as *Fun with Plagiarism*.

Part IX, "Finding, Identifying, and Discovering the Significance of Primary Sources Games," includes games that invite students to work with digital and physical primary sources whether searching for information on the Internet for *Ellie Jones and the Raiders of the Lost Archives*, using the World Digital Library in *Where in the World*, or identifying and finding the significance of primary resources in *What Am I?* Part X, "Games to Assess and Wrap Up Information Literacy Instruction Sessions," offers a series of games that can be used as culminating activities at the end of a class or a semester, including using the Internet tool Wordle, and requiring presentations in the *Three Cs*.

Finally, in Part XI, "*LOST in the Academy*: Library Orientation Session Techniques Help Students Navigate New Territory," the *LOST in the Academy* series of six interwoven games take students from library orientation in *A Treasure Map*, through discovery and evaluation of resources, to an overview of the research process in *How Not to Find It Fast in the Library*. The book concludes with "Game On," which offers a few tips on how to get started with games and a short annotated list of articles, books, and websites to assist the would-be gamer to get started.

The games included here have been crafted to create energy and excitement in the classroom and result in learning while avoiding frustration, stress, and disappointment. When teachers and learners play *these* games, everyone wins.

References

Association of College & Research Libraries. 2000. *Information Literacy Competency Standards for Higher Education*. Chicago: ACRL. http://www.ala.org/ala/mgrps/divs/acrl/standards/information-literacycompetency.cfm.

Avedon, Elliott M., and Brian Sutton-Smith. 1971. *The Study of Games*. New York: John Wiley & Sons.

Chandler, Heather Maxwell, and Rafael Chandler. 2010. *Fundamentals of Game Development*. Sudbury, MA: Jones & Bartlett.

Acknowledgments

Any successful project relies upon the help of others. A book of this nature, made up of the contributions of more than 50 separate authors, could not have been assembled without the help of dozens of people. An acknowledgments page is absolutely necessary here.

First, I must thank the large number of contributors who eagerly responded to the call for contributions and enthusiastically supported the project through its development to its successful conclusion. I must also thank Dr. Kelly Heider, Education Librarian at Indiana University of Pennsylvania, who assisted me as the book was conceived and the call for contributors sent out. Ryan Sitler, Instructional Technology/ Information Literacy Librarian at California University of Pennsylvania and co-editor of two similar volumes on information literacy instruction activities, offered considerable advice and assistance as the project was developed and also contributed two excellent games to the volume. Dr. Rosalee Stilwell, Professor of English at Indiana University of Pennsylvania, must also be thanked. A dear friend and always willing collaborator, she brought her love of student-centered learning techniques to the project, helped expand the scope to include contributions of nonlibrarian fac-

ulty in the book, and contributed two games. Maura Smale, Information Literacy Librarian, New York City College of Technology, also generously assisted the effort by putting out the call for more games to her CUNY Games Network. To the final chapter, Jen Jones, Maura Smale, Ryan Sitler, Tracey Johnson, Christina Sheldon, and Dr. Laurel Johnson Black all contributed their thoughtful suggestions on getting into gaming.

Nan Berkey, the executive assistant to the Library Dean at Indiana University of Pennsylvania, offered her invaluable assistance as the manuscript was assembled, as did Sandy Wood, the Neal-Schuman development editor for the project.

The idea for this book was conceived the afternoon following a session on using games in instruction offered by Indiana University of Pennsylvania's Reflective Practice Faculty Teaching Group, so this connection is acknowledged, with this book being counted as one of the outcomes of that group.

Finally, I must also thank my daughter Elizabeth, who inspired me to begin using games when she told me about how much fun it was to play games in school and asked me why I didn't use them in my classes.

"Everybody Wins": Energizing Information Literacy Instruction with Educational Games

The use of traditional and digital games is growing in physical and virtual classrooms across the nation. Interest in educational games is not new. For centuries those interested in effective methods of teaching have been using games of one type or another. From ancient Romans who used tabletop war games to teach military tactics to twenty-first-century professors who argue that digital games offer fertile opportunities for reaching students in new ways, the call to let the games begin for effective instruction could and can be heard (Prensky, 2001).

Why games? Games are the most natural and enjoyable of learning vehicles. Entertaining as they allow for practice and challenging as they allow students to explore, when they are designed around learning objectives, they can give a positive boost to almost any instruction session. Advocates of educational games of all kinds have for years testified with evangelistic zeal to their benefits. In recent years college and university professors have increasingly realized the limitations of teach/test didactic methods of instruction and turned to more student-centered active methods of teaching, whether in person or from a distance. They have come to believe that when games are played in the classroom students are challenged, learning deepens, instructors are energized, and everybody wins. Educational theorists of active learning and motivational learning and constructivist theorists all support the contention that educational games offer great promise in enriching college and university instruction and learning outcomes.

Active learning advocates argue that active learning techniques, which are defined as "instructional activities involving students in doing things and thinking about what they are doing" (Bonwell and Eison, 1991: iii), can have a significant impact on learning. They suggest that games and other active learning techniques are much more appealing to students, are particularly successful in developing student skills, can challenge students to engage in "higher-order think-

ing," and appeal to diverse learning styles (Bonwell and Eison, 1991: iii, 2). They note that games, in particular, positively impact learning by providing practice through mirroring real-life experience, increasing enthusiasm and motivation, encouraging group work, and enhancing material delivered in lecture format (Bonwell and Eison, 1991: 47).

Motivation theory suggests that "when students are motivated, they have more interest and desire to learn" (Jacobson and Xu, 2004: 4). Games that challenge and entertain the players can be intrinsically motivating, stimulating learning and leading to deep and long-lasting learning experiences (Jacobson and Xu, 2004: 6). Jacobson and Xu offer a word of caution concerning the use of external motivators, such as rewards and punishments, with game play though. They contend that studies have found that extrinsic motivation, whether positive rewards (prizes or bonus points) or negative consequences (lost points or lower grades), result in motivation becoming linked to the material rewards or punishments rather than to the process itself. In these cases, the learning that does occur is not what it might be (2004: 6). Therefore, the use of prizes with games should be minimized, because it may not result in the best learning outcomes.

Constructivist theorists also applaud the educational benefits of games, particularly well-designed digital ones. Constructionist theories of learning suggest that learning should be student centered and active and stress the importance of experience and of students' interaction with the environment. They argue that students should not just receive knowledge but that they should also construct their own understanding of the world (Grassian and Kaplowitz, 2001). They endorse games that are goal oriented, challenging, and interactive and have the potential to shift the focus from the instructor to the student. Proponents of digital gaming, most notably Marc Prensky and James Paul Gee, strongly suggest that digital games offer great promise for enhancing learning (Prensky, 2001:

Gee, 2004). Jong et al. (2008: 7) agree that digital games have great potential and urge the "adoption, implementation and evaluation of game-based learning within school and institutional settings."

Librarians who have experimented with the use of games in their instruction have discovered significant benefits associated with including educational games. For example, Neda Zdravkovic of the University of Auckland Library integrated games and other activities into her instruction and was delighted with the results. In her article on the topic she encouraged others to make similar modifications of their teaching methods, declaring it was a "rewarding risk students will positively and enthusiastically respond to" (Zdravkovic, 2010). Felicia Smith came to similar conclusions when she used simple games such as word searches and crossword puzzles to engage students in a Chemical Skills Research Information Literacy class. One of her students reported that the addition made "an otherwise boring and painful course . . . not so boring and painful" (Smith, 2007). Many other studies of the use of games in information literacy instruction have supported this positive view of the efficacy of these instructional tools.

Articles discussing the use of *Jeopardy!*-like games written between 1995 and 2008 suggest that using some version of this game is beneficial. A 1995 study by Ury and King examined the impact of using a *Jeopardy!* game and a word search game after orientations with freshman students to reinforce material presented. They found that both methods improved the scores of students on post-session tests (Ury and King, 1995: 154).

A 2002 article by Krajewski and Piroli outlined how the librarians at Simmons College used a *Jeopardy!* game with first-year students, combining it with a self-guided tour. They concluded that it was successful in orienting students to the librarians and library resources and services in a positive way (Krajewski and Piroli, 2002: 181). Holly Heller-Ross wrote about her successful use of a different version of the *Jeopardy!* game. She assigned students to groups and challenged them to decide which questions could be answered with which finding tools (Heller-Ross, 2004: 114–115).

Leach and Sugarman (2005: 200) also discussed the use of a *Jeopardy!* game and concluded that, when designed to be "enjoyable" for the students, they had "definite learning outcomes," and they declared that games allowed students to "have fun and learn at the same time." Finally, Billie Walker echoed their findings in her discussion of the use of a *Jeopardy!* game with students from freshmen to seniors in disciplines from English to kinesiology. Walker concluded that the use of games created a "fun" atmosphere that increased the participation of students in class, and added stimulating variety to the sessions (Walker, 2008).

Games have also been used to replace traditional library orientation tours, which have been criticized for trying to cover "too many topics in too short of a time" and because "information gets lost in the onslaught of orientations" (Resnis, Butler, and Barth, 2007). Librarians at institutions from Niagara University to Queensborough Community College have found positive results by substituting more engaging library mystery or treasure hunt orientations, like the one included in this book, for traditional tours (Kasbohm, Schoen, and Dubaj, 2006; Marcus and Beck, 2003). At Trinity University in Texas, librarian gamers have even used alternate reality games to orient students to the library in meaningful ways (Harris and Rice, 2008).

Online alternatives to traditional information literacy instruction sessions also offer promise. Many librarians have made efforts to create digital games, either comprehensive games or ones based on specific principles, to teach information literacy skills. *Gaming in Academic Libraries* (Harris and Rice, 2008) discussed online minigames designed at Carnegie Mellon University to teach call numbers and selection of sources, standalone information literacy games designed at the University of Florida and the University of North Carolina at Greensboro, and alternate reality games used at Trinity University in Texas.

Researchers at the University of Michigan carried out two studies to determine students' reactions to online games designed to teach information literacy skills. In the first study, a single multipurpose game, *Defense of Hidgeon*, was used in an undergraduate history of technology class (Markey et al., 2009). Their findings suggest that students were not terribly attracted to a single comprehensive game that was played by individual students and not directly related to classroom assignments. In the second study, they tested a new game called *BiblioBouts*, which included shorter, more targeted games directly related to classroom assignments that allowed collaboration with peers. The researchers found it far more successful with students, who gained confidence and competence in doing library research. Students found the process so entertaining that they did not realize that instruction was going on (Markey et al., 2010).

Conclusion

The learning theorists and studies mentioned in this chapter suggest that games can have a positive impact on learning outcomes, in general, and in information literacy instruction, specifically. Whether as a result of reading research studies praising the inclusion of such learning activities, because of their own successful personal experience with games, or just hearing about what other libraries are doing—instructors of information literacy are including games in their instruction more and more! Students are increasingly embarking on library mystery orientations, participating in alternate reality games that take place in the library and use library resources, playing *Jeopardy!* games in classes, and engaging in other simulations, hunts, and contests. Games are making their way into libraries and information literacy classrooms as never before and with positive results!

References

Bonwell, Charles C., and Eison, James A. 1991. *Active Learning: Creating Excitement in the Classroom.* 1991 ASHE-ERIC Higher Education Report No. 1. Washington, DC: ERIC Clearinghouse on Higher Education.

Gee, James Paul. 2004. *What Video Games Have to Teach Us About Learning and Literacy.* New York: Palgrave Macmillan.

Grassian, Esther S., and Joan R. Kaplowitz. 2001. *Information Literacy Instruction: Theory and Practice.* New York: Neal-Schuman.

Harris, Amy, and Scott E. Rice. 2008. *Gaming in Academic Libraries: Collections, Marketing, and Information Literacy.* Chicago: Association of College & Research Libraries.

Heller-Ross, Holly. 2004. "Empowering Students with Games." In *Empowering Students II: Teaching Information Literacy Concepts with Hands-On and Minds-On Activities*, edited by Carol Anne Germain and Deborah Bernnard, 113–116. Pittsburgh: Library Instruction Publications.

Jacobson, Trudi E., and Lijuan Xu. 2004. *Motivating Students in Information Literacy Classes.* New York: Neal-Schuman.

Jong, Morris S.Y., et al. 2008. "Harnessing Computer Games in Education." *Journal of Distance Education Technologies* 6, no. 1: 1–9.

Kasbohm, Kristine E., David Schoen, and Michelle Dubaj. 2006. "Launching the Library Mystery Tour: A Library Component for the "First-Year Experience." *College & Undergraduate Libraries* 13, no. 2: 35–46.

Krajewski, Patricia R., and Vivienne B. Piroli. 2002. "Something Old, Something New, Something Borrowed, Something Blue: Active Learning in the Classroom." *Journal of Library Administration* 36, no. 1: 177–194.

Leach, Guy J., and Tammy S. Sugarman. 2005. "Play to Win! Using Games in Library Instruction to Enhance Student Learning." *Research Strategies* 20, no. 3: 191–203.

Marcus, Sandra, and Sheila Beck. 2003. "A Library Adventure: Comparing a Treasure Hunt with a Traditional Freshman Orientation Tour." *College and Research Libraries* 64, no. 1: 23–44.

Markey, Karen, Fritz Swanson, Andrea Jenkins, Brian Jennings, Beth St. Jean, Victor Rosenberg, et al. 2009. "Will Undergraduate Students Play Games to Learn How to Conduct Library Research?" *Journal of Academic Librarianship* 35, no. 4: 303–313.

Markey, Karen, Fritz Swanson, Chris Leeder, Gregory R. Peters, Jr., Brian J. Jennings, Beth St. Jean, et al. 2010. "The Benefits of Integrating an Information Literacy Skills Game into Academic Coursework: A Preliminary Evaluation." *D-Lib Magazine* 16, no. 7/8. http://www.dlib.org/dlib/july10/markey/07markey.html.

Prensky, Marc. 2001. *Digital Game-Based Learning.* New York: McGraw-Hill.

Resnis, Eric, Betsy Butler, and Jennifer Barth. 2007. "Follow the Silk Road to Orientation Success: Promoting Miami University's Brill Science Library." *Issues in Science and Technology Librarianship* (Summer). http://www.istl.org/07-summer/article1.html.

Smith, Felicia. 2007. "Games for Teaching Information Literacy Skills." *Library Philosophy and Practice.* http://www.webpages.uidaho.edu/~mbolin/f-smith.htm.

Splegelman, Martha, and Richard Glass. 2008. "Gaming and Learning: Winning Information Literacy Collaboration." *College and Research Libraries News* 69 (October): 522–525.

Ury, Connie J., and Terry King. 1995. "Reinforcement of Library Orientation Instruction for Freshman Seminar Students." *Research Strategies* 13 (Summer): 153–164.

Walker, Billie. 2008. "This is *Jeopardy!* An Exciting Approach to Learning in Library Instruction." *Reference Services Review* 36: 381–388.

Zdravkovic, Neda. 2010. "Spicing Up Information Literacy Tutorials: Interactive Class Activities that Worked." *Public Services Quarterly* 6, no. 1. https://researchspace.auckland.ac.nz/bitstream/handle/2292/5746/zdravkovic.pdf?sequence=2.

PART I

Icebreakers: Engaging Games for Beginning Information Literacy Sessions

Part I includes Games 1–3. Each can be used to jump-start information literacy sessions, whether one shot or semester long, or to start other courses off with an information literacy twist.

Let's Play *Information Literacy Jeopardy!*

David Magolis and Linda Neyer

Introduction

Jeopardy!, trademarked as "America's Favorite Quiz Show," can also be used as an instructional game to enhance information literacy instruction. *Jeopardy!* is a method for information literacy instructors to integrate multimedia and interactivity, promote active learning, establish learning objectives, analyze needs, and provide an opportunity to fully engage students in the learning process. *Jeopardy!* can be played in a computer lab prior to the instruction as a means of needs assessment with students in a variety of disciplines at the upper undergraduate and graduate levels.

Objectives

The objectives will vary depending on the goals for the instruction. The following objectives are examples of ones that can be used and that are aligned with the five information literacy standards objectives of the Association of College & Research Libraries (2000). They will assess the degree to which students can:

* identify a research question and translate it into keywords and concepts for searching and map question/strategy to the most relevant resources;
* use the library's webpages, catalogs, databases, and reference tools effectively to find desired print and electronic documents;
* evaluate sources using criteria (e.g., currency, coverage, authority, accuracy, etc.) appropriate to discipline and assignment;
* use information effectively to accomplish a specific purpose and incorporate it into one's own knowledge base (e.g., quoting and paraphrasing appropriately); and
* select an appropriate documentation style and use it consistently to cite sources.

Information Literacy Competency Standards Addressed

This game can address any of the ACRL Information Literacy Competency Standards, depending on which questions are included in the game: #1; #2; #3; #4; #5.

Game Background

The abundance of professional literature summarizing the multiple methods of information literacy instruction in higher education illustrates the importance of this topic to librarians, who are constantly searching for ways to improve their instruction. To enhance information literacy instruction, librarians can use the popular educational game *Jeopardy!* to increase classroom interactivity, to pre-assess students' knowledge, and to initiate faculty–librarian collaborations in specific disciplines at both the upper undergraduate and graduate levels.

Maybee (2006) suggests that traditional information literacy pedagogy does not adequately address the needs of learners for a variety of reasons. The author contends that students value learning in a subject area to build their knowledge base, and creating an interactive learning environment through gaming encourages students to participate in active learning and generally improves their knowledge base. *Jeopardy!* is a traditional game that has been adapted to many educational settings, including general chemistry, organic chemistry, biochemistry, analytical chemistry (Grabowski and Price, 2003), management (Benek-Rivera and Mathews, 2004), obstetrics and gynecology (O'Leary et al., 2005), and even library instruction (Walker, 2008). However, our pedagogical approach to using *Jeopardy!* categorizes the game questions according to the *Information Literacy Competency Standards for Higher Education* (ACRL, 2000) while also incorporating subject knowledge. *Information Literacy Jeopardy!* is an instructional game that provides for a friendly, interactive environment with competitive banter while combining knowledge across disciplines and anchoring the game to literacy standards.

Creating *Information Literacy Jeopardy!* questions facilitates collaboration both among librarians and between librarians and teaching faculty. *Information Literacy Jeopardy!* questions and answers can be created collaboratively by librarians working together to establish a "question bank," which can then be tapped for use in different sessions. As questions are written, they should be mapped to both the information literacy standard they address (this will make it easier when searching the question bank) and the library tutorials or library webpages where users can learn more about the topic.

Jeopardy! games can also easily be modified for specific disciplines by working with the classroom instructor to tailor the questions. For instance, the instructor should be consulted when developing questions that identify a discipline's primary journals, databases, citing style(s), and professional organizations.

Audience

This game is designed for college students in an upper undergraduate or a graduate class scheduled for an information literacy instruction session at the beginning of the semester before they have begun working on their assignment.

Time Required

The game runs approximately 15 to 25 minutes for 25 questions. The number of categories and questions can be reduced if less time is available.

Materials and Equipment

The game requires:

- a computer with PowerPoint viewer and
- a projection screen.

The PowerPoint file can also be published as a stand-alone game file to the Internet.

Preparation

The game template is freely available from a variety of online sources to adapt to specific information literacy instruction goals by doing a web search for "jeopardy template." If using a *Jeopardy!* template, the amount of time to adapt the game instruction will be based on the number and availability of game questions. Basic PowerPoint skills are necessary to update and modify the PowerPoint. Librarians can be aided by teaching faculty, students, and library colleagues to generate categorical questions for the game (see Figures 1.1 and 1.2 for sample *Jeopardy!* game boards).

Playing the Game

The game is introduced based on its use as either a pre- or post-assessment. Once the game is introduced, divide

---

Figure 1.1.
Information Literacy Jeopardy! Board

Our Library	Scholarly Journals	Library Databases	Searching Basics	Citation Stuff
$100	$100	$100	$100	$100
$200	$200	$200	$200	$200
$300	$300	$300	$300	$300
$400	$400	$400	$400	$400
$500	$500	$500	$500	$500

Figure 1.2.
Library Databases Category Board

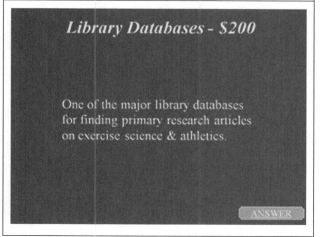

Library Databases - $200

One of the major library databases for finding primary research articles on exercise science & athletics.

ANSWER

the classroom into two competing teams. It is essential to state at the beginning of play what the reward will be for the winning team, as a reward-driven game is thought to increase interaction. Provide the students with an overview of the rules of *Jeopardy!* (for the sake of brevity this is eliminated here; the various templates available and articles cited will provide ideas).

Evaluation

Throughout the game play, the facilitator should note whether or not students comprehend the information literacy concepts in the game. If the game is used as a pre-assessment and the students do not understand the concepts, the subsequent instruction can be adjusted on-the-fly to meet students' needs.

It is also good pedagogy to encourage students to note those questions they do not understand themselves and to consult the additional tutorials and resources mentioned by the librarian during instruction. In our experience, the game may also be an "eye opener" for the instructor who has assumed that the students are proficient in library research but discovers they have some deficits.

To evaluate the effectiveness of the game during the session, in the last five minutes have students fill out an online form (using Google Docs or a similar form) and answer questions about the session as shown in Figure 1.3. Overall, feedback from students and faculty has been that *Jeopardy!* is an effective learning activity.

Tips for Introducing Subject Faculty to the Game

Faculty should select the information literacy standards students will address. The faculty member and the librarian will no doubt refer to the course syllabi and assignments to begin, but to assist the process the librarian can develop a needs assessment using a resource like a Google Docs form, asking the class instructor to identify the specific outcomes to be included in the instruction.

References

Association of College & Research Libraries. 2000. *Information Literacy Competency Standards for Higher Education.* Chicago: ACRL.

Benek-Rivera, J., and V.E. Mathews. 2004. "Active Learning with *Jeopardy!* Students Ask the Questions." *Journal of Management Education* 28, no. 1 (February): 104–118.

Grabowski, J.J., and M.L. Price. 2003. "Simple HTML Templates for Creating Science-Oriented *Jeopardy!* Games for Active Learning." *Journal of Chemical Education* 80, no. 8 (August): 967.

Maybee, C. 2006. "Undergraduate Perceptions of Information Use: The Basis for Creating User-Centered Student Information Literacy Instruction." *Journal of Academic Librarianship* 32, no. 1 (January): 79–85.

O'Leary, S., L. Diepenhorst, R. Churley-Strom, and D. Magrane. 2005. "Educational Games in an Obstetrics and Gynecology Core Curriculum." *American Journal of Obstetrics and Gynecology* 193, no. 5 (November): 1848–1851.

Walker, B.E. 2008. "This Is *Jeopardy!* An Exciting Approach to Learning in Library Instruction." *Reference Services Review* 36, no. 4 (Special Issue): 381–388.

Figure 1.3.   Game Evaluation Form

List the various portions of the instruction session, and ask students to rank them.

Scale: 1 = Very effective;
       2 = Effective;
       3 = Somewhat effective;
       4 = Not very effective

1. How effective were the learning activities used in the session?

2. What are the three most important things you learned during the session?

3. What questions do you still have about library research?

4. What is one thing you learned that you'll definitely use in the future?

5. How can the library session be improved for future students?

Online Jigsaw Puzzles: Using Puzzles to Break the Ice in Information Literacy Instruction Sessions

Toccara Porter

Introduction

The online jigsaw puzzle game (http://www.crea-soft .com/online-jigsaw-puzzle/) is a new way to teach students how to recognize a bibliographic citation. The objective is to have the students complete the puzzle as an analogy for putting the parts of a bibliographic citation together. This is a simple and fun way for library instructors to begin the conversation with students about why bibliographic citations are relevant in the research process.

Objectives

The student will be able to:

- recognize a bibliographic citation.

Information Literacy Competency Standards Addressed

This game addresses this ACRL Information Literacy Competency Standard: #3.

Game Background

The jigsaw puzzle is a free online game that is accessible from a computer with Internet access from the following URL: http://www.crea-soft.com/online-jigsaw-puzzle/. Users can choose from a range of puzzle types, including Mickey Mouse, cars, and animals. Each puzzle has a level of difficulty from Easy to Average and Hard.

Audience

The game is suitable for high school or undergraduate students and can be structured for classroom sizes of 5 to 25 students.

Time Required

Students should be able to do at least two puzzles in five minutes. Keep in mind there are three levels of dif-

ficulty: Easy, Average, and Hard. Therefore, the level of difficulty selected will impact the time required to play. The more difficult the puzzle, the longer it will take the student to complete it.

Materials and Equipment

The game requires:

- computers with Internet access for each instructor, student, and subject faculty.

Preparation

The instructor should play the game prior to class in order to understand how it operates. It is also a good idea to check the website immediately prior to the class period to make sure there is no problem in accessing it.

Playing the Game

The instructor can introduce the concept of bibliographic citation and then have the students play the game. Instructors can also use the reverse approach and have students play the game first and then segue into explaining bibliographic citations.

To begin, direct the students to the online website where the puzzle can be played (http://www.crea-soft. com/online-jigsaw-puzzle/). Encourage the students to complete one or two of the puzzles of their choice. Students can select from a wide range of puzzles, such as cars and animals.

After completing the puzzle, explain to the students that the puzzle can represent another way of thinking about the concept of a bibliographic citation. How? The individual pieces have to be connected in the correct places in order to complete the puzzle. The same is true of a bibliographic citation (at this point, you can also show some sample bibliographic citations). For example, the parts of a bibliographic citation for a book entry include author, title, publisher, and year of publication. For a journal article the bibliographic citation parts include author, article title, journal title, volume and issue numbers, pages, and date. Then explain why it is beneficial for students to be able to recognize and create correct bibliographic citations using a particular citation style (APA, Chicago, etc.).

Evaluation

Instructors can informally evaluate the reaction of the students to the game by asking their opinion and taking note of whether they continue to play after the required game is over. They might also ask questions about the comparisons between a puzzle and a bibliographic citation and see if the students are able to highlight some basic points that are important in a bibliographic citation.

Tips for Introducing Subject Faculty to the Game

Faculty will be more likely to use the game as a part of their class if they have already seen the website and played the game. Also, when the class plays the game, the subject faculty should also be given the opportunity to play.

Tinkertoy Towers: Building Research Projects in Teams
Jen Jones

Introduction

Tinkertoy Towers provides students a visual understanding of performing research in teams through the construction of a Tinkertoy tower. This activity has been used with undergraduates with great success. Students easily recognize how a team research project is constructed and gain skills for working cooperatively.

Objectives

Students will:

- realize how a team research project is more than the sum of the parts,
- learn to appreciate team members' contributions to the research project,
- be able to differentiate between a "group" project and a "team" project,
- engage in discussion of their roles for the team project, and
- gain a deeper understanding of how research projects are organized.

Information Literacy Competency Standards Addressed

This game addresses this ACRL Information Literacy Competency Standard: #4.

Game Background

Students are often placed in "group" projects without any guidance or skills training to perform well in this environment. At the beginning of this activity, when asked whether they enjoyed doing team projects, two students raised their hand; when asked how many disliked team projects, immediately many students raised their hand. The goal for the class was, by the end of the semester, to get students to enjoy working in groups and produce excellent team projects by providing them with the skills necessary for success.

As a former corporate trainer, I know that team skills are fundamentally needed, and, no matter where students find employment, they will be required to work in teams. Furthermore, in the marketplace, even while working individually on a project, students need to realize that they will often rely on others for information. Thus, a course team project is a great opportunity for students to learn and practice team skills through a research project.

During this activity, many students have said, "This is cool" or "I see now how we're supposed to put this together." The activity provided here is just one team-building activity that can be used; adding other activities throughout the semester promotes team, interpersonal, and communication skills.

Audience

This activity works well with all levels of undergraduates. Juniors and seniors will be able to relate the activity to past group work experiences, so they seem to grasp the concept better. However, freshmen and sophomores will be able to apply the concept in future group projects throughout their academic career.

Time Required

This activity ranges from 15 to 30 minutes, depending on the class size and the time the instructor wants to devote to discussion afterward.

Materials and Equipment

The game requires:

- two cans of Tinkertoys, each a 102-piece count for a total of 204 pieces for a class size up to 40 students; and
- large flat areas to work on (desks may be used for the individual portion, but larger areas are needed during the team construction phase, such as a table or floor).

Preparation

Before class the instructor should determine how many Tinkertoy pieces can be allocated to each student. For example, 204 total pieces/25 students = approximately 8 pieces per student. No fewer than 5 pieces and no more than 10 pieces should be allocated to each student, because 5 is just enough to make something creative individually and more than 10 pieces adds too much time to construction during the individual phase. Students should already be organized in research project groups. This activity is most effective if used toward the beginning of the semester or group project.

Playing the Game

As students arrive to class, ask them to choose eight pieces (number of pieces varies depending on number of students); do not tell them what they will be doing with the pieces. You may tell them that it does not matter which pieces they choose. Note: Getting them to choose pieces as they arrive to class helps to conserve class time.

After all students have selected pieces, ask them to construct something creative with them. Tell students that they have approximately three minutes to complete this task. Students are not permitted to exchange or give pieces to others. While they are working, walk around the classroom giving positive reinforcement and asking whether their constructions represent something.

When students are finished with this task, recognize their efforts. Pose the question to them, "You all did a great job with the pieces that you have, but did you feel limited with only [eight] pieces?" Whether they respond "Yes" or give no response, state to them, "I wonder what you could create if each team could combine pieces?" Before they combine pieces, state that all pieces in each team must be incorporated into the structure and that each person is responsible for adding his or her own pieces, which means that they cannot put all their pieces on a pile and allow one person to do all of the construction; everyone must be involved, and all must agree on what is being constructed. Give them seven minutes to complete the activity; the first two minutes should be used for planning.

Although the activity is called *Tinkertoy Towers*, it is not necessary for them to build a tower; it just needs to be a structure that represents their creativity. During the construction, walk around the classroom offering positive encouragement and making sure that every-

one is involved. Sometimes students get competitive during this stage, so remind them to stay focused on their own project and that each will be unique and special in its own way.

When the structures are complete, debrief with the class by asking general open-ended questions. If they do not offer responses right away, remind them that this is not a quiz, prompt them with other questions to get at the responses that you're seeking, or ask them to answer the question within their team first and then share their answers. You could begin with the question, "How does this activity represent your research projects?" Responses that you're seeking include: "This activity represents all of our input"; "We worked together to build the tower like we will when we build our project"; "Everyone's pieces mattered and were part of the tower"; or "We talked together about what we were going to build and how to build it."

Then you might ask, "What is the difference between a *group* and a *team* project, and how would the Tinkertoys look if you worked as a group instead of a team?" Responses that you're seeking include: "A group is just a bunch of people doing their own thing; a team is a group of people who have a common goal"; "We created something better than we could have individually" (this is called *synergy*—the result is more than the sum of the parts); or "A group project would have just been all of our pieces pushed together without any cohesion or group creativity, or it could have been the individual shapes we made just placed side by side."

The next question you might pose would be, "What lessons from this activity will you use while working on your research project?" Responses that you're seeking would include: "We won't let one person do all of the work"; "We will talk about the roles that we'll have while working on the project; for example, since we know that we're doing a team project from the start, we all can 'choose the pieces' that are best for us"; "We will meet to talk about how the project is going during the course of the project and be open to discussion about the use and appropriateness of the information that we've found"; "We will be detailed about our research agenda, what is going into the report, and who's doing certain jobs"; or "We will be positive and have fun working on this project."

Ask the students to talk in their groups about good and bad experiences working in groups (remind them not to specifically identity anyone by name). After they have talked in their groups, ask them to share an example or two with the class.

Finally, apply this activity to the process of finding, evaluating, and using information. This might include talking about how the "strong base" of the tower is like using reliable and authoritative sources in a paper. You might also suggest that carefully choosing keywords when they begin their searching is like choosing the right pieces for their tower or that formulating an interesting research question at the beginning of their search is important and saves time during the construction process. Finally, you can talk with them about how these skills are important in the fields that they'll be entering. Subject faculty might be asked to add their own general debriefing questions or targeted questions related to your particular lesson.

Evaluation

Evaluation might consist of listening to students' debriefing responses and following up with additional questioning to drive at the lessons that instructors wish for them to take away from the activity. A short reflective writing assignment could also be made part of the debriefing. If time allows, to reinforce the concepts instructors can add a reflective portion at the end where the teams each share how their tower represents the research process and team work.

When feedback was requested, students generally gave positive responses, such as, "I wish I was taught how to work on a group project before my junior year"; "I am happy that I made friends with people I would not have otherwise"; "I realized that I was a bossy person, but I learned to value others' work"; "I am very proud of our project"; and "I can tell an employer at an interview that I can work well in a team environment and show my project as an example." The value of this game is also documented by the fact that students were able to submit team projects that demonstrated that they were able to effectively synthesize information to produce excellent work.

Instructors who want to reward the team(s) who made the best connection with the concepts and their construction can ask the teams to vote. When they share their votes, students should also explain why they voted for a particular team; this will help to reinforce the concepts. Students should be encouraged to respond honestly, as some teams may want to vote for their own tower just to claim winner status. The reward can be a simple recognition or a small prize. Note: Adding a competitive nature to the activity will require more involvement from the teacher to keep students focused on constructing their own project and avoiding negative talk about other teams.

Tips for Introducing Subject Faculty to the Game

Faculty members often comment on students complaining about group work; now they can be offered this fun activity to try.

PART II

Games to Energize and Engage in One-Shot Library Orientation Sessions

This section consists of Games 4–9. These games can be used in place of traditional library orientation sessions. The *Library Mystery Scavenger Hunt* and *Library's Best Beach Ball* games are active scavenger hunt activities. *Go Explore!* offers students five challenges to orient them to the library. *Its Alive!*, *Information Literacy Game*, and *Nightmare on Vine Street* are digital games that teach students information literacy concepts and allow them to practice until they gain mastery.

Go Explore! Discovering, Selecting, and Appraising the Jewels of Your Trade

Susan Nelson

Introduction

Go Explore! requires students to complete five tasks as they identify, access, and use research tools and resources from their major field of study. A wiki website serves as the explorers' base for accessing task instructions (http://explorediscipline.wetpaint .com/). The game is best suited for freshmen or other undergraduate students in a discipline's introductory course.

Objectives

Using the library map, students will be able to:

- locate resources through the library's website, including the online catalog, A-to-Z list, library map, subject guide webpages, the library's citation style webpage, and the reference resources webpage;
- identify library locations and retrieve books in a particular call number range;
- identify library locations for print journals in both the browsing and bound journal collections; and
- identify library locations for retrieving a citation style manual for their major field of study.

On a multiple point review quiz, students will be able to:

- identify library research tools to use for specific purposes: citation style manuals, journals, subscription databases, and print books (reference or general collection); and
- identify locations, both physical and electronic, of research tools and resources.

Students will also be able to:

- evaluate information sources (a book, citation style manual, print journal, and electronic database) used in their major fields of study.

Information Literacy Competency Standards Addressed

This game addresses these ACRL Information Literacy Competency Standards: #1; #2; #3; #4.

Game Background

This game-like activity was created for two sections of English106 Composition. Two writing assignments center on students developing an understanding of and appreciation for discipline-specific resources. The first assignment is to write an exploratory essay that includes the students' reason for their choice of a major and a description and evaluation of the research tools and resources used by its scholars: a style guide, print journal, subscription database, and book from the reference or general collection. The second assignment is to create an annotated bibliography of 12 sources on a topic of interest in their field.

Go Explore! teaches students about the tools and resources they will be using for research in their major field. Students contribute evaluations of their sources to subject-specific pages of the wiki, and they can also add conversation threads to ask or answer questions and make comments. They become participants in an ongoing research conversation.

Teaching freshmen and students in introductory classes about discipline-specific resources will increase their awareness of scholarly sources and point them toward sources they should be using in their research as they progress in their field.

Audience

The game is geared toward freshmen and students in introductory level courses. Approximately 15 to 20 students are ideal for this activity, because it requires individual monitoring and assistance. If the class size is larger, an option is to group students by discipline and have them work together.

Time Required

Minus the session introduction, which is approximately 10 minutes, this game-like activity takes approximately 55 minutes.

Materials and Equipment

The game requires:

- one scholarly or trade journal and one popular magazine per table;
- a brief PowerPoint presentation that reviews the two writing assignments for the course and discusses source evaluation criteria;
- one computer per student or one computer per group if students are grouped by discipline;
- a wiki website (e.g., http://explorediscipline. wetpaint.com/);
- a field guide instruction booklet (see Figure 4.1);
- instruction sheets for locating each type of information source: a style manual, a print journal, a subscription database, a book, and a multiple choice assessment;
- a READ® poster or other image made into a puzzle of six pieces and printed on cardstock (identical pieces should be placed in envelopes numbered for each task and final assessment); and
- Nestlé® Treasures or some other reward.

Preparation

The librarian should construct the wiki website, instruction sheets for each task, field guides (print copies), and puzzle pieces in advance. This is time intensive, but the activity can be reused, and students enjoy it.

Wetpaint (http://www.wetpaint.com) open source software was used by this librarian. It is free, requires no knowledge of code, and offers unlimited space. Instruction sheet and field guide content require careful thought so that all instructions are very clear, and students will have a path back to the resources that they will later evaluate. Figure 4.1 offers a sample *Go Explore!* field guide that librarians can adapt.

If students work in pairs or are grouped by discipline, tables should be arranged to accommodate groups. Otherwise, this is an individual exercise; after the introduction students are seated at the computer stations or at tables with their laptops.

Playing the Game

Introduce the activity with a PowerPoint presentation, which serves as a quick reminder of the two writ-

ing assignments: an exploratory essay that includes students' reasons for their choice of a major and a description and evaluation of its research tools; and an annotated bibliography of 12 sources about a topic of interest in their field.

Make sure each table has one scholarly or trade journal and one popular magazine. Discuss the criteria for source evaluation using the PowerPoint, and ask students to discuss the differences between these types of sources. This introduction takes approximately 10 minutes.

After the introduction, pass out the field guides and have students go exploring by completing the five tasks. During the exploration, which is self-paced, be available, along with the course instructor if possible, to assist as necessary. Review the field guides as students complete each task, and hand out the reward puzzle pieces.

After students have completed the tasks, give them a print copy of the multiple choice assessment. When they hand in the assessment, give them their last piece of the READ puzzle. As they finish the puzzle, give them their reward.

Evaluation

The multiple choice summative assessment informs the instructor of those tasks that need further clarification or emphasis. For example, on one occasion, the assessment revealed that the students should have been informed that the print journal collection is arranged alphabetically by title rather than by subject and that the instructor should also have emphasized that general collection books are those that can be checked out of the library.

An informal evaluation based on observation that compared teaching the same class with this game and without it suggested that the activity made the class more fun. Students were all active participants, worked at their own pace, and gained practice and mastery in the processes involved. The READ poster puzzle added a touch of humor as well.

Tips for Introducing Subject Faculty to the Game

This game was designed specifically for one instructor's course based on the assignments. Instructional librarians can introduce it to other faculty who teach introductory level classes by explaining its goal of leading students to develop an understanding of discipline-specific resources used in their field.

Figure 4.1. *Go Explore!* The Five Tasks Field Guide

Your Assignment: Identify, Find, Browse, and Evaluate the Usefulness of Resources Appropriate to Your Field of Interest

Record your field of interest here: _____

Directions:

1. Take this *Go Explore!* field guide with you as you complete each task. This is your "notebook" in which you will identify materials and their locations as you complete each task so that you will be able to retrieve the same items later for your in-depth evaluation.

2. Be sure to ask questions of your librarian and instructor guides, as necessary!

3. This is the URL on the World Wide Web where you will receive your instructions and start your expedition: http://explorediscipline.wetpaint.com/.

TASK 1: Identify an Appropriate Style Guide

Purpose of this resource:

Through writing and publication in your discipline, you are contributing to the conversation of scholarly research. You must give credit to authors who have published the sources that you have used in your own research.

    The citation style and format of your paper depend on the field in which you research and write. Subject-specific *citation guides*, handbooks, or manuals contain formatting rules for both the citations and the structure of your paper.

Record the results of your exploration:

1. What style manual is appropriate for your field? Write its title.

2. Use Snowden Library's *Online Catalog* to FIND the CALL NUMBER for the citation guide in the library's collection. You can use the search box on the library's homepage. *(Please write "not available at Snowden" if not in the catalog—check with the librarian first!)*

Show this field guide to your professor or the librarian to collect a puzzle piece; then continue to #2 on the *Go Explore!* website.

Library Mystery Scavenger Hunt

Kawanna M. Bright and Hyun-Duck Chung

Introduction

Library Mystery Scavenger Hunt provides students with the opportunity to learn how to navigate a new physical space (the library) or new resources (subject-specific databases, websites, or print resources) within the context of solving a mystery or completing a challenge. It has been used successfully with both lower-division and upper-division undergraduates and has been applied to both general and subject-specific course curricula. At the completion of the activity, students have been able to demonstrate their newfound research skills and have shown their appreciation for the fun nature of the activity.

Objectives

Students will:

- apply new information about using a research library in order to navigate physical locations and utilize key online tools and resources;
- practice using library resources to "solve" a mystery or respond to information-finding "challenges";
- build experience working in teams to successfully complete a meaningful task; and
- develop positive attitudes about using the library and establish relevant points of contact for getting further help with research.

Information Literacy Competency Standards Addressed

This game addresses these ACRL Information Literacy Competency Standards: #2; #4.

Game Background

Library "scavenger hunt orientations" are not new. The *Library Mystery Scavenger Hunt* activity differs from traditional hunts in that it strategically applies pedagogical principles of active learning and problem solving for the purposes of basic library orientation and beyond.

Library Mystery Scavenger Hunt is a team-based activity. In it, teams of three to six students work together to gather clues and solve problems along the way. Once the activity and rules are introduced from a "home base," teams are given their first clue and must find each successive clue to finish the activity and report back to home base. Clues are hidden throughout the library, and hiding places can include relevant physical volumes with call numbers or manned stations where staff release the next clue upon receiving the correct prompt from the approaching team. Each clue, in conjunction with a hint sheet, introduces new information about the library's resources or the research process. Clues also prompt the students to either apply that information to solve a riddle or practice using a particular resource to find the correct information. At the end of the activity, student answers are scored for correctness or reviewed verbally as a group. Winners can be determined by a point system, and prizes are awarded for first, second, and third places, depending on the number of teams in play.

The activity originated as a response to a logistical challenge: a large class of 60 students needed to learn how to use a research library for their course assignments. Because of timing and scheduling constraints for both the course and the library, the class could not be broken up into smaller groups for separate sessions, and the library's instructional spaces could not accommodate such a large group at once. This activity allowed the students to receive their library orientation and at the same time allowed the instructional services librarian to work with the class without requiring too many additional helpers. Also, by breaking away from a more traditional computer lab–based library session, the instructional services librarian could combine aspects of using online resources with a physical library tour—something that is not always easy to do with computer lab–based sessions.

The inspiration for the design of the activity came from the instructional services librarian's love of the game *CLUE* and a desire to include some aspects of the classic board game into making the activity interesting and engaging. These aspects included the use of a theme, a background story, and characters. Although these aspects of the activity are not necessary, they do play an important role in helping students recall the tasks and processes of the activity when later conducting their actual research in the library.

Audience

This activity can be adapted for either lower-division or upper-division undergraduate students. In either case, the activity will introduce students to skills in a practical way that they will be able to build on in the future when doing research.

Time Required

The recommended amount of time for implementing the activity from start to finish is one and a half hours. Depending on the learning needs and competency levels of student groups, this timing may be shortened to one hour at the minimum or extended for two hours at most.

Materials and Equipment

This game requires:

- **Clues**: Each team will require a set of clues. The number of clues in each set will depend on how many locations and/or resources will be covered in order to meet the learning needs of the student participants. At the lower-division level, eight locations/resources were used, which called for eight clues—one for each resource/location. Multiply the number of clues in each set with the number of teams completing the activity to determine the total number of clues that must be created. For example, 6 teams using 8 locations/resources will require 48 clues for the activity (or, a set of 8 clues per team). Using a grid to map out the various teams, clues, and locations/resources can help organize the process and minimize frustration. If using a theme, be sure to make the wording of the clues consistent from clue to clue.

- **Library Map**: Use an existing map of the library or modify the map to highlight the specific locations that the activity requires the participants to visit. One map per team should be sufficient.

- **Hint Sheet or Help Guide**: Whether working with incoming freshmen or upper-division students, create a hint sheet or help guide to correspond with the activity. This sheet replaces the 20 to 30 minutes normally required to show students how to use specific online tools and resources or to navigate the library's webpage. The handout also serves as a useful reminder or reference that is tied to the experience of playing the game, and a copy should be available for each student. In addition, assigning students to watch a screencast or a recording of a short narrated presentation that covers information on the resources/library prior to the activity can help make the game a more meaningful and less confusing learning experience. This recommendation is especially true for upper-division classes that require highly specialized and more sophisticated databases in a particular discipline. The screencast/recording would then also be available as a reference for the student following the activity.

- **Scoring Card (optional)**: If points are to be allotted for correct responses and order of completion, preparing a clear scoring card with correct answers and designated number of points arranged in grid formation will make the process of determining the winners much more efficient.

- **Slide Presentation**: Use simple but clear slides to "present" the activity to the students in a visual as well as verbal way. The slides also replace the need for additional handouts that describe the game and the rules for the students. Instead of printing out a large number of copies, simply put the information into the presentation for the whole class. If a room with projector and screen is not available, a marker-drawn flip chart may serve the same purpose.

- **Laptops or Computers**: The activity requires students to use online resources as well as the physical library, and therefore students will need to use a computer with Internet access.

- **Prizes**: Use prizes to enhance motivation and fun for the participants. Non-monetary prizes may include offering extra-credit or points for students in the course (this will of course depend on the permission of the instructor). Gift certificates have also been well-received, especially for local establishments that the students may often frequent, such as restaurants near or on campus. Cookies or candy work well, especially for third-place prizes where the team is given the option of sharing this prize with the rest of the class. Note: Though gift certificates tend to sound more appealing, candy and cookies are just as well-received by the students.

Contact the authors for sample clue sheets, help guides, and scoring cards.

Preparation

To ensure a smooth implementation, the materials and locations must be well-prepared before the start of the game. A checklist can be very useful especially for a first implementation of the game so as not to leave any loose ends.

Selecting a Theme or Scenario

Using a theme can help simulate the research process that students will later need to engage in, thereby making the game more relevant and interesting to the students. Also, make sure to select a theme that can easily work with each clue. For the upper-division students in the entrepreneurship program the overarching scenario was that each team was gathering information for a business plan competition, which was being hosted by a local venture capital firm interested in wireless technologies. When working with lower-division students it is usually possible to pick themes that are more fun and less curriculum focused. For the first iteration of this activity the theme was a murder mystery that the students had to solve. Each clue included a reference to the "murderer's" purpose for visiting a particular location or using a specific resource. The reverse side of each clue also displayed a visual clue as to who the murderer was. If students collected all eight clues, the backs of the clues could be assembled together like a puzzle to display the identity of the murderer (which was the school mascot). In the second iteration of the activity the murderer was replaced with an art thief who had left behind clues related to art. This art theme was applied to the locations used in the activity where students had to locate service points for color and large-format printing, as well as how to find journals related to art

in the current periodical section and books about art in the library catalog.

Locations

Determine which locations in the library will be used as clue stations as well as the home base. The home base must be large enough to hold all student participants at the start and end of the game and should be reserved ahead of time if possible. This home base location should also include the technology needed to introduce and run the game (if technology is being used). Remember that a variety of locations can be included and that a mixture of both "useful for research" and "useful for relaxation" can be beneficial. For the basic orientation, locations included the circulation and reference desks but also two places within the library where students could buy food or drinks.

Clue Stations

Determine whether the locations that will hold the clues will be staffed or unstaffed. If locations are to be unstaffed, determine how the clues will be hidden. For instance, will they all be in plain sight or hidden in specific books, journals, etc.? Using unstaffed resources will require selecting specific monographs or volumes ahead of time. Using the same book for each group is not recommended, because clues may be taken by accident (or on purpose!), which can derail the learning experience of some teams. Hide the clues as close to the start of the game as possible to minimize the impact the game may have on the library. If using a staffed location (e.g., the reference desk), make sure that the staff at the location know about the activity and are also on board. It is also a good idea to communicate with other public services staff about the event so that they will know what is going on and be able to help the students if necessary.

Playing the Game

Plan to meet the class in a central location in the library at a designated time. Once everyone is there, make brief introductions and then lead the students to the location that will serve as home base. Once at home base, divide the students into the desired number of groups needed. If the class is already divided into groups for a course project, maintain these groups, as it will work well with the activity. Once students are in their groups and sitting together, introduce the activity using the prepared presentation.

The introduction should include the rules, objective(s), and what the students will need to do to successfully complete the game. If prizes are being awarded, explain the scoring system and what the prizes are. The final part is to make sure the students are aware of timing and to give them a designated time to return to home base regardless of whether or not they have completed the activity. At this point ask the students if they have any questions, and make sure that everything is clear to them before officially starting the game. Once all questions have been answered, start the game by giving out the first clue to a representative from each team.

While the students are working on solving the clues, either stay at home base and wait for them to return or, as extra staffing permits, roam the library to keep an eye on the students as they work. Provide guidance if they ask for help, but attempt to do so without giving away the answer.

Return to home base before the completion of the game so that the first group to finish will not return to an empty home base. As the groups come in, check to see if they have solved the mystery or completed all of their tasks, and award points if a scoring system is being used. Once the final group completes the game (or returns to home base at the required time), announce the winner and review the clues used for the activity. Once the review has been completed, a more formal evaluation can be issued, either online or on paper, and then the prizes can be awarded to the winning team(s). This time can also be used to have the students focus on specific resources, tools, or skills from the game, assess student skill levels, and identify gaps in learning that may continue to exist. If technology is available, demonstrate some of the skills used to complete the activity to the students. Recorded notes from this discussion can also be helpful for making changes to the game for future offerings.

Evaluation

Evaluation can take place during the recap or debrief of the activity once all teams have returned to home base. Evaluation can also take on a variety of formats, from informal observations and verbal communication to more formal written feedback using an online or paper form. No matter what specific format is utilized, evaluation should aim to gauge student learning according to the objectives set out at the start of the activity, as well as the implementation of the activity itself.

Evaluative prompts may be asked in an informal manner and include questions such as asking students to describe how they did or did not find the information they needed, what continues to be confusing, or if they have further questions about the library or the activity. More formal methods of gathering feedback include using a short form asking questions such as which of the resources used during the activity were new to the students or what aspect of the activity they found to be the most useful or appealing.

Tips for Introducing Subject Faculty to the Game

This game requires a significant amount of time and work to plan and implement and is not infinitely scalable. It is not suggested that the activity be offered to all faculty or classes, although it can be used in a variety of curricular contexts. It is best with faculty with an interest in active learning techniques or those who specifically request "something a little different" from a traditional session. Be prepared for requests for the activity upon a successful implementation— word of mouth from one enthusiastic instructor to another tends to be a powerful way to promote programs offered at the library. If actively seeking additional participants or trying to sell the idea to a faculty member, make the most of images and feedback collected from past activities as a way to communicate the value of the activity.

Library's Best Beach Ball
Theresa McDevitt and Rosalee Stilwell

Introduction

This active investigation game uses a beach ball to randomly assign library places and services to student teams for exploration. Teams consult background sources, search out library places and points of service, observe what goes on there, and report their findings to the class. For those who don't like the ball but like the activity, this game can be played without the beach ball.

Objectives

Students will:

- be introduced to important library places and services,
- investigate at least one library place or service and determine its value, and
- present their findings to the class.

Information Literacy Competency Standards Addressed

This game addresses these ACRL Information Literacy Competency Standards: #1; #2; #3; #4.

Game Background

For many years, librarians at Indiana University of Pennsylvania have taught a one-credit library instruction class. One session has always been devoted to orientation to library places, collections, and services. In the past, these sessions were rather dull, as students listened passively as instructors lectured, showed virtual tours and PowerPoint presentations, or provided a traditional walking tour of the building. These methods were found wanting, because they did not engage students or allow them to do their own investigations of library places or services. This game was developed to provide students with an active, discovery learning experience that allows them to teach one another about the treasures in the library.

Audience

This game has been used with groups of up to 30 undergraduate students with considerable success. The number of students/players easily accommodated at once depends on the number of library places and services assigned. If students are broken into teams, more students could be included.

Time Required

This game requires less than 10 minutes at the beginning to assign places to student teams and then 5 to 10 minutes per student team at the end to present their findings. The exploration part of the game can take place in or outside of class. If it takes place outside of class, it will not take as much class time.

Materials and Equipment

The game requires:

- beach ball,
- Sharpie marker,
- list of library places or services that student teams will explore and report on,
- method of recording places/services,
- slips of paper for voting and method of recording votes, and
- small prizes or certificates for winners.

Preparation

Prior to class a list of library spaces and services should be created. These can be selected from library orientation materials, virtual or video tours, or other materials but should include the most frequently visited library places and the most popular services. On a beach ball, write the names of the services and places, separating them as much as possible.

Playing the Game

Begin by providing printed, video, or Internet-based orientation information about the library so that students have some sources to fall back on to begin their quest. To begin the game, instruct students that they are going to be sent out to find places and services in the library. They will be required to investigate what happens at each place and then provide a five-minute presentation to the class on why that place or service is valuable and possibly the best in the library.

Create teams of two to four students, depending on how many students and how many places/services are on the list. Teams should have the same number of students, as much as possible. To create the teams and assign places/services to investigate, throw the beach ball with places/services written on it around the room. When a student catches it, assign him or her to investigate the place/service that the right thumb is touching on. Repeat this until each student has a place/service and partners for the quest. Record the students' names, places/services they are investigating, and team they are on. (Often the teams will not be equal using this method, so you should intervene to equalize the groups.) This process can be done in a less active, more controlled manner by writing the names of the library places/service on pieces of paper and putting them in a container. Students then pull slips of paper from the container.

Then send the teams out to investigate the places/ services. Have them answer three questions about each: "Where is [place/service] located?" "What happens there?" "Why might this be considered the best place in the library?"

You can include the investigation part in a class session, but it takes far less class time if it is a homework assignment. When the investigations have been completed, the teams pick a reporter for the team to present to the class why the place/service they have investigated is the library's best place or service.

When the presentations are completed, give students a slip of paper and ask them to vote for what they think is the library's best place or service. You can tally the votes during the session or later to build the suspense. When votes are tallied, announce the library's best place award and declare the team that reported on it the winners. Small prizes can be distributed if desired.

Evaluation

Although no formal evaluation of this educational game has been made, instructors have observed that students enjoy the discovery learning process and appreciate hearing the evaluations of other students. In addition, instructors almost always gain some insight into what the students value about the library.

Tips for Introducing Subject Faculty to the Game

When suggesting this novel way of doing a library orientation to subject faculty, the librarian might stress that the students generally enjoy this exercise much more than the traditional version, whether they are on the winning team or not. Even better, they are required to actively participate in finding and presenting the information, and it is therefore likely that more significant learning occurs.

It's Alive!

Mary J. Snyder Broussard

Introduction

It's Alive! is an online game (http://www.lycoming .edu/library/instruction/itsalive.html) designed to be played in a computer lab by introductory biology students. It introduces students to the research materials and methods involved in locating background information for lab reports on exercise physiology.

Objectives

It's Alive! teaches students:

- the appropriate databases in their field,
- how to select effective keywords,
- database tricks such as Boolean operators and truncation,
- how to find the full text of the citations found in the databases,
- how to identify peer-reviewed articles (a requirement of the assignment), and
- how to cite the articles in their lab reports in the CBE format.

Information Literacy Competency Standards Addressed

This game addresses these ACRL Information Literacy Competency Standards: #1; #2; #5.

Game Background

Biology 111 students at Lycoming College have an assignment to research and create an experiment to look at how exercise affects the body among various groups of people. After the first year of teaching the library instruction session for the Biology 111 students, the librarian began looking for a more engaging activity to teach the resources the students needed to complete their assignment. There are four sections of Biology 111 offered every spring, and it is one of the few times during the biology major that librarians have the opportunity to teach research strategies in a biology classroom.

The game took approximately two months to develop, although the librarian was still learning the necessary programming skills throughout the development process. It was built using Macromedia Flash with the aid of a basic Flash instruction book and *Beginning Flash Game Programming for Dummies* (Harris, 2006). A small group of students (only one of whom was a biology major) was consulted periodically, and other Lycoming librarians helped test the game for glitches. When the game was near completion, it was sent to one of the Biology 111 professors for approval.

It was first introduced in January 2008 and repeated in January 2009. In the game, students work in pairs to play a mad scientist who wants to build a monster to use for his exercise experiments. The character Moe sells body parts but wants to be assured that the players know enough about research in biology before accepting parts. Students select which body part they want to obtain, each one leading to a section of related questions. They are allowed to miss only one question in each section to get the body part; otherwise, they are sent back to Moe's Body Shop to select a body part again. If they earn the body part, that part is added to the growing monster on the right side of the screen. The goal is to answer enough questions correctly to obtain all of the body parts and create a complete monster.

Feedback is given after each question is answered so that students learn from their mistakes, and links to resources and clues are provided throughout. The game is therefore designed so that carefully reading each question and following the clues will allow students to finish more quickly than students who guess. Students are instructed to let the librarian know when they have reached the final screen so that she can pass out evaluation cards. A small prize is awarded to the group who finishes first.

It's Alive! was accepted for inclusion in the Association of College & Research Libraries' PRIMO database in June 2009. Editable Flash files are available upon request for librarians wishing to adapt this game for their students.

Audience

This game has been used primarily with traditional freshman biology majors but could work with any group of students enrolled in an introductory biology class.

Time Required

The game requires approximately 30 to 45 minutes to play.

Materials and Equipment

The game requires:

- enough computers with Internet access so that students can work in pairs and
- two $1 gift certificates to the campus café for each class section.

Preparation

Because the game uses live databases, it needs minor updating each year to represent the databases' changes. In January 2009, the updating took approximately three hours, but that included adding section labels and correcting a misunderstanding about the desired citation style from the previous year.

Playing the Game

The introduction and closure are as important to any educational game as the game itself. Students often do not read written instructions carefully enough, which causes problems later in the game. To avoid this problem, you should introduce yourself during the first few minutes of class, explain why the students are playing a computer game, and point out the clues and links in the game. Students then play the game, which takes 15 to 25 minutes. The game requires students to answer questions relating to topics such as using the online catalog, database searching, and interlibrary loan. If they give correct answers, they will get the body parts they need. If not, they will be given tips and chances to try again. Students then fill out a short, anonymous evaluation form that asks what they learned, what they are still confused about, and if they feel prepared for the assignment. Once you collect the evaluations, address the areas where students are still confused. After you discuss all of the issues, the students can leave.

Evaluation

Fifty-five evaluation forms were collected in the four sections of Biology 111 in January 2009. The form asked three questions:

1. Name something new you learned from the game.
2. What is one area you still have questions about?
3. Do you feel this game prepared you for your assignment?

Forty-eight respondents answered the third question with "Yes." Only two said "No," two said "Somewhat," and three offered positive information but did not indicate if they felt prepared for the assignment. One student wrote that the game was "better and more interactive than past presentations." They indicated they had learned a lot about the databases and special features such as the MeSH (the thesaurus in MEDLINE). Few students asked any questions, and those who did seemed mostly confused about the benefits of using the MeSH or where to find information about citing in CSE. These were addressed at the end of class.

While the librarian is content with the results of this game in comparison to previous activities, this game continues to be a work in progress. Future implementations will ideally include more real-world involvement with the physical library to provide more context for the online content. Currently, there are several reasons why the class must take place in the biology computer lab rather than in the library classroom. However, the minor adjustments made before the second implementation, including the labels to each section of the game and changes to the introduction and closure activity, made this year's classes run much more smoothly, and the materials seem more relevant to the students in comparison to last year.

Tips for Introducing Subject Faculty to the Game

As a librarian at a small college who has used online games in classes, previously established relationships with the professors paved the way for the game's acceptance. Faculty should be notified if the game will deviate from what has been done in past instruction sessions. In this case, the professors were asked before starting the game development if they would be open to trying something new. When the game was nearly complete, the link was sent to one of the professors so that she could preview the activity. After seeing students interact with the game, she was very pleased and requested to repeat it in future years.

References

Harris, Andy. 2006. *Beginning Flash Game Programming for Dummies*. New York: John Wiley/For Dummies.

Information Literacy Game
Amy Harris Houk

Introduction

The *Information Literacy Game* is an online board game that introduces students to library services and research skills. It is available at http://library.uncg .edu/game/.

Objectives

Students will be able to:

- select appropriate keywords from a research question,
- select an appropriate resource (book, website, scholarly journal article, or magazine article) based on an information need,
- evaluate websites, and
- cite sources properly.

Information Literacy Competency Standards Addressed

This game addresses these ACRL Information Literacy Competency Standards: #1; #2; #3; #5.

Game Background

The idea for the *Information Literacy Game* came from Scott Rice, who was at the time the Networked Information Resources and Distance Education Librarian at the University of North Carolina at Greensboro (UNCG). He approached the author, who was then the First-Year Instruction Coordinator, about creating an online game geared primarily to first-year students. The result was an electronic board-game-style game in which students could compete against each other using one computer or play alone. The game was intended to reinforce the concepts students were learning in face-to-face library instruction sessions, namely, choosing keywords, choosing appropriate types of sources, citing sources, and navigating the physical library. Being able to reinforce these concepts is vital because librarians see students in a classroom setting for only one class period during the semester. The game provides the opportunity for students to review the concepts without taking additional class time.

Scott envisioned a game that would be freely available for other libraries to download and adapt for their own uses, so the game was released under a Creative Commons Attribution-Noncommercial-Share Alike 3.0 United States License. This allows libraries (and other noncommercial entities) to adapt the game as long as they credit UNCG and allow their own games to be adapted by others.

Audience

The game is designed to be played by one to four players, although it can be played by more students in teams. In its unaltered state, it is designed for first-year students, although upper-level and graduate students have also played it. The questions are relatively easy for the more advanced students, but they have still enjoyed playing it and reported learning from it. People at other institutions have changed the questions in the game so that it can be played by children in elementary school or by hospital employees.

Time Required

The game is designed to be played outside of the classroom, but it can also be played in groups during class time. A typical game lasts between 10 and 30 minutes, depending on the number of players. A single-player game goes more quickly than a multiplayer game.

Materials and Equipment

The game requires:

- a computer with Internet access and a web browser.

Preparation

The *Information Literacy Game* was designed to be adapted by librarians at other institutions. The author was fortunate to work with a librarian with programming skills and the desire to help students learn information literacy skills, but not all librarians are in this position. Therefore, the creators produced a game that other librarians could easily adapt for their own institutions. The downloadable .zip file located on the website contains everything a librarian needs to customize the game, including question files, sounds, images, and step-by-step instructions.

To use the game at another institution, the most important changes are customizing the library logo on the game board and the link to the library's help service. Some of the questions in the Library Wild Card category are also UNCG specific and should be changed for other libraries.

Playing the Game

The game is typically played in library instruction sessions with librarians. Show students how to access the game, and briefly demonstrate how it works. If desired, teach students how to e-mail their results to their professors.

Evaluation

The creators conducted extensive play-testing of the game before it was released. They asked student workers and librarians to play the game and provide feedback. The feedback resulted in changes to specific questions and other minor improvements. Several new versions of the game have been released to correct bugs and other issues. Feedback from students and other librarians who adapt the game for their own institutions is always welcomed.

Tips for Introducing Subject Faculty to the Game

The librarians at UNCG have marketed the *Information Literacy Game* to faculty as a way to enhance library instruction. Because the players have the ability to e-mail or print results, faculty can require students to play the game outside of class time and turn in proof that they played.

Nightmare on Vine Street: Librarians, Zombies, and Information Literacy

Bo Baker, Caitlin Shanley, and Lane Wilkinson

Introduction

Nightmare on Vine Street is an online escape-the-room style video game designed for freshmen and other new library users (http://www.youtube.com/watch?v=_3U39lwpWyU; YouTube video capture). In the game, the player awakes in a library study room after the library has closed and, when attempting to leave, gets blocked by zombies. To escape, the player must appease the zombies by gathering the materials the zombies request and descending the library floor by floor. This requires players to collect objects such as a book, a special collections manuscript, an online journal article, a library Kindle, and more. Players who escape successfully are awarded a certificate.

The game environment is constructed from a combination of video, still photographs, titles, music, and sound effects. Players navigate the environment by using a mouse-manipulated cursor to click on objects and move in general directions. The game complements a video tour of the library available on library-owned iPods and reinforces many of the tour elements.

Objectives

Students will:

- be oriented to the physical layout of the library and the various available resources,
- learn what types of resources are available at the library, and
- be introduced to reference librarians (as the mildly threatening members of the undead).

Information Literacy Competency Standards Addressed

This game addresses these ACRL Information Literacy Competency Standards: #1; #2.

Game Background

Nightmare on Vine Street is part of a revision to Lupton Library's original iPod video tour. The tour is required for all sections of a one-credit University Studies course offered primarily to freshmen at the University of Tennessee at Chattanooga (UTC). Students check out an iPod preloaded with the video tour, take the tour, and are directed to play the video game on a library PC. Completion of the tour and game are a required assignment for the course.

The choice to develop a video game is the result of a librarian enrolling in a programming course and generously offering use of her video game assignment as a library instruction tool. Reference and instruction librarians jumped at the opportunity to integrate a more active component into the video tour and designed the game.

While development of the game was a complex process, a small team of librarians, working on the game sporadically, produced a working game over the course of two months. First, two librarians printed library floor maps and walked through the building identifying areas, services, and materials to highlight. Librarians then met to storyboard the narrative, work with the librarian programming the game to translate game objectives into programming objectives, and generate a list of needed props and images. To capture the video footage and images, librarians donned zombie costumes and stayed after work on two separate occasions, totaling about six hours. After filming, one librarian completed postproduction tasks, such as creating sound effects, editing photographs and video, and producing a simple score. Meanwhile, another librarian programmed the game using XNA Game Studio. When the media elements and programming were complete, librarians tested the game, revised as needed, and loaded the game onto library PCs.

The entire production—including scripting, acting, makeup, audio video production, photography, and programming—was completed by librarians over a period of two months. The game was programmed in C# using XNA Studio. Development of the game required the following: Visual Studio Express (free), XNA Game Studio 3.1 (free), digital camera, digital camcorder, microphone, video, photo and audio editing software (e.g., Adobe Premiere, Photoshop, and Sound Booth), music creation software (e.g., Apple Garage Band) and zombie makeup and costumes.

Audience

The estimated number of students enrolled in the University Studies course in a typical semester is 325. Students are generally freshmen. However, the game is available to all university students.

Time Required

The video game generally takes 10 to 15 minutes to complete.

Materials and Equipment

This game requires:

- library PCs loaded with the game and
- certificates of completion.

Preparation

This game uses still images of a particular institution, so librarians may want to create their own versions based on the unique qualities of their libraries. As such, the original source code and planning documentation will be of the most value to anyone wanting to replicate the game.

The librarians who created *Nightmare on Vine Street* are happy to assist with tips for creating game-friendly storyboards, organizing the photo sessions,

understanding the source code, and troubleshooting programming issues (see the List of Contributors for contact information).

Playing the Game

Nightmare on Vine Street uses a point-and-click interface for navigation. Players use a mouse to explore the library and select items to pick up. Trying to descend to another floor of the library triggers a zombie encounter and creates a new task for the player based on what resources are available on each floor of the library. Wrong moves, such as trying to descend a floor without completing a task or trying to complete a task out of order (i.e., trying to get a book on the shelf without first getting a call number), trigger another zombie encounter. Once the player appeases all of the zombies on a floor he or she is free to descend to another floor of the library and, ultimately, leave through the front door.

Evaluation

Players either complete the game or not—there is no scorekeeping. Upon completion, players receive a certificate to turn in for course credit. Because all students enrolled in the University Studies course must complete the game to fulfill their course requirement, the game has been designed in a mostly linear fashion that encourages completion.

Tips for Introducing Subject Faculty to the Game

Librarians at UTC maintain a collaborative relationship with the University Studies department and involve faculty when planning library-related activities. In addition, librarians arrange visits to University Studies classes where they introduce basic library services and explain how to complete the iPod tour and video game activities.

PART III

Organization of Information Sources Games

This section contains Games 10–12. These games teach and provide students practice and challenges with the concepts of library classification systems and call numbers.

Name That LCSH!

Christina Sheldon

Introduction

Name That LCSH! is a traditional game developed to introduce and reinforce the organization of library materials, specifically book classification systems. The game asks student-players to guess an appropriate Library of Congress Subject Heading (LCSH) for a given set of book titles as they are revealed to the class, one at a time, in a slide show.

Objectives

In playing *Name That LCSH!* students will:

- be introduced to the idea and application of controlled vocabulary within library catalogs,
- analyze a set of book titles to consider what topics and subjects they share in common, and
- consider and volunteer an appropriate LCSH that might be assigned by a cataloging librarian to the set of books and by which they might access similar books in an online catalog.

Information Literacy Competency Standards Addressed

This game addresses this ACRL Information Literacy Competency Standard: #2.

Game Background

Anyone remember *Name That Tune*? The game was televised in America from the 1950s through the 1980s, so librarians might, but students probably will not. Still, many people can identify with the reflex to guess what pop song is playing on the radio, television, or computer after hearing only a few seconds of the work. This spontaneous act draws upon a human instinct to access one's knowledge base and assign a recognizable label to any newly introduced object: to categorize and organize. As such, *Name That Tune* supplies a light-hearted model by which to introduce students of all ages to the categorization and organiza-

tion of books using systems of bibliographic control. In the instructional adaptation of the game—enticingly titled *Name That LCSH!*—instead of feeding game players a song one second at a time so that they may guess its title, the game feeds students one book title at a time so that they may guess the collective set's LCSH. Following a few rounds of game play, students whose eyes would normally glaze over at the mention of "controlled vocabulary" and "authority records" will nonetheless be more familiar with the utility of both and will possess a set of useful book titles for consultation on their research projects.

Audience

Name That LCSH! is targeted for use in a classroom of 10 to 30 students. The titles of the books used in the game can be customized for each class, so the game is appropriate for lower-division, upper-division, or graduate-level courses in any discipline for which a research project is assigned and/or as a single class session in a research methods or information literacy course.

Time Required

Total game play (of four rounds) takes 15 to 30 minutes, but partial game play (one or two rounds) can take less than 10 minutes and prove beneficial to students.

Materials and Equipment

The game requires:

- *Name That LCSH!* PowerPoint presentation (see sample slides in Figures 10.1 through 10.5);
- computer, video projector, and projection screen; and
- prizes (suggestions include pencils, stickers, temporary tattoos, candy, bookmarks, or points for extra credit).

Figure 10.1.
Name That LCSH!

Name That LCSH!

A game of classifications

Created by Christina Sheldon, 2010

Figure 10.2.
Name That LCSH!
Motion Pictures—History

- *The Flicks Or, Whatever Became of Andy Hardy*
- *Multimedia Histories: From the Magic Lantern to the Internet*
- *Radical Hollywood: The Untold Story Behind America's Favorite Movies*
- *Icons of Film: The 20th Century*
- *A Short History of the Movies*
- *Light and Shadows: A History of Motion Pictures*

And the LCSH is ...
Motion Pictures — History

Figure 10.3.
Name That LCSH!
Presidents—United States—Biography

- *American Dynasty: Aristocracy, Fortune, and the Politics of Deceit in the House of Bush*
- *Dog Days at the White House: The Outrageous Memoirs of the Presidential Kennel Keeper*
- *Martin Van Buren and the American Political System*
- *Ike: His Life and Times*
- *In Search of Bill Clinton: A Psychological Biography*
- *The Presidents, First Ladies, and Vice Presidents: White House Biographies, 1789–1997*

And the LCSH is ...
Presidents — United States — Biography

Figure 10.4.
Name That LCSH!
Family Violence—United States

- *Living Between Danger and Love: The Limits of Choice*
- *Getting Out: Life Stories of Women Who Left Abusive Men*
- *The Battered Elder Syndrome: An Exploratory Study*
- *Domestic Violence in Asian American Communities: A Cultural Overview*
- *Battered Women and Their Families: Intervention Strategies and Treatment Programs*
- *Family Violence in the United Sates: Defining, Understanding, and Combating Abuse*

And the LCSH is ...
Family Violence — United States

Preparation

Before game play, customize the *Name That LCSH!* game template in PowerPoint to reflect subject headings appropriate for the class you will be leading. Optimally, you will solicit from the visiting class's instructor a sample of the topics that the students will be researching. If no samples are available, create your own topics, making sure that they are appropriate to the content and level of the course.

Based on class-appropriate research topics, identify in the library's online catalog a set of five to six book titles that might be helpful for each topic and that share a single LCSH. Consider these tips when assembling the titles:

- The books' LCSH should have no more than one sub- and/or sub-subheading. The complete LCSH will ideally have two "filled slots" and no more than three, e.g., "Presidents—United States—Biography."
- The book titles should range from being vague in their suggested subject matter to being rather obvious.

Figure 10.5.
Name That LCSH!
Bible—Criticism, Interpretation, etc.

- *Out of Order: Homosexuality in the Bible and the Ancient Near East*
- *Age of Reason: Being an Investigation of True and Fabulous Theology*
- *Asimov's Guide to the Bible: The Old and New Testaments*
- *According to the Scriptures? The Challenge of Using the Bible in Social, Moral and Political Questions*
- *Interpreting the Bible: A Handbook of Terms and Methods*
- *The Limits of Literary Criticism: Reflections on the Interpretation of Poetry and Scripture*

And the LCSH is ...
Bible — Criticism, interpretation, etc.

- At least three of the book titles should explicitly include one or more of the words used in the official LCSH.

After you assemble two to four sets of appropriate book titles, input the titles into the game slides of *Name That LCSH!*, dedicating one slide to each LCSH and its correlating book titles. Use PowerPoint's "Fade In" feature to animate every book title so that it will appear only when you reveal it with a mouse click, and the official corresponding LCSH will appear only after all book titles have themselves been revealed. No further modification of the game template is necessary.

Playing the Game

Introduce the game by explaining to students the theory and practice of using controlled vocabulary, such as the Subject Headings assigned by the Library of Congress, to organize published materials in such a way as to improve the ease and efficiency of accessing information. Announce that to familiarize students with the use of LCSHs as they are applied to books, the class will play a game called *Name That LCSH!* in which book titles will be revealed, one at a time, and students will guess what LCSH best corresponds to the book set.

To play the game, reveal one book title on the PowerPoint slide—the one that is most ambiguous in its suggested subject matter. Call on the first student

to raise her or his hand and field the student's guess. If the guess is incorrect, reveal the next book title—one that is slightly less ambiguous in its suggested subject matter—and students may make a reasoned guess as to the corresponding LCSH based on review of the two titles now showing. Call on the first person to raise a hand. If the guess is incorrect, reveal a third title, so students now have three titles upon which to make a reasoned guess. Guessing continues as you sequentially reveal more titles until a student correctly guesses the corresponding LCSH, which is at last revealed to the class.

Reward the student who correctly guesses the accurate LCSH immediately with a small prize, and the class play continues to the next slide with a different set of book titles and LCSH. Continue until all slides/rounds are viewed or time runs out.

As direct follow-up/application, announce that all book titles displayed in the game are available for use in their own class research. You can also demonstrate how to locate a book title using the library's online catalog, and allow students time to identify and/or locate other books of interest that share a relevant LCSH.

Evaluation

Name That LCSH! is intended to be a tool for formative assessment, not summative assessment. As such, students can be asked to complete a short post-test at the close of the class session and/or game play in which they are asked to identify which of multiple choices is the most appropriate Subject Heading for a given book title. After reviewing student responses, and as time allows in the discipline-specific course, additional instruction, play, and/or examples may be offered.

Tips for Introducing Subject Faculty to the Game

To create interest for faculty and relevance for students, solicit from subject faculty sample research topics for the class content, and assure the faculty member that these topics will be used as the foundation for game play. You might also demonstrate the game at a faculty department meeting. Once faculty observe that the game can be tailored to incorporate books appropriate to higher education, they may be more willing to incorporate the game into a library session.

Confectionary Classification

Blaine Knupp

Introduction

The *Confectionary Classification* game gives students practice in classifying everyday items as an introduction to the concept of library classification systems for organizing library materials.

Objectives

Students will:

- appreciate that things can be organized,
- explore their own organization/classification systems, and
- relate their own organization system to various systems used in libraries.

Information Literacy Competency Standards Addressed

This game addresses these ACRL Information Literacy Competency Standards: #1; #2.

Game Background

This exercise was developed for use in a two-credit library skills class as part of a unit on library classification. In this unit, students examine the concepts of organization and classification and have hands-on experience with the Library of Congress, Dewey Decimal, and SuDoc classification systems.

Audience

This game has been used successfully with undergraduate students but could be used with high school or graduate students.

Time Required

The game takes between 10 and 15 minutes.

Materials and Equipment

The game requires:

- a variety of candy—enough for 8 to 15 different pieces for each student; and
- paper bags—small, brown paper lunch bags work great.

Preparation

Before the game, put candy in bags, with one piece of each variety per bag, and seal the bag. Prepare one bag for each student.

Playing the Game

Begin the game by distributing the bags and telling the students not to open them until instructed to do so. Then inform the students that they will be organizing the contents of the bag in some way. Explain that how the students organize the items is up to them but that they need to follow these rules:

- Place the items in an order that has a specific beginning and end.
- The organization order must be expandable (i.e., handle new items).
- The organization order must be able to incorporate each item in a specific place, not just within a subgroup.
- The organization order must be able to handle duplicate items.

When the rules are understood, tell students to begin and give them five minutes to organize the contents. After everyone has finished, ask the students how they went about organizing the items. Discuss why they organized the candy the way they did and notice the variety of methods used. Some schemes in the past have focused on:

- size,
- color,
- alphabet (these are the future librarians?), and
- preference (e.g., the ones least liked to the ones best liked).

After this discussion, give out an additional piece of another type of candy and have the students add it to their group. When the exercise is finished and students have thought about their own classification systems, introduce the idea of organizing materials in a library and illustrate a variety of library classification systems.

Evaluation

This game has been very well-received by the students who participated. Their curiosity is piqued when they receive the mystery bags and instructions, and there are always chuckles when they open the bags. Sometimes the students need to be prompted to think about various organizing schemes, but they are usu-

ally creative once they get into the exercise. Even in small classes, they usually come up with a variety of schemes. As the schemes are discussed, students realize that there are many ways of organizing objects. This leads nicely to a discussion of how library materials are organized and then into an introduction of the concept of library classification schemes. The exercise gets students thinking so that they are receptive to the idea of classification. Students also love getting to eat the candy at the end of the exercise.

Tips for Introducing Subject Faculty to the Game

This game has been used as part of an information literacy course taught by a librarian and was not introduced to subject faculty, but librarians teaching IL instruction classes in subject disciplines that make extensive use of book collections might find subject faculty interested in teaching classification systems in this particularly engaging manner.

Ready, Stamp, Go

Tracey Johnson

Introduction

Ready, Stamp, Go is a timed game to play after lessons on understanding call numbers and title pages. It lets players demonstrate what they have learned and to demonstrate it faster than the other players. This game relies on quick thinking and manual dexterity. It has been used with student employees during National Library Week, but it can also be used in classes in which library classification systems are discussed.

Objectives

The game is a culminating fun activity to follow instruction in classification. Participants will:

- demonstrate knowledge of the Library of Congress Classification System by applying real call number spine labels to images of book spines and stamping pretend "title pages" with the library's rubber stamp, as if indicating library ownership of the book.

Information Literacy Competency Standards Addressed

This game addresses this ACRL Information Literacy Competency Standard: #2.

Game Background

The goal of the game is to demonstrate understanding of the library's classification scheme and of book processing procedures, while under pressure. The game is a reward for learning the basic classification outline, which is essential for library student workers, but it also gives all students a better understanding of how the library is arranged, resulting in more efficient retrieval of library materials from the shelves. This was developed as a fun "field day" activity for library staff and student workers at a small academic library. Everyone knew where spine labels and ownership stamps go, but it was harder to place them neatly while working as fast as possible, and occasionally someone forgot what classification category best represents a book on a specific topic. Potentially debatable choices for book titles to be used in the game were avoided—for example, in Library of Congress classification, a book called *Alcoholism* could easily be in Social Sciences (H) or Medicine (R), so more obvious titles might be, for example, *Social Implications of Alcoholism* or *Medical Therapy for Alcoholism*. The stamping/title page portion of the game is geared more toward student workers; for college or university classes that teach library classification systems, this part can be omitted and emphasis placed on matching call numbers and titles.

Audience

Any number of students, high school or college level, who have been trained in the classification system used by their library can play this game. Small groups of 5 to 15 are best.

Time Required

The game takes about 30 minutes, depending on number of participants. Setup and judging take the most time; the actual game lasts only minutes.

Materials and Equipment

The game requires:

- a packet for each participant (regular paper, 8.5 × 11 inches). The first page is images of book spines, with title, author, publisher's logo, etc., as if the viewer is looking at books on a shelf. Subsequent pages are title pages to match titles on images of book spines, one title page per sheet of paper. The titles are generic, to avoid any copyright issues. Each title must clearly belong in a specific classification category. Examples are *Nutritional Needs of Common Farm Animals* (S, in LC), *Review of Nursing* (R), *Anthropology Understood* (G), *Great Music from the Beatles* (M), *Learning about Art for College Students* (N), etc.;

- a selection of self-stick call number spine labels (still attached to backing) to correspond with titles of books, cut apart and placed in an envelope, one complete set per participant;
- ink pads and rubber stamps, one set per participant (any stamp will do if not enough proper library ownership stamps are available);
- a stopwatch; and
- prizes: one full-sized chocolate bar and a selection of miniature chocolate bars or similar items. The fastest person gets the chocolate bar, and everyone else gets a smaller treat per whole point earned.

Preparation

A review of the library's classification system and standards for book processing would be appropriate, or this game can serve as the review. The information found on a title page can be reviewed again. The game leader can decide whether or not to provide a basic outline of the classification system (e.g., each major category by letter in Library of Congress classification—see Figure 12.1) for reference during the game. Each student receives a packet (face down), a set of labels, a rubber stamp, and an ink pad. Ink pads are open, and rubber stamps are at the ready before the stopwatch is started.

Playing the Game

Say the word "Go," start the stopwatch, and have participants turn over packets and open envelopes. Participants sort labels and apply them to the "spines" of books shown on the first page of their packet. The spine labels must be placed on the correct title by subject, and neatly done. If you provide a classification outline, players must remember that glancing at the outline takes time. Title pages must be stamped in the location indicated by that library's practices. The fun comes in when people are really trying to hurry, flipping page after page, and smacking the rubber stamp down. For more hilarity, participants can have two stamps and alternate between them for each page; how many stamps actually manage to be right side up? Note the time when each player puts down the stamp and declares "Done."

Evaluation

Evaluation is based on time and performance. Every spine label attached to the correct title gets two points. If the label is upside down, minus one point; if the label is crooked or sloppy, minus half a point or more as the judge decides. Ownership stamping must be neat, level, and in the library's approved location. Half-points are deducted for sloppy, upside-down, or poorly placed stamps. Winners are determined by shortest time and highest points, and small prizes are awarded.

Tips for Introducing Subject Faculty to the Game

This game has been used for library student workers. However, subject faculty who discuss library call number classification systems in their classes might be interested in this game, which allows students to demonstrate their mastery of library classification systems.

	Figure 12.1. Library of Congress Classification Mnemonic Sheet
A	General Works: The beginning; **a**lpha
B	Philosophy, Psychology, and Religion: To **B** or not to **B**
C	Auxiliary Sciences of History: **C**ulture and **c**ivilization
D	General and Old World History: The ol**d** country
E	History of America: **E** pluribus unum
F	History of the United States and British, Dutch, French, and Latin America: **F**riends and **f**oreigners
G	Geography, Anthropology, and Recreation: **G**o! (go visit, go learn, go play)
H	Social Sciences: It's all about **h**umans
J	Political Science: Studying **j**ustice
K	Law: **K**ings used to make the laws
L	Education: **L**earning
M	Music: **M**usic
N	Fine Arts: Fi**n**e arts
P	Language and Literature: **P**oetry and **p**rose
Q	Science: **Q**uarks and **q**uantum leaps
R	Medicine: **R**x, of course
S	Agriculture: **S**heep, **s**oils, and **s**ustainability
T	Technology: **T**ools and **t**ricks of **t**rades
U	Military Science: **U**ncle Sam wants **U**
V	Naval Science: Na**v**al science
Z	Bibliography, Library Science, and General Information Resources: Libraries are E**Z** to use!

PART IV

Research Races and Processes Games

This part includes Games 13–21. These games challenge students to show their mastery of finding information. Games range from one that asks students to find information with their cell phones to those where students give their answers with clickers or even act things out.

Research Relay
Emily Missner

Introduction

Research Relay is an interactive classroom game that encourages students to delve into specific library resources to find the answers to interesting and quirky questions and to compete against each other in an exciting relay. It has been used successfully with both undergraduate and master's-level business students.

Objectives

Students will:

- be introduced (in a fun way) to the kinds of information and sources the library offers;
- develop goodwill and a light tone so they will remember the library when they actually have a research project;
- be encouraged to begin using library resources without a lot of handholding or step-by-step instruction; and
- practice working in teams and develop teamwork skills (important as many students complete team projects in their classes).

Information Literacy Competency Standards Addressed

This game addresses this ACRL Information Literacy Competency Standard: #2.

Game Background

This game was developed to provide a library orientation for incoming students. Such orientations can be dry and generally take place before classes actually begin. Students participating might not have received any assignments that they know will require library research and are not as motivated to learn about the library as a student with an assignment at hand. This game motivates students by challenging them to use library databases and introduces them to the depth and breadth of the resources available through the library, from articles in magazines and scholarly journals to industry reports, company directories, statistical sources, and much more.

The game was based on scavenger hunts, but the questions were not designed to be difficult. An effort was also made to create questions that could not be easily answered via a Google search. The objective was to provide students with a positive experience in searching library resources without the frustration that might result from difficult, poorly worded, or tricky questions. The result was a game that allowed students to have fun while becoming oriented to the library and comfortable using library resources.

Audience

This game has been used successfully at the undergraduate and graduate levels. It has been used for orientations for MBA students as well as undergraduate business and sport management students. If students have a competitive drive, it can be a fun and successful orientation to the library.

When used with international students, the questions should be worded more carefully and be more direct. Incoming international students are already dealing with language barriers and cultural differences, so it will help to be straightforward in both explaining the game and creating the questions.

Time Required

This game requires 45 to 60 minutes.

Materials and Equipment

The game requires:

- paper and laptops/computers for the teams,
- places for groups to huddle in teams, and

- prizes. (The idea of prizes seems to be more motivating than what the prizes actually are; examples include tote bags, T-shirts, and even library-branded key chains.)

Preparation

Create five questions. This is the most time-consuming part of the process. *Research Relay* is not an exercise in stumping the students and making the questions impossible to answer. Instead, strive to create a small list of intriguing, quirky questions that the students may actually be interested in answering as well as using the tools they need to actually find the information.

For each question, you'll want the following:

1. The question
2. Any tips or tricks for using the database ("Registration is required"; "Here's how to navigate it"; etc.)
3. A paragraph describing the database

Questions should vary in their difficulty. Several should have specific answers, and others should be more ambiguous. Here's an example of a straightforward question:

Question: Please provide 10 years of quarterly income statements for Burger King in an Excel spreadsheet. And I want it reported in kroners. And I need it, like, yesterday.

Database: Mergent Online

About: Mergent Online is the place to go for any kind of research on companies. It contains detailed company overviews. Search for a company overview by company name, ticker symbol, location, size, or SIC code. Use the tabs across the top of the screen to view the company's annual reports, history, SEC filings, and highlights.

Here's an example of a more ambiguous question:

Question: Compare and contrast the characteristics of rabid pro football fans (meaning American football) to the characteristics of hard-core college football fans. Who would you rather sit next to on a transcontinental flight?

Database: Mintel Reports

Note: To use Mintel Reports, you'll have to create a profile. It will take about a minute to set it up.

About: Mintel Reports offers a wide variety of market research reports on consumer products and consumer behaviors. It is an essential resource for marketing classes.

Make sure you know how many students are in the class. You'll want to divide them into teams with four or five students per team. Print out a set of questions for each team. Each question should be printed out individually so that teams will get only one question at a time.

Mix up each set of questions so that the teams are not working on the same questions at the same time. This will cut down on cheating and add to the drama of the game, because some questions will be easier to answer than others.

Playing the Game

Divide the students into teams. Explain the rules, which are the following:

1. Every team will get the same set of questions, but they will be in a different order for each team.
2. A team member must come up and answer each question to my satisfaction before getting the next question. Bring up a laptop to show me the answer and where you found it.
3. If questions are not answered to my satisfaction, teams will be sent back to work on the question for a little longer.
4. Creativity counts!

Ask each team to send up a representative to get the first question. Teams will bring their answers to you. If you think they've answered the question well, give them the next question. If not, send them back to work on the question for a little longer. When all the teams have worked through the questions, you can announce the winner. It's up to you how you want to award the prize, but suggestions include awarding the prize based on teamwork, creativity in their answers, speed, and stealth.

Evaluation

This game has not been evaluated formally. If the students are working together, finding the answers, and having fun doing so, then it is a success. It means that you've done a good job in setting a good first impression of the library and that the students are getting into the resources and are figuring out how to use them.

Tips for Introducing Subject Faculty to the Game

This game has been used for general orientations and introduced to program managers and other administrators with great success. The game has not been used for subject-specific classes, because in classes there is usually a specific research need that must be addressed.

Fact-Finding Races: Using Cell Phones in the Classroom to Define Terms and Locate Sources

Rosalee Stilwell

Introduction

Cell phone races allow students to use their hand-held devices to race to find information on the Internet and then evaluate the results. It is great for undergraduate students.

Objectives

Students will be able to:

- retrieve definitions from the Internet,
- recognize reliable and useful sources, and
- record bibliographic information accurately.

Information Literacy Competency Standards Addressed

This game addresses these ACRL Information Literacy Competency Standards: #1; #2; #3.

Game Background

Teachers are becoming increasingly annoyed with students who text message on their cell phones during classes about writing research papers but often feel that nothing they say can diminish the practice. One semester, instead of desperately and fruitlessly punishing students for using cell phones in class, this instructor decided to put their skills to work by having them compete in "cell phone races" to find the definitions of basic, broad terms related to the general class session. It started with a simple contest: "The first person to locate the definition of the abbreviation 'MLA' in Google wins five bonus points."

The answer, of course, was "Modern Language Association," a fact that took about 15 seconds for the winner to find. The students liked participating in a competition that used their phones and that had a concrete reward attached, and even the most inveterate text messagers sat up and took notice.

The students were then sorted into teams. To reinforce basic search methodology by sharpening group decision-making skills about judging the usefulness of sources and polishing extemporaneous presentation skills, students were given this challenge: "You have five minutes to locate, define, and present two useful Internet sites on the subject of how to apply MLA to college research papers. The team with the most useful information described in the clearest way wins 10 bonus points." Judging the winning team's entry was done by "instant online verification," that is, by following each team's directions as they presented them via the classroom large LED screen and the classroom Internet connection. It was apparent to all which team won, because their directions to the sites they thought would be valuable and the information provided by the site itself was clear to all. It became a victory by consensus, with everyone benefiting by having access to the winning team's information.

Although extraneous text messaging in class has not completely disappeared, this fact-finding race via cell phone connections has at least focused the majority of the students' attention on ways to use the Internet for beginning their research writing process.

Audience

A cell phone race with the goal of defining basic academic terminology has worked well with first- and second-year college students. At the junior and senior levels, students need more challenging races, such as questions that require more discernment or experience in answering. "Which databases in our library are accessible by your cell phone connection?" or "What is the call number for books about safety management?" are basic questions for more advanced students.

Time Required

Races to define simple words or concepts can be completed in about three to five minutes, including the initial set of directions, the actual search, and the discussion of findings. Using more complex race questions and small groups will take longer. One race can take a full class period (50 minutes) if the automatic online verification process is included and the class as a whole gives some sort of rating (a simple thumbs-up/thumbs-down sign works well) after each team presents its findings.

Materials and Equipment

Cell phone races require:

- cell phones with an Internet connection,
- an overhead LED screen connected to a classroom computer for group viewing, and
- paper with pens or pencils.

Preparation

Cell phone races work at any level of content if the student can see the connection between the questions ("What does MLA stand for?") and the class content ("research writing"). If you have presented some concept that the students must have investigated before as the basis for the race, then students can easily see how the race question is connected to the real world. The complexity of the question and thus the success of the activity itself, then, depend on the background information you have provided over the course of the semester. Race questions should reflect what you know to be your students' background schema on the topic.

Playing the Game

Use a fact-finding race in a class that includes a general review of a previous reading assignment. Introduce the game, and announce a pop quiz on the last reading assignment's major concepts (e.g., "Using MLA citation format in college-level papers" or "Using MLA in-text citations").

Students will appear alarmed and then delighted when you tell them to take out and turn on their cell phones and get paper and pencil ready for note taking. Tell them that the first person to answer a two-part question gets a reward. Instruct them to raise their hand and shout out "Bingo!" (or something relevant) when they want to answer. The first person to do so and receive verification by having the site checked out on the class computer will win a simple prize, such as bonus points. Be ready at the class computer to verify answers as soon as students are ready to give them.

Usually it takes about a minute for a student to find the answer and then another minute for the teacher to verify it. The race can be extended by including discussion of the reliability and authority of the sites discovered. This is also a good opportunity to point out that not all information is equal and invite students to apply evaluative criteria to the websites visited. Conclude with a discussion of any difficulties encountered in finding information about MLA and what MLA means in the research process. Contrasts will naturally arise between MLA and other citation systems, and these contrasts should be discussed.

Evaluation

Cell phone races have had the immediate and obvious effect with students to curtail (but not stop!) "extra-curricular communications" (text messaging) while class is in session. Including cell phones in a class activity allows the students to share ways to use this particular Internet connection for "serious" purposes like research, which pleases them. Assigning them to write a (very) short reflective essay on their personal evaluation of the game can be a way to assess whether or not students feel the game is worthwhile. Students with the most helpful and concrete suggestions can win the right to conduct the next race in the following class period, with a little oversight beforehand to guide their choice of question, timing, and presentation. Bonus points are always appreciated. Finally, by instructing the students to incorporate one site or text reference that they learned about during a race into a term paper creates another reason to stop texting and start racing to the information literacy finish line.

Tips for Introducing Subject Faculty to the Game

Any question about the use of cell phones by students in class is almost a universal entre into the game. Just ask, "Cell phones in class a problem?" and you're there. Be sure to tell them to tell their friends about it, though, so they can text someone soon.

The Biggest Researcher Competition

Jennifer M. Woolston

Introduction

The Biggest Researcher challenges students in an introductory undergraduate English class to search library databases, find the most relevant sources, and win the title of "The Biggest Researcher."

Objectives

After playing the game, students will be able to:

- identify databases that will be beneficial to their research project;
- correctly identify peer-reviewed scholarly articles and differentiate between other sources (such as newspaper or magazine articles);
- independently find relevant articles or essays that speak to their larger research project;
- accumulate a large collection of research materials that they can read through (and hopefully cite from), effectively making their own tailor-made personal research database about a given subject; and
- hone their research topic (if needed) or realize the need to continue searching for relevant sources through other avenues (interlibrary loan, requesting copies of articles unavailable online, etc.).

Information Literacy Competency Standards Addressed

This game addresses these ACRL Information Literacy Competency Standards: #1; #2.

Game Background

The game was developed in the fall of 2009 to add a fun and engaging lesson to a class on research writing that focused on building basic research skills and utilizing library databases for students at Indiana University of Pennsylvania. Many students in the course had never used databases before and expressed some trepidation. This game was designed to give students hands-on researching experience while allowing them to learn about which features of the databases were most useful to their endeavors. It was also intended to dispel some of the "fear of the unknown" that surrounded this component of the research process. Because students seem enthralled with game play outside of the classroom (video games, online games, etc.), it seemed like a great way to grab (and hold) their attention during a pivotal class session.

Audience

This game is crafted for groups of up to 25 undergraduate or graduate students to be played quickly and easily. Although it has not been tried with elementary through high school students, it's possible that they can also play it successfully.

Time Required

Allot 5 to 10 minutes for setup, which includes aiding students with log-in information, explaining the location of the printer, and covering the rules and objectives of the game. Then spend 10 minutes to quickly walk the class through the searching methods of a selected database. The game will take 30 to 40 minutes, depending on how quickly students apply themselves to using the databases.

Materials and Equipment

The game requires:

- one computer per student (or team) and
- a research topic for each student—either selected by students or assigned.

Prizes are optional. They were not used when the game was developed, but they may be a welcome addition. Students are likely to enjoy "winning" something small as an acknowledgment of their efforts during the game play. Pencils, erasers, candy, or even printed "Biggest Researcher" certificates are appropriate prizes.

Preparation

The instructor should reserve a computer-networked classroom before the class session so that each student can have his or her own computer to search with. If this is a problem, students can be divided into pairs or teams so fewer computers will be needed.

In a prior class the instructors should discuss using research databases and what databases may be the most useful for the research interests of the class as a whole. Commonly used databases such as EBSCOhost, Project Muse, and MLA can be recommended. Instructors should then demonstrate how to search the database with a "sample" search. Instructors can cover keyword searching and how to narrow results by date, publication medium, library's holdings, etc. Topics should be assigned or selected by students before the game.

Playing the Game

Inform the students that they will be playing a game designed to improve their research skills called *The Biggest Researcher*. Tell them that this game is an inversion of the television show *The Biggest Loser*. Rather than attempting to lose weight, students are encouraged to "bulk up" their secondary sources for a given research topic. The object of the game is to see which student can locate and print the most articles on a given subject. They can then use these articles as source materials for their ongoing research projects. This is both a skill-building exercise and a chance for students to find and locate relevant research material.

Then explain the rules of the game. Students will begin looking for source materials in a database and have until the close of the game to accumulate as much information as possible. (They will want to print out documentation references and subsequent information for each article as well. This will allow them to properly cite the articles in their later research papers.) If students find a source that they wish to use but need to order via another medium (such as interlibrary loan), they should print out the citation information as proof of their "findings."

During game play, feel free to roam the room and answer student questions as they arise. Students hav-

ing trouble may need suggestions on how to hone their topic, vary their keywords, explore an alternate database, and so forth.

When the allotted time is up, declare an end to the searching process. Students will take a moment to tally up how many sources they have found about their subject. Students can then share how many sources they have located. The student with the most sources is decreed the "official" winner and earns the title of "The Biggest Researcher" for the day! (Of course, each student involved in the activity should feel a sense of winning accomplishment once they have completed the game and printed a fair amount of source material.)

Praise every student for trying the game and for utilizing the databases. If you decide to use prizes, hand them out at this time.

As a follow-up, ask the class if any additional questions about database usage persist. You might also ask "The Biggest Researcher" to provide their classmates with searching tips or examine "The Biggest Researcher's" results and evaluate them for relevancy and authority.

Evaluation

This game has not been formally assessed. Often, playing the game is the first time many students have attempted to use a database. Once students are guided through the process and have some time to "test drive" the databases, they seem much less nervous about searching for relevant source material. Additionally, students express a sense of gratitude at having some supervised class time to begin conducting research that will benefit their later coursework.

Student responses to this activity have been positive, energetic, and full of questions. Once students begin to locate relevant articles, they seem to feel a sense of empowerment about the research process as a whole. There is a strong sense of accomplishment in being able to use databases efficiently.

This game can be a very valuable component of a research writing course, because it allows students hands-on experience navigating library databases. There is no pressure, because the game (and subsequent "fun" attitude) dispels a lot of the initial fear students have about using these tools. Moreover, every student should walk out of the classroom with at least a few sources, so this allows for an additional sense of accomplishment. (If a student cannot locate source material, this may be a valuable moment for the instructor to suggest a topic shift or change.)

Tips for Introducing Subject Faculty to the Game

Games are rarely a requisite component of English classes, and instructors should examine their personal course objectives prior to adopting this activity. If the instructor wishes to create a student-centered environment and believes that it is important to alleviate student jitters surrounding topics such as database usage, they may wish to try it. The game is easy to construct and implement and can be recommended to anyone interested in meeting the game's proposed objectives. It is most useful during the middle of a course focused on research and academic writing as a hands-on follow-up to the instructor's introduction of the subject matter. Once students know how to properly take notes from source material, cite works in text, and construct Works Cited lists, they may be ready to begin conducting research via the databases. This is a great way to encourage students to begin that process, as it places them at the center of the lesson.

Library Quest: A Game for Understanding Database Searching

Lyda F. Ellis and Andrea Falcone

Introduction

Library Quest teaches general database searching in a competitive environment. The game is intended for a traditional one-shot session and is best suited for college freshmen.

Objectives

Students will:

- learn the skills needed to search and locate articles in a general database—in this case ProQuest Research Library; and
- become familiar with the library's website, choosing keywords, browsing suggested topics, identifying various source types, and locating full-text copies of articles.

Information Literacy Competency Standards Addressed

This game addresses this ACRL Information Literacy Competency Standard: #2.

Game Background

During *Library Quest*, a goal-oriented game, students are ignited by the sense of competition and enjoy tackling the research process with their peers. *Library Quest* was created to support the Core Library Instruction Program (CLIP) at the University of Northern Colorado (UNC) where instruction librarians regularly teach Database Searching (CLIP 3) sessions to undergraduate students. Reasons for constructing the game were twofold: to minimize student boredom and to alleviate the frustration instruction librarians often experience when students attend library sessions without research paper assignments or topics.

Prior to creation of the game, students were exposed to database searching skills through a demonstration, but there was not an immediate connection to their coursework. Students were often disinterested because they were not expected to readily apply the skills learned during the session. *Library Quest* eliminates the need for assignments or topics, yet it achieves the same overarching goal as the demonstration.

Audience

Library Quest has been used to engage second-semester freshmen and sophomores in classes of 25 to 30 students; however, the game can easily be modified for an experienced audience by adding more complex questions. Alternatively, *Library Quest* can be simplified to serve elementary, middle, or high school students. While the game centers on a general database, ProQuest Research Library, it can be modified for any other general or subject database owned by the library.

Time Required

To give students adequate time to complete the questions, the library session should be at least 75 minutes long.

Materials and Equipment

Each team requires:

- a flip chart (suggestion: use a flip chart with a sticky back),
- colored markers,
- computers (at least one per team),
- a set of eight questions, and
- an item displaying the library's URL (e.g., a library pencil).

The instructor requires:

- rules of play,
- answer key,

- score card, and
- prizes for the winning team. (Winners have been awarded with a library-branded lanyard or koozie. Prizes are not necessary, but they amp up the competition.)

Preparation

The first step in preparing *Library Quest* is to create the game questions, which will vary depending on the chosen database. (Figure 16.1 shows the questions for the original *Library Quest.*) Make enough copies of the questions for each team, and laminate the questions to increase the longevity of the materials. Put each question in a separate envelope, and number envelopes one through eight. Prepare the questions in sequence for each team. Set flip charts and colored markers at each group's computer.

Playing the Game

Divide students into groups of four to maximize the participation of each member. Typically, a class of 25 students is divided into 6 teams; however, the number of teams will vary by class size.

Next, show the rules of the game with a projector. Be sure to stress that this is a race to find correct answers, not just any answers. Only correct answers will earn points. Then, hand out Question One in envelopes to each team, and tell them not to open them until you say so.

Instruct the students to begin searching. When all teams have finished, have them post the answer sheets on the front wall. Assign one student to mark off incorrect answers with a marker. Go over answers together and tally the scores. If there is a tie, use the prepared bonus question. Finally, announce the winner(s). Those on the team with the highest score are the winners. You can then hand out the prizes and do the assessment quiz.

Evaluation

The assessment will vary depending on the time remaining in class. If there are at least five minutes left in the session, students will take a short five-question quiz. The quiz serves two purposes: it tests the student's knowledge in using ProQuest Research Library, and it informs the librarians about the success of the game and the type of information students are retaining. The librarian discusses the answers at the end of class, collects the quizzes, analyzes them, and sends them to the course instructor for use as extra credit or participation.

If time is limited at the end of the library session, students will be given one minute to write about any concepts that may still be confusing. The librarian can use this information to improve future sessions.

Tips for Introducing Subject Faculty to the Game

This game, which allows students to develop database searching skills in a guided, but self-directed manner, would appeal to subject faculty who wish their students to acquire these skills but have noticed that students often find instructor-led demonstrations of these skills to be boring and not meaningful.

Figure 16.1.
Library Quest **Questions**

---

1. I am interested in researching about Chinese immigration into the United States. The main search terms for this topic are **Chinese immigration** and **United States**. What are some alternate search terms for this topic? List all that apply.

   (a) U.S. and Chinese immigration

   (b) America and immigration

   (c) United States and Chinese immigration

   (d) America and Chinese immigration

2. I am interested in researching about human trafficking. I want to concentrate on sex trafficking of girls under the age of 18. I would like to find journal articles and newspaper articles about this topic. What are the main search terms?

   (a) journals and human trafficking

   (b) girls and sex trafficking

   (c) sex trafficking and women

   (d) articles and human trafficking

3. Find the pencil located in your envelope

   Follow the URL printed on the pencil.

   Go to the **Articles & More** link listed on the webpage.

   Find the database *ProQuest Research Library.*

   Enter the database.

   Conduct the following search: girls and sex trafficking.

   How many results are returned? _____

4. If you cleared out your search from the previous question, redo that search now (**girls and sex trafficking**). Which of the source types listed below are available for this search? List all that apply.

   (a) Trade publications

   (b) Magazines

   (c) Newspapers

   (d) Reference/reports

   (e) Scholarly journals

5. If you cleared out your search from the previous question, redo that search now (**girls and sex trafficking**). When you select **girls and sex industry** from the *Suggested Topics* box:

   How many scholarly journals are returned?

   _____

6. Search for this article in *ProQuest Research Library*: "Female Criminal Victimization and Criminal Justice Response in China" from *The British Journal of Criminology*. Is the entire article available in full-text from *ProQuest Research Library*?

   Yes *or* No.

7. Find the database Academic Search Premier.

   Enter the database.

   Search for this article: "Sex Offender Clusters." This article is not available in full-text in Academic Search Premier. Which database has this article in full-text? (*Hint*: review the attached sheet.)

   (a) Journal

   (b) ScienceDirect Journals

   (c) *ProQuest Research Library*

   (d) Sex Offender Clusters

8. Which of the following keywords are listed at the beginning of the PDF copy of the article "Sex Offender Clusters"? List all that apply.

   (a) Sex offender

   (b) Applied geography

   (c) Spatial analysis

   (d) Trafficking

Race for the Facts

Laura Krulikowski

Introduction

Race for the Facts is a hunt in which students race to find answers in print reference sources. Players at the college level will compete in small teams to navigate selections of reference materials to answer questions posed by the instruction librarian.

Objectives

Players will:

- learn about the various types of print reference resources available in the library,
- learn that print reference sources in libraries are authoritative and sometimes contain information that is not available online,
- use resources chosen from a selection of materials arranged by library staff, and
- access the needed information efficiently in order to receive the next question to continue to race against other teams.

Information Literacy Competency Standards Addressed

This game addresses these ACRL Information Literacy Competency Standards: #1; #2.

Game Background

Today's students are most likely to begin their research with Google or Bing and too often make it through their college years with little or no exposure to print sources. Professors and librarians wage a tireless battle against unreliable informational resources; the ease and speed of Internet searching removes students from the stacks and places them firmly in front of their computer screen. Without intervention, they might not learn how to access information not available electronically or miss out on the benefits of the library as a learning place. This library fact hunt game challenges students to find the answers to questions in traditional reference sources, sometimes not available online. The experience of using print reference sources is one that enriches students' information-seeking repertoires and increases their ability to find information on any topic.

Audience

The players may be graduate or undergraduate students from a class requiring library research for assignments, campus organizations, or a drop-in workshop. It is most effective when the information located has some relevance to a research project the participants are or will be carrying out. This could also be used as part of a faculty orientation or a National Library Week celebration.

Time Required

Time required to play this game depends on the number of questions, the difficulty of those posed, and the location of sources that must be consulted. Age, level of education, and experience of participants will play major roles in determining the complexity and number of questions.

Materials and Equipment

The game requires:

- questions printed on index cards so that only one question is answered at a time,
- a list of reference sources to be consulted,
- envelopes containing the correct answer and where it was found, and
- prizes.

Preparation

Choose reference sources and locate entries that will interest and engage players. The best questions will be those that include information that students need or want to know. Choose questions that can be logically found through using reference sources in the way they are meant to be used. Questions that can be answered only by looking for hours and serendipity will frustrate students and create a negative impression of library research.

After the questions have been written, the appropriate reference works should be pulled and grouped separately to ensure access to all the players during the game. Each team of players will be assigned a selection of resources. For example, provide a cart holding one dictionary, one index, one yearbook, a few volumes of an encyclopedia, an atlas, and so forth—a few extra resources could be added for a greater challenge. By housing these resources separately for the duration of the game, players are guaranteed access to the required resources, and game play can be confined to a specific section or room of the library. It is a good idea to do a test run with library workers or other students to be sure that the uninitiated can locate the information without experiencing frustration.

Provide players with some orientation, such as a traditional lecture, online tutorial, or readings, that introduces them to print reference sources and their use. This will give students some background knowledge to draw upon to select the proper resource to answer the question.

Playing the Game

After players are schooled in "how to use the library" and teams are formed, distribute the first questions to each team. The game can be played as a race to answer a set number of questions or a race to answer the most questions in a set amount of time. A librarian or other staff or faculty member assigned to each team is responsible for evaluating submitted answers and for distributing questions. If additional staff members are not available to assist, a centrally located referee could oversee the progress of the game. Envelopes with the answers should be available to assist with this.

When multiple teams are in competition, prizes may be awarded to the first team to answer their entire sent of questions or to the team that answers the most questions within a time limit. Prizes could be college/university merchandise, gift certificates to the campus coffee shop, or extra credit awarded by course faculty.

Evaluation

Players can evaluate the game through a written survey administered following game play, but, with the excitement of competition, responses may be limited. Evaluation can also be based on the enthusiasm and participation of players during game play. Course faculty, if involved in the event, can also prove helpful in gauging student reaction to the activity.

Tips for Introducing Subject Faculty to the Game

Race for the Facts will be popular with professors who are concerned that students do not have experience using traditional print resources and could easily be marketed to that population. Introduction of the game to faculty should emphasize that participation in the game will introduce students to reference materials and serve to improve research tactics for future projects.

QuickDraw Shootout

Randy Christensen and Richard Eissinger

Introduction

QuickDraw Shootout is a competitive game in which students try to be the first to give an answer. It is similar to an Old West shootout in which cowboys quickly draw their pistols from their holsters and fire. The game can be adapted for use in many situations or subject disciplines by using a different set of questions. This game has been popular with classes from tenth grade to upper-division college students. It has the advantage of being easy to set up with a minimum of technology, and it can be easily enhanced with audience response systems such as clickers or SMS response programs.

Objectives

Students will:

- gain experience determining the purpose and audience of potential information resources, especially in choosing popular versus scholarly and current versus historical sources;
- learn to appreciate the need to use an appropriate documentation style and use it to cite sources;
- understand the need to access a variety of reference or historical information sources to understand the background of their topic; and
- gain experience in evaluating information sources for potential reliability, validity, accuracy, authority, timeliness, and point of view or bias.

Information Literacy Competency Standards Addressed

This game addresses these ACRL Information Literacy Competency Standards: #1; #2; #3; #5.

Game Background

This activity is easy to set up and can be very competitive. It has the possibility of being set up sponta-neously and can be used with or without technology, such as PowerPoint or clicker support.

Audience

This game has been used with students ranging from tenth-grade high school students to upper-division college students. It can be used with small groups of 6 to 12 students or an entire classroom.

Time Required

Depending on the number of participants and questions, *QuickDraw Shootout* can take from 10 to 30 minutes.

Materials and Equipment

The game requires:

- classroom space for 6 to 12 students in a panel with students standing, seated, or at a table;
- participant selection devices such as a beanbag, rubber chicken, paper airplane, balloon, a cowboy hat, or just about anything that can be easily and safely passed between students; and
- optionally, clickers, cell phones, or PowerPoint slides for evaluation purposes.

Preparation

As an example scenario, seating can be moved to create some open space. Select participants by throwing a cowboy hat. The person by whom it lands closest throws the hat to someone else and then goes to the front of the room. The next person throws the hat again and also goes to the front. This continues until 12 participants are selected. They are placed in two columns of six each, with people in one column facing toward the people in the other column. A shootout situation is thus created, with six people on one side facing six people on the other side. The six people on one side are the first team. The six people on the other side are the second team. Other options to accomplish this include the following:

- Anything can be tossed around the room to randomly select the participants, including a beanbag, a paper airplane, or even a rubber chicken.
- Instead of the teams standing and facing one another, players can sit at desks facing the class with team members lined up behind each desk. Only those at the desk can answer the question. Team members rotate forward so new members can answer the next question.
- The entire class can be involved, with each person defending himself or herself from all the others.
- In one situation, the authors established groups from people seated at circular tables, with each table constituting a team.

Playing the Game

Tell the participants that they are in a competition. They draw and fire by being the first to raise a hand (or, if sitting, slap or knock on the desktop.) If the answer is correct, their team receives a point. However, these are single-shot weapons. Players can answer only once; then they must rely on other team members for protective cover. The team that has the most points at the end of the questions is the winner. The winning team receives a reward, such as Hershey's miniature candy bars or chocolate kisses.

Following are sample questions and answers about the development of the atomic bomb and nuclear testing for an English 2000 composition class writing about the effect of radioactive fallout. (Note that other questions would be used to fit the specific information literacy instruction provided.)

1. Development of the atomic bomb was initiated with a letter from Albert Einstein to President Franklin D. Roosevelt stating that the Germans were about to develop such a bomb. What type of information source is the letter? (Students were introduced previously to primary and secondary information sources.)
2. The first nuclear bomb was exploded at White Sands near Alamogordo, New Mexico. Would you need to cite this fact in your paper? Explain.
3. The Manhattan Project was so secret that the only mailing address for thousands of employees was Box 1663, Santa Fe, NM. The actual name, Los Alamos, was prohibited from appearing anywhere. Where would you look to confirm this fact (reference, history books, Google)?
4. Following the test explosion J. Robert Oppenheimer quoted from the Bhagavad Gita, "Now I am become death, the destroyer of worlds." How would you attribute this quotation in your paper?
5. An early indicator that radiation exposure could damage or kill occurred in 1953. Sheep owned by Kern and McRae Bullock were trailed from Nevada to Cedar City, Utah. Burns appeared on the animals' lips; wool fell off in clumps; new lambs were stillborn with deformities; and a third of the 18,000 sheep died. The U.S. government denied any responsibility. Where would you find historical information on a topic such as this, and how would you determine its point of view or bias?
6. During a government effort to resume nuclear testing at the Nevada test site in the late 1990s, articles in *Newsweek*, *Atlantic Monthly*, and the *Journal of the American Medical Association* reviewed the increased incidence of cancers and malformations in downwind populations affected by the original testing. Justify which source might provide the most accurate information.

Evaluation

Immediately after the game, students can be asked how they liked the game, what they learned from the activity, and how it could be improved. Students can be polled by a hand count, by using clickers or online polling software, or by providing them with a brief online survey that they can complete after class. Follow-up with faculty can be accomplished with an e-mail or brief online survey.

Tips for Introducing Subject Faculty to the Game

To encourage a visiting classroom instructor to incorporate this game in their library orientation, point out that the game can be used as an icebreaker at the beginning of a class or as a review of major points covered. Emphasize that active learning activities will improve the instruction.

YouTube Detectives:
Working Backward to Sources

Judith Villa

Introduction

YouTube Detectives is designed to help students recover from "research fatigue" and to practice their research skills in a low-stress, supportive learning environment. They begin the game by researching information they glean from an artifact on YouTube. Then they progress to using popular research tools and, finally, to more traditional research tools. In the process, students discover a variety of research sources, ideas, and skills.

Objectives

Students will be able to:

- create a research question,
- discover both popular and scholarly sources that attempt to answer it,
- evaluate the sources,
- put them in correct bibliographic format, and
- present their findings to their classmates.

Information Literacy Competency Standards Addressed

This game addresses these ACRL Information Literacy Competency Standards: #1; #2; #3; #4; #5.

Game Background

I believe that each classroom is a laboratory belonging to both the students and myself and that we are free to try whatever methods might help us enjoy what we are doing and (Surprise! Surprise!) learn something that we are able to use to good effect after the class ends. I have learned the hard way, both from sitting in deadly classes and from teaching a few, that it isn't "anti-academic" for learning to be a pleasure and that I just never know exactly how we are going to make a class pleasurable until it is all over at the end of the semester.

Besides a flicker of interest in the topic, researching also requires a fairly intense focus, and most students, though very capable of focusing, resist it and surf around in a horizontal search on the web rather than digging deeper into library and other authoritative, trustworthy sources in a vertical search. So the question is: how do we put this random surfing to good use? This is where the game begins. And what will most likely spur students to actually complete the assignment is that they will either get interested in what they are doing or they will not want to make a poor showing in the required class presentation, which, although short, will be evaluated by their classmates. The spectacle of eye-rolling, tepid applause, and glazed looks from their peers is often a compelling reason to take the research plunge, and, once they are in the game, they (hopefully) find that it is not quite as daunting and as dull as they once experienced.

Audience

This game has been used in two different General Education writing classes for first- and second-year students, both of which require varying degrees of research. The game works best for this group because they are still pretty new to performing university-level scholarly research. At the same time, most students have bad cases of "research fatigue" due to being veterans of the 20-page high school research paper (including index cards) on "old news" topics in which they are uninterested and uninvested (think global warming, gun control, the death penalty). Many students seem to have lost their intellectual curiosity, and even when encouraged to choose a topic that interests them they remain balky and resistant to researching beyond page one of a Google search because the process seems meaningless and tedious. A beginning research assignment needs to be either crucial (as in, they *really* want to find the answer to something) or fun or quirky (all three is best) for most of these students to get interested.

Time Required

This game can be played several ways:

- You can assign it as homework and include all components of the game except for the class presentation, with the next class period as the due date. It can take anywhere from an hour, for the decisive and motivated, to two hours, if the student gets lost in her surfing of YouTube.
- If you are lucky enough to have a computer classroom, you can successfully play this game during a single class; bring a timer, allow a specific amount of time for each component, and instead of a class presentation, ask each student to shout out her question and whether or not she was able to find a reliable answer.
- Follow the directions for the first bulleted item. Then during the next class period assign a five-minute presentation for the following class(es). The components of the presentation are described below in "Playing the Game." You may need more than one class period depending on the size of the class.

Materials and Equipment

Students will need an Internet connection, library database access, and access to a word processing program and a printer. They also need to have attended an "Introduction to Research Sources" workshop.

Preparation

The person coaching this game needs to be familiar with YouTube and credible library database research sources, and she must have an open mind as well as a flexible definition of success. Because this is an introduction to research methods game, some students may stumble down an alluring bypath (such as Wikipedia). Be flexible and encouraging so that you can turn this bypath into another discussion of the vast variety of sources and some ways to distinguish whether or not they are trustworthy.

Playing the Game

For example, I would say to students in my Research Methods and Writing class: You are given an assignment to find something on YouTube that you are curious about. As you surf around, you happen to take time to listen to the ever-wonderful Bob Marley sing "Buffalo Soldiers." Even though you have heard it a thousand times, all of a sudden you realize that you aren't sure what the heck he is actually singing about.

You decide on this for your research question: "What is a Buffalo Soldier, and why is Bob Marley singing an entire song about one?" Good job! Phase One of the assignment is complete! You have a question.

Next, you look around quickly, using a Google search, to see what is "out there" in the world of popular culture about Buffalo Soldiers. You type Buffalo Soldiers into the Google search box and click on the first thing that comes up, which is a site that lists some names and events and dates and includes a video titled *Wal-Mart Honoring the Buffalo Soldiers*. You click on the icon to enter the next level of the site and find out that it is all about retail, although there is one line that says: "Buffalo Soldiers, African American troops in the U.S. forces 1866–1945." You go back to the main page and click on "1866: Who are the Buffalo Soldiers?" and a brief two-paragraph history comes up. Okay! Phase Two of the assignment is complete; you have located a popular source, belonging to http://www.buffalosoldiers-lawtonftsill.org/history.htm.

Phase Three requires that you find an authoritative source that answers the first part of your question. You feel somewhat confident about this because you have recently been to two classes showing you how to do this. You take the plunge and log on to your library's website, and you are off to the races!

Now that you have completed this, the most difficult phase, you make sure you have the web addresses correctly typed up, and you write your impressions of their trustworthiness, again using what you learned in your library classes.

Finally, you prepare for your class presentation: you will talk about your detective work as you show the class the two sources you found. You will also briefly discuss whether or not it was an example of successful investigation and what you will do differently next time so that it is not only quicker, but better.

Evaluation

Students not only enjoy this game and get a lot of laughs from some of the wacky but interesting topics people come up with, but they also learn something about research as long as there is no grade attached to it. Why no grade? They do not want to worry about choosing a "stupid" topic, nor do they want their game coach to think they are "slackers" because they used the first thing that came up in their Google search for Phase Two. Best results come with a "Great. You did it!" or with an "Uh-oh. You forgot part of the assignment; for credit, you need to complete it by the next class period." What markedly improves the quality of this game is the class presentation component along with some kind of a reward. Students can vote for most intriguing topic, silliest topic, best digging around, etc. There is nothing like a little peer group accountability to up the quality of the game performance!

Tips for Introducing Subject Faculty to the Game

Invite one or two open-minded, pleasant, nonjudgmental colleagues to the class for the presentations, and be sure to e-mail them a copy of the assignment beforehand.

Interactive Forum Theatre for Research Questions

Kimberly Ramírez

Introduction

This game transforms the classroom into an interactive theatrical forum that generates different creative responses to a single research problem. Instead of leaving the writer to a solitary research and writing process, he or she engages a collaborative audience in the early stages of a project rather than waiting to deliver the finished project to readers.

Objectives

Student writers will:

- have the opportunity to propose to a forum the conflict they intend to explore,
- collectively stage this conflict to experiment with multiple outcomes, and
- engage with future readers/audience earlier in the process (thus better anticipating potential readers' reactions).

The class will collectively:

- improvise staged responses to the research problems classmates present (such as, "Are there enough healthy places for students to dine near campus?" or "Does this novel perpetuate cultural stereotypes?");
- invent two or more "characters" to stage the research conflict and cast classmates to enact these roles (e.g., roles might be a restaurant worker and a hungry student or a trio of characters in the novel);
- reach a response, course of action, or even a proposed solution, to the conflict; and
- refine one or more of the responses generated in the forum into a thesis (and may easily continue to imagine audience reactions when they defend this thesis in written form).

Information Literacy Competency Standards Addressed

This game addresses these ACRL Information Literacy Competency Standards: #3; #4.

Game Background

This game was inspired by Augusto Boal's Theatre of the Oppressed techniques, which were in turn inspired by Paolo Friere's Pedagogy of the Oppressed. In Boal's theatre, participants behave as "spect-actors" (both spectators and actors) in order to collectively stage and solve oppressive conflicts that victimized individuals or societies. The author began employing Boal's techniques in a learning community themed around improving New York City neighborhoods. Watching the students interact made it easy to conclude that it might have a wider application, and the game has proved a success in all classes in which students conducted any form of composition and/or research.

Audience

The game will work with a group of five or more students, and it is suitable for all class types, including remedial through advanced college writing.

Time Required

Scenarios may be played once or repeated with different "actors" for alternate outcomes. A typical scenario plays from 5 to 10 minutes, excluding interjections from the "audience" and post-scenario feedback. Two to four scenarios may be played per one-hour class period.

Materials and Equipment

The game requires:

- students and
- prepared research questions.

Enhancements include:

- media for recording and exchanging ideas,
- a whiteboard for posting the research question being staged and/or recording audience feedback, and
- a video recorder to capture interactions and post them to students' e-portfolios or other interactive Internet forums to expand the possibilities for feedback.

Preparation

For students: Before playing the game, all students should conduct an initial phase of independent research related to a topic they select (or one that is assigned). Students must conceive a conflict, or identify a problem, within the realm of what they have investigated and pose this conflict in the form of a question. The question should resemble a "research problem" that might lead to the formulation of the thesis.

For instructors: Instructors may want to review Boal's basic tenets in his *Theatre of the Oppressed* (Theatre Communications Group, 1993), *Rainbow of Desire* (Routledge, 1995), or *Games for Actors and Non-Actors* (Routledge, 2002), but an understanding of Boal is certainly not imperative to playing or implementing this game in the classroom.

Playing the Game

Before the class period during which the game is to be played, each student is asked to develop a research problem based on a topic that he or she would like to investigate. This assignment should be given when students are in the early phases of research and before they have begun the writing process. The game begins once the first research question is shared. The class then collectively conceives and "casts" the characters required in ordered to enact each situation. For example, one problem may involve two characters (i.e., a husband and wife); another may require a city councilperson, a mayor, and several citizens.

The center or the front of the classroom may be used as an acting area so that the remaining students witness the improvised scene. But the audience is not

a passive one; they can exclaim "Freeze!" to pause the action at any point in order to interject an observation, comment, question, or request from the actors. They can also volunteer to switch out roles in the middle of the scene in order to deliver a different interpretation or alter its course. The writer will get the most out of this game by not "directing" the action beyond the posing of the research question. He or she is advised to remain silent, temporarily ceding control to the actors and the audience. The writer should be further cautioned that "vetoing" proposed exchanges or challenging comments before the scenario has been played to a solution will limit what he or she gains from this collective experience.

The game can also be conducted in digital realms, on websites or e-portfolios, where students may generate an archive of snapshots—videotaped interactions juxtaposed with a research question for spectators to answer. This can work as either a substitute for or a supplement to the in-class game. The classroom forum, the digital forum, or both together allow students to "stage" their ideas beyond the constraints of the traditional text-based research process. Students dialogue with each other as well as with their resources, manipulating and publishing unresolved "plots" for classmates to review.

Evaluation

Students leave the interactive forum much better prepared to begin writing and, in almost every case, much more enthusiastic about the writing process. Opportunities for feedback are widened considerably from more traditional composition methods in which students complete work on their own or exchange drafts only with the professor. The forum is also much more dynamic and involved than a typical peer critique or review.

Both during and after the game, students behave simultaneously as "teachers" and "learners," though they are usually too engaged in the spirit of community generated by the theatrical exchange to always realize this. For example, a student writing a paper in response to Barack Obama's *Dreams from My Father* (Text Publishing, 2008) posed the question, "Why do Obama and his sister Auma refer to their father as 'Old Man'?" Before the forum, this student expected to work toward a thesis that cited this nickname as prime evidence of the "distance" that the children must have felt from their father. However, during the forum, one student from the "audience" shared his knowledge that "Old Man" is a very common term of endearment in Kenya. This shared observation influenced the way the scene was played by the "actors," expanded the class's perceptions about the memoir, and ultimately informed and strengthened the student's thesis before the writing process began.

Tips for Introducing Subject Faculty to the Game

Emphasize that this lively physical and oral interaction is intended as a way of jumpstarting the research and writing process, as well as a way of allowing the writer to engage with his or her readers/audience from the beginning. Point out that the game may be played successfully with or without adding a multimedia dimension to the forum. Introduce the process with examples of how it might be useful in writing classes across various disciplines. Because the game is intended to closely examine a conflict that will serve as the impetus to a research project, this student-centered game can be utilized as a launching pad for almost any writing assignment.

Topical Full Monty

Tracy Lassiter

Introduction

In this activity, students are assigned a mock research topic. They then have to use *all* library places and points of service to prepare a sampled list of book and journal titles, databases, e-books, multimedia, and other holdings that support that topic.

Objectives

Students will:

- be exposed to a library's full offering of materials (e.g., government documents, archives, special collections, etc.), thus exploring a library "top to bottom";
- recognize other kinds of material as potential sources of information rather than defer to the most readily available (e.g., Internet sources or library books); and
- turn in a folder of materials and/or present their findings to the class.

Information Literacy Competency Standards Addressed

This game addresses these ACRL Information Literacy Competency Standards: #1; #3; #4.

Game Background

During my years of teaching at a two-year college, I noticed when students approached a research project they typically defaulted to the "easiest" or most-familiar resources, either information gleaned quickly through an Internet search or by just borrowing library books. They often overlooked other sources of information, such as documentaries, archives, government publications, and the like. This game requires students to survey holdings at greater depth, researching an imaginary topic to find resources from across the library that ostensibly could provide information for a research project on that topic.

Audience

Topical Full Monty would work well with a research writing undergraduate class or with first-year graduate students.

Time Required

This game requires about an hour's worth of preparation before class. Instructors prepare a worksheet of the various library holdings for the students so they are aware of the different areas and sources available. The worksheet should provide a box or line so students can check off places they've already researched. It is helpful to leave a few blank spaces for students to fill in as they go through the library in case they discover a special collection or other source the instructor was not aware of. Also, the worksheet details what the instructor requires the students to provide from each area—for example, 10 relevant journal titles, a printout of the library's media holdings related to the assigned research area, a list of 5 topical books, including authors and call numbers, etc. Depending on the institution's library size, students may need more than a class period to thoroughly explore their topic; in this case, the game can be assigned for homework. (Alternatively, for undergraduates, instructors might hold class in the library the day this activity is first assigned in order to address questions the students might have.) If instructors require students to report their findings to the class, the presentations could take a class period or two. This obviously depends on the number of students who will present their findings, the time allowed for their presentations, and the length of the class period.

Materials and Equipment

This game requires:

- a worksheet listing the names/locations of various library holdings (perhaps a library map or link to a virtual tour could assist) and the required materials from those areas;

- strips of paper on research topics (e.g., "pediatric nursing," "international business," "education for autistic children");
- folders for the materials students gather during the exploration (e.g., printouts of journal titles, a list of media, such as DVDs, slides, recordings);
- strips of paper for voting on best presentation (if instructor opts to do so); and
- prizes awarded to the best three presentations (as determined by student vote or by highest grades on packets as determined by the instructor). One prize suggestion is a deck of cards, in reference to one of the possible etymological sources of "full Monty" as being a pot won during the card game "Monte."

Preparation

Prior to the class, the instructors should prepare the worksheet that identifies the various library service areas and collections. It may be useful for instructors to take their own tour of the library or to work with a reference librarian to learn more about the library's holdings. For each area/collection, instructors should specify what they want students to provide as resource material on their topics—whether those are a particular number of journal titles, a list of embedded links to e-books, photocopies of documents or images, etc. Separately, the instructors should write on strips of paper the mock research topics students will explore.

Playing the Game

In class, distribute the worksheets and then allow students to draw a topic strip from a basket or large envelope. To help prepare students for their exploration, provide copies of the library's map or show the virtual tour of the library, if the institution offers one.

Explain to students that the purpose of their activity is to explore fully all library holdings on a particular topic. Rather than merely surveying each area for an overview, this assignment asks them to engage with the materials, looking up sample titles and documents in order to more fully realize what is available to them for their own research. Also tell students they must evidence their research by providing examples of their findings, and the students will be judged on their selection of the documents and their rationale for including those documents. For example, a student might include two monographs but one anthology because the anthology includes an essay that provides a useful counterargument to her topic.

At this point, announce whether you will grade the packets to determine the "winners" or whether the students will present their findings to the class for voting. Either way, mention that there will be prizes for the "best" research packets, specifying those criteria, such as student annotations or other rationale, to be used in determining the top projects. Students then begin their in-depth library research.

On the day the projects are due, students either turn in their packets or present their findings to the class for voting. When the packets are graded or the votes are tallied, announce the winners and distribute the prizes accordingly.

Evaluation

No formal evaluation of this activity has taken place yet. However, students seem glad to learn that other materials, such as films, can count as academic research. Furthermore, they often are not really aware of what "archives" and other materials constitute, so working more closely with these documents will provide them a greater understanding of these sources.

Tips for Introducing Subject Faculty to the Game

Student-centered learning results in greater, more profound education for the students. This activity shifts the work from the instructor, who invests time in the preparation and perhaps evaluation of the activity instead of spending a class period lecturing on various types of library sources and research options. The students gain greater insight by working with the materials firsthand and, it is hoped, take away ideas for research sources well beyond this one assignment.

PART V

Online Search Techniques Games

This section consists of Games 22–26. These games help students understand the benefits of Boolean logic or finding "just right" search terms for the most effective searches.

Boolean Bingo!

Christina Sheldon

Introduction

This variant of *Bingo* can be used with anyone from freshmen to faculty to introduce and reinforce the functions of Boolean searching. The activity also supports other values that are important for information searchers to appreciate, not just the importance of how subtly, precisely, and complexly descriptors for databases can be input and/or interpreted.

Objectives

In playing *Boolean Bingo!* students will:

- critically think about objects—and, by analogy, text documents—and consider their constituent elements; and
- practice using the Boolean operators AND, OR, and NOT.

Information Literacy Competency Standards Addressed

This game addresses this ACRL Information Literacy Competency Standard: #2.

Game Background

This game asks student-players to locate candy pieces on a *Bingo* board using Boolean commands called out by the librarian/instructor. When students have cleared a full row on their *Bingo* board, they achieve "Boolean Bingo!" The activity pulls upon a game structure that's instinctive to understand by players of all ages. However, the game's structural simplicity belies the more complex orders of analysis and application that are required for successful play. To put it formulaically: Goofy + thoughtful = fun + effective!

Audience

Boolean Bingo! is targeted for use in a class of up to 30 students. The game is most appropriate for lower-division courses whose students may never have been introduced to the nature or utility of Boolean operators. Alternatively, graduate classes, which may include a number of adult students who are less confident in their skills with information technology, may also benefit from the game.

Time Required

Total game play of 4 or 5 rounds can take 15 to 20 minutes, but partial game play of 1 or 2 rounds could occur in less than 10 minutes and still prove beneficial to students.

Materials and Equipment

The game requires:

- a computer terminal with projection capabilities (alternatively, a whiteboard or chart tablet and pens);
- 20 to 30 copies of the game board, pending session attendance (see Figure 22.1);
- the instructor's guide, "*Boolean Bingo!* Notes & Regulations" (see Figure 22.2);
- the instructor's choice of four or more bags—one bag per candy item—from the following list:
  - ◆ M&Ms
  - ◆ Skittles
  - ◆ Reese's Pieces
  - ◆ Mixed Jelly Belly jelly beans
  - ◆ Starburst
  - ◆ Now'n'Laters
  - ◆ Substitute any candy item that is small enough to function as a game piece and preferably has some variety among individual candy pieces (i.e., Hershey's Kisses may not be a good choice because every Kiss—a single drop of chocolate wrapped in silver foil—is a duplicate of the others and allows for scant variety)
- one large bowl;

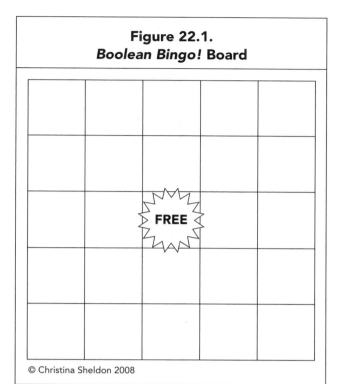

Figure 22.1.
Boolean Bingo! **Board**

FREE

© Christina Sheldon 2008

Figure 22.2.
Boolean Bingo! **Notes and Regulations**

For the purposes of this game and demonstration:

- Randomly distribute candy pieces onto your game board, one per square. Lay candy pieces with any designating mark facing up ("S" for Skittle, "M" for M&Ms, etc.). If playing with Reese's Pieces, beware: They have no designating mark! And also take care with yellow M&Ms—it's difficult to see their "M" mark.
- As each search string is called, review your board. Remove any candy pieces that satisfy the entire search criteria.
- Where color descriptors are concerned, if the color exists on the candy piece, then consider it fair game to be played should that color be called out. For example, with multicolored Jelly Bellys, whatever color you can see, consider that its color.
- For the purposes of "chocolate" as a descriptor, Reese's Pieces have none: Theirs is a "candy" coating (per the bag's description).
- When in doubt, ask your neighbor to serve as judge/witness.
- When one entire row on your board— vertical, horizontal, or diagonal—is empty of pieces, call out "Boolean Bingo!" You'll be the winner! Prizes!!!

- 20 to 30 plastic cups, depending on session attendance; and
- one to six main prizes for game winners and a selection of consolation prizes for the remaining students. (Solicit and/or create prizes as an extension of library outreach: gift certificates to the campus bookstore; a coupon good to exchange for one book formally withdrawn from the library collection; pencils, bookmarks, stickers, or other items that advertise library services, etc.)

Preparation

Before the session begins, the librarian/instructor will:

- make copies of the game board in sufficient quantities that all expected class participants will have one board (alternatively, have one game board available for every two students to share in pairs);
- mix chosen candies together in a bowl to achieve a random variety of candy types and candy colors; and
- have a computer and projector system running, with easy access to a blank document in

Microsoft Word or another text-editing application into which session commands/search strings are typed (alternatively, use a whiteboard or chart tablet and pens).

Playing the Game

Before introducing the game, distribute to every student one plastic cup and one game board: one per student if game play will proceed individually or one per pair of students if game play will proceed among teams. Then pass the bowl of mixed candy pieces among players and instruct them to fill their cup with candy so as to have one cup of candy per game board.

While the bowl of candy is being passed around, introduce the theory and practice of using Boolean operators. You may want to describe how Boolean operators are derived from logic and math formulas conceived in the 1800s by George Boole and to explain that they are used to search through large sets of information and retrieve either more specific results by using the operator AND or more broad results by using the operator OR. Tell the students that to familiarize them with using Boolean operators in searching an online catalog or database for relevant information, they will play a game called *Boolean Bingo!*

Display or read the Notes & Regulations handout (see Figure 22.2). Pause while students lay individual candy pieces on individual board squares. After answering any student questions, play one to two practice rounds to familiarize students with the game's proceedings and to clarify their understanding of search strings using Boolean operators. Search strings are randomly chosen. Display them by typing them directly into a computer that can project them onto a screen or write them on a whiteboard or chart tablet for the entire class to see.

You can combine basic descriptors in search strings of increasing complexity. Descriptors can be chosen from the following: candy types (M&Ms, Skittles, Jelly Bellys, etc.), candy colors (brown, blue, yellow, white, etc.), and candy tastes (chocolate, peanut butter, fruit, etc.). As appropriate to student skill level, you can designate additional qualities (one advanced variant may be to identify consonants and vowels on the candies that have alphabetic symbols printed on them). Escalate from simple strings like "M&M AND red" to more complex and/or selective ones like "(M&M OR Skittle) AND (blue OR yellow)," "(Reese's OR M&M OR Jelly) AND (brown OR black)," or "fruit AND (purple OR pink)."

When you feel students understand the game, begin to call out search strings of escalating complex-ity. Students will identify which of the pieces on their game boards meet the conditions of the called search string and remove such pieces from the board. When a student empties a row on the game board, he or she yells out "Boolean Bingo!" and is considered the winner. Prizes are awarded. After playing a set number of rounds, proceed to demonstrate real-time applications of Boolean operators in an advanced search utility of your or a student's choice: a database, online catalog, or the Internet at large.

Evaluation

Boolean Bingo! is intended as a tool for formative assessment, not summative assessment. As such, students can be asked to complete a short post-test at the close of the class session and/or game play in which they are asked to identify which of multiple choices is the most appropriate application of a search string using the Boolean operator AND or OR. Upon reviewing student responses, and as time allows in the discipline-specific course, additional instruction, play, and/or examples may be offered.

Tips for Introducing Subject Faculty to the Game

Make explicit to faculty that *Boolean Bingo!* is a short activity intended to actualize the use of Boolean operators, which in turn is a foundation of advanced research strategies. Assure faculty that students, immediately following the game, will apply their improved understanding of Boolean operators to advanced search techniques for information of relevance to the course. You might also demonstrate the game at a faculty department meeting. Once faculty observe that the game requires spontaneous and critical thinking that is analogous to higher orders of evaluation, they may be more willing to incorporate the game into a library session.

Shuffle Up and Deal: Boolean Logic Game

Blaine Knupp

Introduction

The *Shuffle Up and Deal: Boolean Logic Game* gives students a concrete example of set theory and Boolean logic. Through the use of prepared cards, each student is given a set of characteristics (in this version, their "pets"). Based on these characteristics, students can then place themselves in the various sectors of a Venn diagram and observe how the diagram can be used to represent the universe of characteristics. Students then use Boolean operators to create statements similar to database search statements to identify specific groups with particular characteristics.

Objectives

Students will:

- be introduced to the concepts of Venn diagrams and set theory;
- use the Boolean operators AND, OR, and NOT to manipulate variables; and
- construct basic search statements that incorporate Boolean operators.

Information Literacy Competency Standards Addressed

This game addresses this ACRL Information Literacy Competency Standard: #2.

Game Background

The *Shuffle Up and Deal: Boolean Logic Game* was developed for a two-credit information literacy course to introduce Boolean logic and the construction of search strategies using Boolean operators in a unit about online searching concepts. It has been very well-received. I had heard of instructors using "Human Boolean," in which the instructor would demonstrate a search strategy using characteristics of the class members (e.g., "All those with 'blond hair'

AND 'glasses', stand up."). While that exercise is fun, it is hard to control (Can you, on the fly, find some set of characteristics that all students have?) and can be confusing for the students. Using prepared cards works better by making the variables easier to control and makes the concept clearer to the class.

Audience

This game has been used successfully with groups of 25 to 30 undergraduate students.

Time Required

This game takes from 15 to 20 minutes.

Materials and Equipment

This game requires:

- 4 × 6–inch note cards on stock that can be run through a printer (I used standard business form postcards that come on perforated 8½ × 11–inch sheets), enough for at least three cards per student;
- clip art of dogs, cats, and fish (or whatever objects you desire, but at least three clearly differentiated items);
- a blackboard, whiteboard, or smart board;
- writing equipment; and
- small prizes (pencils, erasers shaped like animals, etc.)

Preparation

Prepare the cards. Print one clip art image on each card. You should have enough so that each student will receive at least three cards.

Draw three large, intersecting circles (the Venn diagram) on the board. Label the circles A, B, and C. Then label each sector within the circles with a number from 1 to 7.

Playing the Game

Shuffle and deal the cards randomly, giving at least three to each student. Tell the students, "Congratulations! You've just become pet owners. What kind of menagerie do you have?"

Label the Venn diagram circles to correspond with the images on the cards: Circle A is for people who have dogs, Circle B is for people who have cats, and Circle C is for people who have fish. Then label the Venn diagram segments to identify the images on the cards (make sure your segment numbers match the categories appropriately):

Segment 1 is for people who have only dogs.

Segment 2 is for people who have only cats.

Segment 3 is for people who have only fish.

Segment 4 is for people who have dogs AND cats (no fish).

Segment 5 is for people who have dogs AND fish (no cats).

Segment 6 is for people who have cats AND fish (no dogs).

Segment 7 is for people who have dogs AND cats AND fish.

Have each student write his or her name in the Venn diagram segment corresponding to the cards they have. Alternatively, you can write a representative name in each segment. Then introduce search statements using Boolean operators, and have students identify themselves (raise hands or stand up) if they match the search strategy (e.g., "All those who have a cat OR a fish stand up." "If you have a dog AND a cat, raise your hand." "Hands up all those who have a cat OR a fish, but

NOT a dog."). Be sure to cover all three operators and cases of mixing operators (ANDs and ORs in the same statement). The searching concept can be made more generic or abstract by referring to the sets by letter and the segments by number (e.g., "Which segments would I get with the statement 'A AND B OR C' or 'A AND [B OR C]'?").

Identify specific diagram segments (or combinations of segments), and have students develop search statements that will result in those segments. Those who are able to successfully complete a search statement with appropriate use of Boolean operators (hopefully the entire class) get a small prize. End by discussing how the concepts learned here can be applied to searching in online databases using keywords and Boolean operators.

Evaluation

Students win the game by applying the concept—if they can successfully write a search statement using Boolean logic representing their hand of cards, they win! In talking with students who have participated in the game over the years, many indicate that they had a better understanding of set theory and Boolean operators after working with the game. They appreciated the concrete examples and could relate the examples to the concepts better than just working with standard Venn diagrams with only set letters and numbers.

Tips for Introducing Subject Faculty to the Game

This game is most appropriate for a semester-long information literacy credit class and has not been offered to faculty in subject disciplines.

Research Feud

Christina Sheldon

Introduction

As an instructional variation of the television game show *Family Feud*, *Research Feud* is intended to introduce and reinforce online searching skills, in particular the application of keywords and related terms within a library database.

Objectives

In playing *Research Feud* students will:

- consider and volunteer appropriate synonyms and related terms for a given keyword and
- learn that results retrieved from a database or catalog can differ significantly depending on what terms are input to a search screen.

Information Literacy Competency Standards Addressed

This game addresses this ACRL Information Literacy Competency Standard: #2.

Game Background

Whether hosted by Richard Dawson in the 1970s or Steve Harvey in the 2010s, *Family Feud* is a game show that has pleased generations of television viewers. Balancing individual effort with team collaboration, the game poses a unique analogy for the process of information collection; just as *Family Feud* players attempt to guess the "best," most popular answer hidden on a board of survey responses, so do novice researchers attempt to locate the "best," most perfect resource hidden within a catalog or database. In this instructional version of the game, student-players are asked to guess the most "popular" related terms for a research topic—those key terms that retrieve the most articles on a given topic while searching an appropriate database. In playing the game, students engage in the process of brainstorming appropriate key terms for a search string and also benefit from seeing (when they are revealed) some of the best-advised key terms for a given search topic. Students further begin to recognize that although there may be no singularly correct approach to undertaking a research task, some approaches are—in context—better than others.

Audience

Research Feud is targeted for use in a classroom of 10 to 30 students. The content of the game may be customized for each class by the librarian/instructor, so the game is appropriate for lower-division, upper-division, or graduate-level courses in any discipline for which a research project is assigned and/or as a single class session in a research methods or information literacy course.

Time Required

Total game play of three or more rounds can take 30 to 50 minutes, but partial game play of one or two rounds could occur in 15 minutes and prove beneficial to students.

Materials and Equipment

The game requires:

- a *Research Feud* PowerPoint presentation (see sample in Figures 24.1 through 24.8);
- a computer, video projector, and projection screen;
- a whiteboard or scratch paper for tabulating team points; and
- prizes (such as pencils, stickers, candy, bookmarks, or points for credit).

Preparation

Before game play, the librarian/instructor must customize the *Research Feud* game template in PowerPoint to reflect research topics appropriate for the class (see Figures 24.1–24.8).

Figure 24.1.
Research Feud

Figure 24.2.
Research Feud—Start

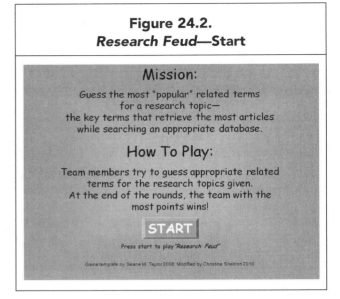

Figure 24.3.
Face-Off Question

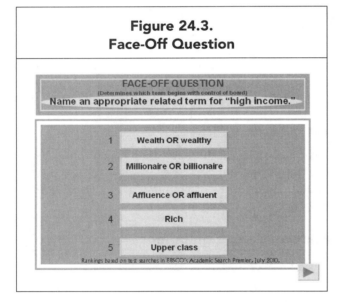

Figure 24.4.
Appropriate Related Terms for "Teens"

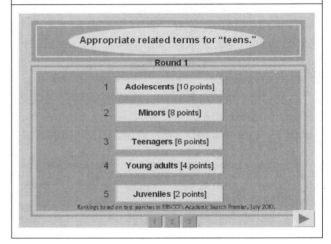

Optimally, the librarian solicits from the visiting class's instructor a sample of the topics upon which class students will perform research. If no samples are available, the librarian must create her or his own model topics, taking efforts to ensure that the model topics are appropriate to the content matter and level of the course. After compiling model topics, the librarian identifies key terms within each of four topics—one for the face-off round and three for remaining rounds of play.

The librarian conducts sample searches within one discipline-appropriate database, inputting considered synonyms and related terms (or those recommended by the database's subject thesaurus) one at a time, conducting a keyword search for each term, reviewing the number of results that each term retrieves, and ranking related terms from those that retrieve the highest number of results to those that retrieve the lowest number. By means of this rough "survey" of a word or phrase's "popularity" as a relevant related term, the librarian constructs a ranking of the top five related terms for any given keyword.

The librarian inputs these ranked terms (and a citation for the database used to retrieve the ranked results, including date of retrieval) into the appropriate game

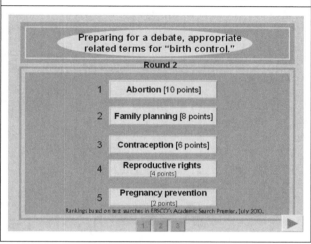

Figure 24.5.
Preparing for a Debate, Appropriate
Related Terms for "Birth Control"

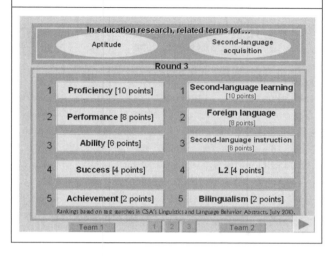

Figure 24.6.
In Education Research,
Related Terms For . . .

Figure 24.7.
Congratulations Team 1

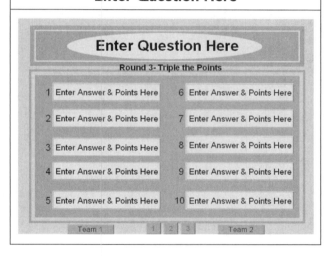

Figure 24.8.
Enter Question Here

slides of the *Research Feud* game template. Upon updating the slides with appropriate key term rankings for the face-off round and three game play rounds, no further modification of the template is necessary.

Playing the Game

Introduce the game by explaining to the students the importance of brainstorming relevant related terms for a research topic and of using an appropriate disci-

pline database to increase the likelihood of retrieving relevant search results. Announce that to practice and reinforce these points the class will be playing a version of *Family Feud*.

Divide the class into two separate groups, identifying one group as Team 1 and the other as Team 2. Ask for a volunteer from each team to start the game by answering the face-off question.

Display the first two slides of the *Research Feud* PowerPoint presentation, which display the game's mission and basic rules of play. Announce what prizes are at stake for the winning team.

To start the first round of the game, two opposing team members "face off" to determine which team will gain control of the board. Tell volunteer team members to respond to instructions when they are displayed and to slap their desktops when they have an appropriate answer. Then display the face-off question by clicking the appropriate slide. Whichever student guesses the answer ranked highest on the board automatically earns control of the board for her or his team. If neither player gives a valid answer, the next member of each team gets a chance to answer, with control again going to the team giving the highest ranked answer. The team who wins the face-off question gains control of the board, and play proceeds to Round One.

Starting with the next team member in line, each team player gets a chance to give one answer. Team members may not confer with one another while in control of the board. The team gets a strike if a player gives an answer that is not on the board or fails to respond within five seconds. Three strikes cause the team to relinquish control of the board, giving the other team one chance to steal the points in the bank by correctly guessing one of the remaining answers.

Allow the second team 10 seconds to confer and offer its guess. If the team guesses a remaining answer correctly, the team receives the points accumulated by the prior team and gains control of the board for the following round. Other options for play are to alternate teams for control of the board or insert additional face-off questions at the start of every round.

After determining who takes the bank of points for a round, any remaining answers are then revealed. Per tradition in *Family Feud*, the assembled class may yell each unrevealed answer in a choral response. At the close of three rounds or partial rounds, as time allows, review the points earned by both teams, identify the game-winning team, and award the winning team its prizes.

Evaluation

Research Feud is intended as a tool for formative assessment, not summative assessment. As such, students may be asked to self-report at the close of the class session and/or game play on their confidence level with the task of brainstorming appropriate related terms for their research topics. Upon reviewing student responses, and as time allows in the discipline-specific course, additional instruction, play, and/or examples may be offered.

Tips for Introducing Subject Faculty to the Game

To introduce the game to subject faculty, stress the instructional advantages offered by games, and note that the research topics used as the foundation for game play are those used by instructors in their classes. You might also attend a subject faculty departmental meeting and demonstrate the game. Once faculty members observe that the game may be tailored to address topics and databases appropriate to higher education, they may be more willing to incorporate the game into a library session.

Twitter and Tagging Your Research Paper

Linda L. Plevak

Introduction

In this activity, students use their texting skills to determine search terms and search strategies for a research paper. It is designed for first-year students in English but can be adapted to use with other disciplines and both higher and lower grade levels.

Objectives

Students will be able to:

- define a manageable focus for a research assignment,
- create several search strategies for their research topic, and
- understand how to narrow or broaden their topic using Boolean operators.

Information Literacy Competency Standards Addressed

This game addresses these ACRL Information Literacy Competency Standards: #1; #2; #5.

Game Background

This game combines what students would rather be doing, texting their friends, with their research assignment. Students are also familiar with online tagging, although they may not fully understand how it relates to finding information. In this activity, students pretend they have already completed their research paper and choose a few descriptive words to tell their friends about their topic. These words are then combined to create effective search strategies. Students apply newly acquired skills to broaden their research topic using truncation and/or to narrow it using the AND Boolean operator.

Audience

The game works successfully with freshman and sophomore students in English, but it can be modified for other grade levels. The activity in the example is designed for a Current Events or Controversial Topic research assignment.

Time Required

Allow one class period of 50 to 80 minutes. You should first demonstrate how to do a search in the online databases. Then distribute the game and give students a defined amount of time to complete the game. The time may vary based on the assignment. For the activity in the example, allow students 10 minutes to come up with search terms, find a relevant article, and cite it correctly.

Materials and Equipment

This game requires:

- a computer lab,
- a projector, and
- an in-class activity, one copy per student (a sample is provided in Figure 25.1).

Preparation

Choose a topic and search strategies that you will use in an online database. Think about related search terms that you could use to tag a research paper on that topic. Test the search strategies in one or more databases, including the library catalog, according to the requirements in the assignment.

A sample of the in-class activity is provided in Figure 25.1. Adapt the activity to fit the assignment by modifying the examples given. You could also customize the assignment by directing the students to a specific database or set of databases (e.g., use the Literature Resource Center to search for a literary criticism assignment). Make a copy of the activity for each student.

Ask the instructor if he or she would be willing to give extra points to students who complete the assign-

Figure 25.1.
Twitter and Tagging Worksheet

Start your research today!

This exercise is designed to help you prepare an effective **Search Strategy**.

Searching in a database is similar to Twitter. When you twitter, you use special vocabulary and very few words. In a database search, you will get the best results if you use "controlled vocabulary" and a limited number of words in your search strategy.

1. Write down your search topic or thesis in a **complete sentence**. (*Example:* Puppy mills in Texas should be outlawed.)

2. Pretend you have already written your research paper. What words would you use to "tag" your paper and send it to a friend?

   Use the Twitter grid below and write down **at least 6 words** or **short phrases** you would use to "tag" your paper. Remember to think of both synonyms and antonyms when you tag. (Example: Puppy mills, dog breeding, purebred breeding, AKC breeding, Texas laws, Texas legislation, legal breeding, illegal breeding.)

   _____

   _____

   _____

   _____

   _____

   _____

3. Take **one** of the terms above and show how you would search using truncation. (*Example:* Breed* will find breed, breeds, breeder, breeders, breeding.)

   _____ will find

   _____

4. Use one of the **electronic databases** and try your search combining two of your search terms. (*Example:* Dog breed* and Texas legislation.)

   What database did you use?

   _____

   How many "results" did you get?

   _____

5. Too many results? Try adding another term.

   Too few results? Try a related word or truncation of the other word.
   (*Example:* Dog breed* and Texas laws.)

   Still too few results? Take away a word.
   (*Example:* Dog breeds and laws.)

6. Look at the abstract or summary of the articles. **Find an article that is relevant** to your research project.

7. **Cite the article in correct MLA format** (or other format as required by your instructor). Some databases will cite the article for you. If so, e-mail both the article and citation to yourself and to your instructor.

   You will receive **two points for an appropriately relevant article** and another **one point for a correct citation** if you complete this activity within the allotted time.

ment by finding and citing an appropriate source in the time allowed. You will need to share the assignment with the instructor and agree on a time limit. Explain that the activity works best if the students come prepared with possible topics or ideas for their research. The teacher should give students their research assignment before the class but should not share the Twitter exercise with them. You will distribute that exercise in class.

Before class, decide who will determine (the librarian or the instructor) if the student has earned the points. If the teacher is willing to grant the extra points, include this information in the instructions on the student worksheet. Otherwise, delete it.

Playing the Game

Demonstrate how to do a search using the AND Boolean operator with your first strategy. Before you continue, talk to students about how they use text and Twitter. Compare how they use a "controlled vocabulary" and few words to communicate. Explain how these same concepts apply to the use of controlled vocabulary and that use of words or short phrases is better than a full sentence (gets better results).

Then tell students they are going to learn how they can text their friends about their research paper. Ask them if they can come up with search terms that are similar to the ones you already demonstrated. Prompt them with one or two examples as needed. Hopefully, they will come up with one more of the search terms you have prepared ahead of time. Use one of their terms or one of your own to do a new search. Point out how the results change when the search terms change. Also show how some databases include related terms and subjects with the results.

Discuss how to narrow a topic using specific concepts with the AND operator. Share examples and have students suggest examples, such as:

- Place (Texas or college):
- Age group (children or teens):
- Population or specific group (women or students):
- Time frame (past three years):
- With an additional topic.

Remind and demonstrate how to add *one search term at a time* when working at narrowing the results. Also, demonstrate a search strategy that yields too few results and show how to broaden the results, such as eliminating a search term or changing to a larger

category. Using one of the search terms, show how truncation can find more results (see Figure 25.1 for a more detailed explanation).

Finally, look at a selection of satisfactory results and ask students how they would choose a relevant source for the topic. Show them how to cite the source in the correct format as required by the instructor.

Give them the exercise with a few verbal instructions. Tell them it is important to use real words (not abbreviations or symbols) and correct spelling when they use the databases. The only exception is using the correct symbol to truncate a word. Tell them they will have a set amount of time (e.g., 10 minutes) to determine the search strategies, complete the search, and e-mail the results. Be sure to mention they will receive points toward their grade if the instructor has agreed.

Evaluation

Students can relate to texting. They are surprised at how something they do every day relates to doing research. The game helps them pause to develop their search strategies before they begin their search. This should correlate to an improvement in results from the database and saving time for the student.

Tips for Introducing Subject Faculty to the Game

This activity is very versatile, because its primary focus is developing appropriate search terms. If a teacher assigns a specific research prompt or topic, use those to create the examples on an activity sheet. When collaborating with instructors, ask if they would be willing to give points to students who complete the game within the allotted time period. Students could either e-mail the instructor or the librarian with their article, putting their research topic in the subject line, to determine if they will earn the extra points. They should also correctly cite the article. Suggested point values are two points for finding a relevant article and one point for correct citation information.

Special Thanks

The author would like to express special thanks to Retired Air Force Major Willis Humiston, Teacher of English at Northeast Lakeview College, who provided the inspiration for this game.

Finding "Just Right" Search Terms for Your Research Assignment

Linda L. Plevak

Introduction

This activity uses a hybrid of digital and traditional tools for teaching students how to select manageable research topics using a YouTube video of a commercial as a prompt for discussion. The game works best with controversial topics and current event assignments, but it is adaptable for other types of research. It is designed for students in upper high school through college sophomores, who are new to the research process. It is appropriate for entry-level English and Reading students, but can be used in other disciplines.

Objectives

Students will be able to:

- determine which search strategy from four choices will give them the best results on select research topics ("best" is defined as a limited number of results that is manageable and relevant to the research topic);
- create their own search strategies for their own research topics; and
- understand how to narrow or broaden their topic using Boolean operators.

Information Literacy Competency Standards Addressed

This game addresses these ACRL Information Literacy Competency Standards: #1; #2.

Game Background

Students have a multitude of distractions that keep them from their schoolwork. This game/lesson plan was conceived just before one of the ultimate distractions, Super Bowl Sunday, which comes with the other distractions, Super Bowl commercials. To introduce the activity, ask the students what they would rather spend time doing—watch the Super Bowl or work on their research assignment? During other times of the year, substitute other popular televised attractions for the Super Bowl when introducing the game. Tell them that the objective of the library instruction session is to save them time on searching for good sources, thereby giving them more time to watch the Super Bowl or whatever else they wish to do with their free time. Then, play the "Just Right" Budweiser beer commercial and ask them what it has to do with their "Current Events/ Controversial Topics" assignment. The answer is: picking a research topic that is "just right," not too broad or too narrow and saves time and effort. The commercial and the promise of more free time gets their attention and makes them think about how to narrow or expand their topic to find results with ease.

Audience

The game is best for 25 to 50 freshman or sophomore students. The students are divided into teams, so you could lower the number of students on each team for a class with less than 20 students. Ideally, there will be four or five teams. If there are more than five teams, you will need to allow more time for discussion and/or shorten the time for the in-class assignment. Successful audiences for this game include entry-level English and Reading students with a research assignment about controversial topics or current events, although it can be modified to use with other assignments and other disciplines.

Time Required

Allow one class period of 50 to 80 minutes for the game and the in-class assignment. Use the first 8 to

10 minutes of class to introduce the game and to play the YouTube video. Give students time to think about the video and how it relates to their assignment. Next, demonstrate how to search and narrow a topic in an electronic database (six to eight minutes). Then, introduce the activity (three minutes) and give students five minutes to determine the "just right" search strategy. Allow three to five minutes for each team to present their findings. Use the remaining time for discussion and the in-class assignment. Ideally, the students will complete the in-class assignment before they leave the session, but it can be completed later if needed.

Materials and Equipment

The game requires:

- inkjet white postcards (5½ × 4¼) or equivalent (perforated note cards that can be sent through a color printer, such as Avery® Postcards for Inkjet Printers 8387, 5-½" × 4¼", white, matte;
- a color printer;
- a computer;
- a projector;
- an in-class assignment, one copy per student (a sample is provided in Figure 26.1); and
- candy or other incentive prizes.

Figure 26.1.
Developing a Research Topic That Is "Just Right"

The success you have in writing a research paper begins with **selecting a topic** that will give you the results you need. If you choose a topic that is too broad, you will end up with information overload. Pick a topic that is too narrow and you may find little or nothing at all. This exercise is designed to find a topic that is "just right."

A. **Select a topic.** Pick a topic you are interested in or curious about. Write it here:

_____

B. **Search.** Try a search in **Academic Search Complete** using your topic. How many results did you get?

_____

More than 100? Narrow your topic by adding a search term. In Advanced Search, apply **AND** to combine your topic with another keyword. How many results did you get? _____

OR

Less than 10? Think of how you can broaden your search by using a related term. It could be the larger category or a similar concept. Try your search. How many results did you get? _____

Here are some ways to narrow your topic. **Add one** of these concepts to your topic (examples in parentheses):

- Place (United States or Texas):
- Age group (youth, elderly):
- Population or specific group (women, students):
- Time frame (past three years):
- With an additional topic.

C. **Choose an article that works.** Look at the results list and **read the abstracts (summaries)** of a few of the articles. Choose one that is appropriate (relevant) for your paper. E-mail it to yourself in MLA format.

Preparation

This activity requires a computer and a projector. Prepare sets of postcards in advance. Be sure to shuffle the four postcards within each set. Keep the four postcards in a set together with a paper clip. Also prepare one copy of the in-class assignment for each student.

Students will be divided into teams for this activity, with five to seven students per team, and each team will need a packet of four postcards. Use the number of students to determine how many sets of postcards are needed. Example: Divide a class of 27 students into 4 teams and prepare 4 sets of postcards.

Select four related search strategies (using the AND Boolean operator) for each set of postcards. Test the results of each search in a general electronic database, such as Academic Search Complete. The search strategies should yield somewhat obvious results in one of the following four categories: (1) too many results, (2) very few results, (3) no results or unrelated results, and (4) "just right" number of results (ideally between 5 and 50 hits, but this will vary). Here are some suggested searches for the note cards (answers in parentheses—do not include the answers on the cards):

- Genetically modified food (too broad)
- Genetically modified food AND health (too broad)
- Genetically modified strawberries (too narrow)
- Genetically modified AND berries ("just right")
- Capital punishment (too broad)
- Death penalty (too broad)
- Death penalty AND Texas AND women ("just right")
- Death penalty AND Texas AND juveniles (too narrow)
- Animal cruelty (too broad)
- Animal cruelty AND pit bulls ("just right")
- Animal cruelty AND Chihuahuas (too narrow)
- Animal cruelty AND dogs (too broad)
- Environment (too broad)
- Environment AND water (too broad)
- Environment AND bottled water ("just right")
- Water AND Ozarka (too narrow)

Pick one additional topic and a final set of search strategies that you will use to demonstrate the concepts of too many, too few, and "just right" results. Test the results in the same online database.

Create a document and use postcard template 8387 (Avery template for Microsoft Word). Type in the search strategies you found, one per card, four (related searches) per sheet. Put a border around each postcard. Choose a color for the border and the words (one color per set). The color for each set will keep the postcards organized when handing them out to the students during class.

Print each set of search strategies on the postcards. Tear along perforations. Keep the sets together (paperclip if needed). Tip: Scramble the order of the four cards within each set, so students will need to read and think about each one.

Choose an appropriate "Too Light or Too Heavy" Bud Lite commercial from YouTube. Save the URL in your teaching artifact (wiki, LibGuide, etc.). If possible, embed the link under the phrase, "What does this have to do with research topics?" Here is one example: The Patron—Too Light or Too Heavy? http://www.youtube.com/watch?v=3w5ZsqAqo_A.

Playing the Game

Tell the students you are going to play a YouTube video. Their task is to determine what it has to do with research topics. Play the video. Afterwards, ask the question, "What does this have to do with research topics?" Allow students to guess the answer. Give them hints; tell them the answer has nothing to do with the product, beer, or with a controversial topic, such as drunk driving. If they need an additional clue, tell them it has to do with the slogan.

The correct answer is that sometimes we pick topics that are "too light" or too narrow of a focus, while other times we pick "too heavy" topics, those that have too many results and are too broad for the research assignment.

Next, tell them you are going to show them how they can combine terms (using Boolean operators) in an electronic database to get results that are "just right" for their research. Use the topic and search strategies you prepared, and demonstrate how to add search terms to narrow the results to a manageable topic. Also, show an example that gives little or no results. Explain how it is important to add search terms one at a time when narrowing the results.

Tell them you have prepared sets of topics with search terms. Their task is to determine which topic in the set is "just right" to research. Divide the students into teams. Ask one member of each team to pick a set of four postcards. Tell them they will have five minutes to categorize the search strategies into "too heavy" (too broad), "too light" (too narrow), or "just right." Ask them to pick a leader to share the results with the class. Students who get the right answers will receive candy or other incentive as a prize. Allow them to use databases to test their terms.

After five minutes, ask the team leaders to share their results. As each group shares their answers, encourage them to discuss why some of the search strategies did or did not work well. The group gets candy if they have determined which search strategy works best as a research topic.

After all the groups have presented their answers, project the results of one of the "just right" search strategies on the screen. Ask students which article or articles they would choose for their assignment and why. Discuss how to determine if a source is relevant, including reading the abstract, determining if it is an actual article and not a book review, or other factors.

Discuss how the topics were narrowed using specific concepts and the AND operator. Share examples or have students suggest examples, such as:

- Place (United States or Texas):
- Age group (youth, elderly):
- Population or specific group (women, students):
- Time frame (past three years):
- With an additional topic.

After the discussion, give students the in-class assignment to complete, where they will work on narrowing or broadening their own topics.

Evaluation

"Just right" is a subjective term, and the game is actually most effective when students disagree about what is a "just right" search strategy. As students present their results, ask them to discuss their results and how they determined the "just right" answer. The game encourages students to discuss what does or does not work when searching. You can also discuss how searching is a "moveable feast." If something is currently in the news, it will probably garner more results in a database.

Tips for Introducing Subject Faculty to the Game

Assignments where students choose their own research topics or where they are given broad research topics are a good fit for the game. When collaborating with the instructor, explain how the activity helps students narrow their focus. Do mention you will be using a beer commercial, just in case there are any objections. Usually teachers are pleased with the concept of using a popular commercial to engage students in their research assignment. If the teacher gives you the topics, use those topics to create your search strategies for the note cards.

PART VI

Evaluating the Quality and Authority of Information Resources Games

This section consists of Games 27–35. These games challenge students to evaluate the quality and authority of information sources.

Evaluating Information with the *Trivial Pursuit* Game

Charlene Thompson

Introduction

This game challenges students to find the answer to a trivia question from a *Trivial Pursuit* game card and to evaluate their information source.

Objectives

At the end of the session students will be able to:

- use criteria (authority, audience, accuracy, currency, objectivity) to evaluate information and
- distinguish between scholarly journals and popular magazines.

Information Literacy Competency Standards Addressed

This game addresses these ACRL Information Literacy Competency Standards: #1; #3.

Game Background

Trivial Pursuit, produced by Hasbro, is a game in which players are asked trivia questions. If players answer the trivia questions correctly, they advance their positions toward winning. There have been many different editions of *Trivial Pursuit*. This lesson is based on the 2009 *Trivial Pursuit Team* edition.

If time allows, it can be adapted so that students play the entire game. The *Trivial Pursuit Team* edition even includes 30 cards that can be customized to include library-specific questions. In this lesson, however, only the question cards are used. The question cards provide an easy and fun way to begin discussions about evaluating information sources.

Audience

This lesson was originally intended for classes of less than 30 undergraduate college students, although it may appeal to high school students as well.

Time Required

This game can be played in approximately 60 minutes.

Materials and Equipment

The game requires:

- a computer with Internet access for each student;
- a computer with Internet access and a projector for the instructor;
- a dry-erase board, markers, and eraser;
- directions written on a large sheet of paper or on an extra dry-erase board;
- *Trivial Pursuit* question cards;
- Worksheet One (see Figure 27.1);
- Worksheet Two (see Figure 27.2);
- Evaluating Information Handout (see Figure 27.3);
- Print examples of scholarly journals and popular magazines (optional); and
- YouTube video about scholarly journals and popular magazines (optional).

Preparation

Each student needs one *Trivial Pursuit* question card and one copy each of the worksheets and handout. Cover the answers on the cards with sticky notes. On the large sheet of paper or an extra dry-erase board, write the following directions:

1. Pick a question on the card.
2. Find the answer.
3. Remember where you found the answer (write it down if necessary).
4. You have until [insert time].

Playing the Game

Hand each student a *Trivial Pursuit* card as they enter the classroom. Instruct them to follow the directions

---

Figure 27.1.
Trivial Pursuit **Worksheet One**

How do you know whether you can trust information you read, see, or hear? Write your response on the lines below:

_____

_____

_____

_____

_____

_____

_____

_____

Figure 27.2.
Trivial Pursuit **Worksheet Two**

What is the answer you found?

_____

How did you find the answer?

_____

Where did you find the answer?

_____

Did you get the same answer as what was on

the card? _____

How well does the source you found your answer in do in the following areas and why?

	Poor			Excellent
Authority	1	2	3	4
Why?				
Audience	1	2	3	4
Why?				
Accuracy	1	2	3	4
Why?				
Currency	1	2	3	4
Why?				
Objectivity	1	2	3	4
Why?				

---

on the board. When all of the students have found an answer to a trivia question, begin the session by welcoming them and introducing yourself. Hand out Worksheet One that has the question, "How do you know whether you can trust information you read, see, or hear?" Give students a minute to think about and write down their answers.

Through class discussion, gather their answers and write them on the board. Group their answers on the board into five categories (Authority, Audience, Accuracy, Currency, and Objectivity), but do not write the categories on the board.

Discuss and introduce each of the five evaluating information categories. As you discuss and explain the categories, refer to the answers the students had provided on Worksheet One and show how their answers fit into the categories. Discuss the differences between scholarly journals and popular magazines.

Instruct students to take the sticky notes off of their *Trivial Pursuit* cards to see if they found the correct answer. Hand out Worksheet Two and have students

fill in their answers. After students have completed the worksheet, read each of the questions, ask students for their answers, and lead discussions when appropriate.

Hand out the Evaluating Information Handout at the end of the class so that students can refer to the categories later. As a conclusion, encourage students to think about the categories as they use information sources in the future. Collect Worksheet Two as students leave the classroom.

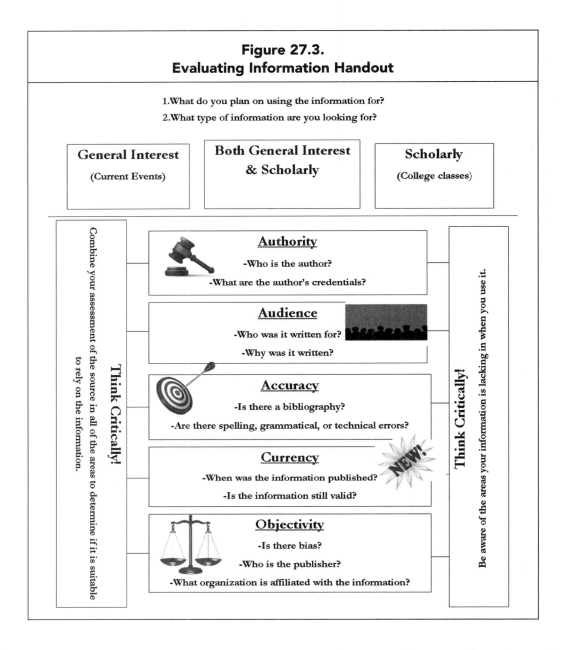

Figure 27.3.
Evaluating Information Handout

1. What do you plan on using the information for?
2. What type of information are you looking for?

General Interest
(Current Events)

Both General Interest & Scholarly

Scholarly
(College classes)

Combine your assessment of the source in all of the areas to determine if it is suitable to rely on the information.

Think Critically!

Authority
-Who is the author?
-What are the author's credentials?

Audience
-Who was it written for?
-Why was it written?

Accuracy
-Is there a bibliography?
-Are there spelling, grammatical, or technical errors?

Currency
-When was the information published?
-Is the information still valid?

NEW!

Objectivity
-Is there bias?
-Who is the publisher?
-What organization is affiliated with the information?

Think Critically!

Be aware of the areas your information is lacking in when you use it.

Evaluation

Evaluate the lesson's success by reviewing Worksheet Two. Look at the sources where students found the answers to their questions, the scores they gave sources in each of the categories, and their answers for why they gave the sources the scores they did. If students gave sources appropriate evaluation scores and reasoning, they understood and the lesson was a success. Make comments on all of the worksheets in order to reinforce the lesson objectives. Return the worksheets either directly to the students or to the teacher who can forward them to the students.

Tips for Introducing Subject Faculty to the Game

If the lesson is introduced in a face-to-face group meeting, give the subject faculty the opportunity to find an answer to a question on a *Trivial Pursuit* card. Ask the group what sources they used to find their answers. Ask them what sources they think the students would use and then explain the lesson. If the lesson is introduced electronically, provide one trivia question to spark interest and then introduce the lesson.

Stock and Trade
Cynthia Akers and Caleb Puckett

Introduction

Stock and Trade teaches students how to evaluate the information they may encounter online during the course of their research papers or projects. This game is quite adaptable and can be used to teach higher order information literacy skills for any discipline and can be played by both undergraduate and graduate students.

Objectives

Students playing *Stock and Trade* will be able to:

- discuss essential criteria for evaluating the quality and applicability of online information;
- thoughtfully engage with a range of online information that is representative of materials encountered in content- and context-specific research scenarios;
- form a foundation for sound decision making regarding the relative value of information and its relevance to specific research scenarios;
- discuss the relative value of information as it applies to chosen research scenarios; and
- apply critical thinking skills to the assessment of information and visiting the library.

Information Literacy Competency Standards Addressed

This game addresses this ACRL Information Literacy Competency Standard: #3.

Game Background

It is well documented in information literacy literature that students struggle with the more advanced concepts of properly evaluating information for incorporation into their research papers and other projects. While students may readily identify the quality and usefulness of some sources, such as the ubiquitously maligned Wikipedia article, they may have difficulty evaluating the subtle but significant differences among less obviously problematic sources. The focus of *Stock and Trade*, then, is to actively promote critical thinking in situations where sources would seem, on a surface level, to have a similar value. *Stock and Trade* employs Jim Kapoun's (1998) criteria for evaluating webpages as a means to address information students might typically encounter online during their research. Kapoun's criteria are adapted into a gaming rubric that addresses the complexities of evaluation and gives groups of students a chance to examine information in authentic content- and context-specific research scenarios.

Audience

This game is appropriate for both undergraduate and graduate students, regardless of major.

Time Required

The game takes approximately 50 to 75 minutes to complete, depending on the number of students involved and the length of the accompanying discussions.

Materials and Equipment

The game requires:

- a handout for each student that contains the game instructions (see Figure 28.1);
- a handout for each student that presents five different research scenarios and five sets of evaluative rubrics/guiding questions;
- an interactive whiteboard for the instructor to review selected sources online and display his or her ratings to the class (this can be optional); and
- information literacy stock certificates to be used as prizes.

Figure 28.1.
Stock and Trade Instructions

For this class activity, you will work with a group of fellow students. Your group will be given a research scenario for a specific class assignment, a bibliography of four articles that might be used for that assignment, and an evaluative rubric. Your group's task is to take stock of each article.

As a group, go online to locate the articles listed in the bibliography and utilize the rubric to examine each of them. Consider the criteria of authority, accuracy, objectivity, currency, and coverage in the context of the topic for the assignment. After addressing all of the criteria, rate the articles and briefly explain how the five criteria informed your ratings.

Your group will have seven minutes to rate the articles for a given scenario. You will then be asked to trade the scenario and bibliography with the next group. You will continue trading until your group has reviewed all of the scenarios and rated all of the bibliographies given to the class. "Stock certificates," which may be redeemed for food or drinks at the library café, will be awarded to groups who most accurately rate their articles.

Preparation

Develop five content- and context-specific research scenarios, and assign ratings to all sources contained within the bibliographies.

Playing the Game

Begin with a brief discussion of the challenges of evaluating information and an introduction to the evaluative process. As part of the discussion, highlight scenarios that reflect common topics for research in specific courses at the university. Review Kapoun's (1998) criteria, and then divide students into five groups. Give each group the same evaluative rubric and a different research scenario. Each scenario presents a description of the topic or information need for the paper or project and contains a bibliography of four sources that may or may not be considered appropriate for the group's particular research needs.

Give students a copy of the game instructions (see Figure 28.1). The basic concepts of game play are actually included in the title, *Stock and Trade*. Groups of students will take stock of each of their sources through formal evaluations. After the groups have completed their scenarios, they trade them with other groups. In particular, students in each group will be asked to address a series of questions that helps them to formulate an informed opinion regarding the quality and applicability of each source in their bibliographies.

The last question in the series asks students to rate the overall suitability of each source using their rubric and to briefly explain the rationale for their rating. In each instance, students will need to examine clues such as the date of publication, author's credentials, and scope of the article before they assign a rating. While some of the sources may be valid in and of themselves, such as websites from credible organizations or peer-reviewed journal articles and books from university presses, the key is to determine the worth of each source relative to the exact scenario at hand. After approximately 7 to 10 minutes, each group will pass its scenario to another group in round-robin fashion until every group has had an opportunity to address each scenario.

Before playing the game, you will have assigned ratings to each source listed in all scenarios. At the conclusion of the game, ask each group to reveal its ratings for the sources contained within a certain scenario. Then display your ratings for the sources and encourage students to discuss any differences in their ratings. Award one credit per source to groups whose ratings match or most resemble yours. Every member of the winning group(s) gets an information literacy "stock certificate" that is valued at one share, which is worth a 10-cent credit at the library café.

In a best-case scenario, each individual in the group would accumulate 20 credits (5 scenarios; 4 sources per scenario), which would amount to $2.00 off any food or drink item at the café. In all likelihood, every participant would receive some credits to apply to discounts at the café, which means that every student would be rewarded for learning how to evaluate information. These credits would, of course, also encourage students to come back to the library.

Evaluation

Give students a short survey regarding their impressions of the game as a learning tool and form of entertainment.

Tips for Introducing Subject Faculty to the Game

Stock and Trade can be used to teach the evaluation of information in all subject areas. Subject faculty may be introduced to the game through their respective librarian liaisons. Librarians should explain that the game will work as a general, standalone exercise for library instruction and as a component of an existing research assignment for a particular course.

References

Kapoun, Jim. 1998. "Teaching Undergrads Web Evaluation: A Guide for Library Instruction." *College & Research Libraries News* 59, no. 7 (July/August): 522–523.

Sources Smackdown: Effectively Evaluating Information Sources

Susan Avery

Introduction

Sources Smackdown is a card game that addresses the need for students to critically evaluate their information sources. Using a "deck" of cards devoted to resources for a specific topic, students apply evaluative criteria to smack down their sources, determining the most credible ones for their assignments.

Objectives

Students will be able to:

- apply evaluative criteria to a variety of resources in order to determine which sources are appropriate for usage in academic research and
- critically examine sources in order to determine for what purposes a particular source is most appropriate.

Information Literacy Competency Standards Addressed

This game addresses this ACRL Information Literacy Competency Standard: #3.

Game Background

The *2009 ECAR Study of Undergraduate Students and Information Technology* notes that the proliferation of web-based information "alters the student's relationship to the familiar physical trapping of a higher education" (Smith, Salaway, and Caruso, 2009). The same conclusion can be applied to the sources students use in their research. The physical cues inherent in print journals and popular magazines are often not present, as libraries opt to provide online-only access to an increasing number of resources. Noting that an increasing number of students arrive at college never having used print periodicals while heavily relying on resources such as Google and Wikipedia is further evidence of the need for a new means to teach students about sources. "Is it a magazine or a journal?," the question that librarians have long posed to students as they evaluate their information, must be expanded to include additional information formats such as webpages, blogs, videos, and digital images. An additional challenge facing librarians is discovering how to best engage students while teaching evaluation skills. *Sources Smackdown* was created in response to these concerns.

Sources Smackdown is a game that consists of decks of cards, each devoted to a specific topic. Each card contains an image of a source retrieved from a database or search engine. During the course of the game play students apply evaluative criteria while examining each source to make the determination as to whether or not a source should be considered. This game has proven to be successful with undergraduate students who are seeking greater confidence in their ability to evaluate and determine the credibility of their sources.

Audience

This game is particularly appropriate for first-year students who are being introduced to source evaluation and beginning to apply criteria to help them determine a source's credibility and its role in academic research. The game can also be used to examine resources and determine in what situation a particular source might (or might not) be appropriate. For example, in communication classes students may be encouraged to select sources that are written in a language easily understood by their audience rather than articles written with significant scholarly jargon. However, when writing a research paper in a history class they may be encouraged to focus exclusively on scholarly sources.

Time Required

Fifteen minutes is generally sufficient to play the game.

Materials and Equipment

The game requires:

- decks of cards devoted to a series of popular research topics (as described in "Preparation") and
- ideally a computer and projector so the librarian can display a source for the entire class to examine.

Preparation

The most preparation goes into creating the decks of cards. Here are some guidelines:

1. Select topics for each deck of cards. "Hot topics" tend to work best, as they are likely to be covered in a variety of types of information sources. The game is played in groups of three to four students, so select enough topics to accommodate the largest class you teach.
2. Search for articles about the topics using library databases and search engines such as Google. From the searches select a variety of sources that represent the following categories. Six sources for each individual topic are suggested.
   a. Scholarly journals
   b. Popular magazines
   c. Credible webpages, such as government sites
   d. Questionable and clearly biased web sites
3. Create screen captures of each of the selected sources. Sources that will fit well on 8 ½ × 11 paper will work best.
4. Select a design for the backs of each deck's cards. (It is best to have a different design for each deck.) Suggestion: Look for interested art students to create unique, interesting, and colorful designs. (For example, the artwork for the back of the Undergraduate Library cards we used was created by Jovanny Varela, student, School of Art + Design, University of Illinois at Urbana-Champaign. Figures 29.1 and 29.2 (p. 92) show the front and back of a sample Undergraduate Library card.)
5. Use a program such as Microsoft Publisher to create the cards in each deck, matching topics to card faces.

6. Print and laminate the cards.
7. Create a handout that contains guidelines for evaluating sources. The information and guidelines should be appropriate for your instruction program and institution. (Online versions of a sample handout can be seen at http://www.library.illinois.edu/ugl/howdoi/pertype.html and http://www.library.illinois.edu/ugl/howdoi/pertypeonline.html.)

Playing the Game

In your introduction, discuss the kinds of sources students will encounter in their research and the qualities of the sources they should use in their academic writing. Examine and discuss the handout outlining evaluative criteria, particularly noting the characteristics unique to specific resource types. Stress the importance of multiple criteria in determining source type and selection; for many students this will be a new expectation. It can be helpful to share physical copies of the various resource types.

**Figure 29.1.
Card Back Image**

To play the game, divide the students into groups of three or four. Distribute a deck of cards to each group. It is now time to smack down sources! Using the evaluative guidelines, have each group examine their cards and arrange them in order of least to most credible. Then ask students some questions about their sources. The exact questions will depend on the individual course and/or assignment; here are some examples:

- Which source is most credible and why?
- Which source is most likely from a magazine?
- Which source is most appropriate if you are giving a speech?
- Which source(s) has no role in academic research and why?

As closure to the game, have students discuss what they observed and learned from examining a variety of resources. Ask them, either individually or in groups, to compile a list of the most important points they learned while playing the game.

Evaluation

Student assessment takes place on several levels. First, did each group correctly smack down the sources? Were they able to identify scholarly sources, magazine articles, webpages, and biased information? Second, did they adequately identify the criteria they used to determine the category and type of source for each card?

Self-evaluation on the part of the instructor will, in many ways, be reflected in the student assessments. Was it clear the students understood the purpose of the game? Were students engaged in the activity? Were they able to adequately describe source type and the criteria utilized in making their determinations? If the responses to questions such as these do not produce the desired answer, self-reflection will help determine how this activity might be introduced and played differently.

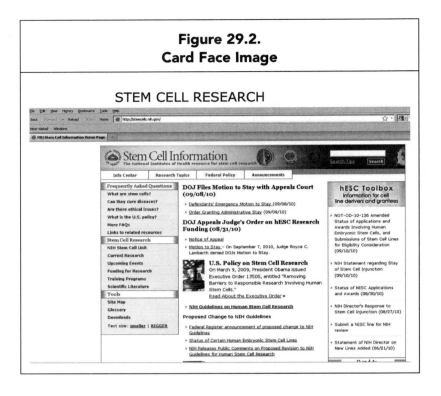

**Figure 29.2.
Card Face Image**

Tips for Introducing Subject Faculty to the Game

Concerns about the resources students use in their research are common among faculty. The proliferation of online sources and easy access to them means that students often lack awareness of the common physical cues of which faculty are well aware. The necessity for developing more realistic means of teaching students evaluation skills, presenting them with resources in the same context in which they encounter them, is crucial. A game such as *Sources Smackdown* not only provides this but also actively engages students in critical source evaluation.

References

Smith, Shannon D., Gail Salaway, and Judith B. Caruso. 2009. *The ECAR Study of Undergraduate Students and Information Technology.* Boulder: Educause Center for Applied Research. http://net.educause.edu/ir/library/pdf/ers0906/rs/ERS0906w.pdf.

Sharing Stories: Research, Technology, and Listening to Student Knowledge

Christine Cusick

Introduction

This game allows undergraduate students to "process" the idea of how they can achieve mastery in a strange environment (research libraries) with a strange language (specialized terminology). Through the use of rhetorical techniques, they practice as a group to discover their own competence at becoming an information education expert.

Objectives

Students will be able to:

- retrieve data from the Internet,
- distinguish reliable and task-appropriate material, and
- identify and locate themselves within a discourse community.

Information Literacy Competency Standards Addressed

This game addresses these ACRL Information Literacy Competency Standards: #1; #2; #3; #4; #5.

Game Background

Instructors of writing do well to be attentive to the ideas and attitudes that inhibit student enthusiasm for and success with engaging in the research process. Particularly in first-year writing classes, students generally feel disoriented by their first encounters with academic discourse and even more alienated by the specialized language that they encounter when immersing themselves in a specific research topic. Too often, this vulnerable position discourages students and in some cases convinces them that they do not have a voice to contribute to academic conversations. In this game, students are empowered as they are asked to identify a topic that they feel that they are an expert on. This topic

may or may not be related to their student life; in most cases, it is not. In the past, students have chosen topics ranging from punk rock to carpentry, from defensive football plays to auto mechanics. Either individually or in collaborative searches, students are asked to find a credible "source" on their topic and then to identify the terminology in the source that they feel is specific to the field. The instructor then asks students to evaluate the relevance and quality of the sources they are finding. As they do, the students often begin to realize that they have a body of knowledge that the general public does not.

Audience

This assignment is designed for first-year writing students. It has been used to introduce Basic Composition students to the rhetorical situation and to introduce students in research writing classes to principles of information literacy.

Time Required

Because this game is designed as a cursory introduction to discourse analysis, it can be completed within a 75-minute class period, including the introduction, game play, a peer quiz forum, and final class discussion. The game, however, is designed to initiate a sustained discussion of how we evaluate the quality of online sources as well as how researchers determine the purpose and audience for their sources.

Materials and Equipment

The game requires:

- Internet access via laptops, cell phones, desktops, or iPads (if multiple technological tools are used, incorporate a comparison and contrast of the tools into the final discussion); and

- a computer or pen/pencil and paper for students to take notes as they research and present to their peers.

Preparation

This game best serves a research writing class when completed in the early stages of the research process. Ideally, the students are already familiar with concepts such as audience, thesis, appeals, and claims so that the task will invite them to apply their understanding of these to topics that they are already familiar with. In most cases, students already will have a few "go-to" websites for their areas of expertise. And so, this activity requires them to evaluate a source in order to determine the expert terminology.

Playing the Game

Provide an overview of a previously discussed research assignment and readings. Ask students to collaboratively define the word "expert," reaching a consensus definition. Based on this definition, invite students to brainstorm their own areas of "expertise."

Using their chosen research tool, they will search the Internet for a single concise "source" that they feel is credible on the topic of their expertise. This source might be an academic article, an informative website, or a video with an evaluative interpretation. The only criteria for their selection are that as an expert on this topic they deem the source credible and that the source is concise enough for them to evaluate within the class period. At this point, walk around to each student, asking them about their criteria for credibility.

After they have chosen the source, students are to make two lists of vocabulary. One list of words should pertain to the topic but should be accessible to a general audience. The second list should be words that pertain to the topic but that they deem as specialized, known only to themselves and fellow experts.

Direct the students to meet in small groups of three. In these small groups they will quiz one another on the terminology they have identified, determining whether or not they were accurate in their assessments. If their peers are able to define the "general audience" terminology, the student earns one point for each word. If students do not know the "specialized terminology," they earn one point for each of these words. Because of the nature of this point system, it is important that

the small groups do not include two "experts" on one topic. Students should keep track of how many terms they accurately categorized, and the small group that collectively tallies the most points earns five extra credit points.

At the end, regroup as a community and discuss the assignment. Students will inevitably have had some disagreements about how well their peers were able to define their terms, and the hope is that these conversations will lead students to a fuller understanding of the interpretive processes that we hone and enact through research. The following questions will help students to see the connections between the game and its objectives:

- What criteria did you use to choose your sources? How did the confines of the assignment affect your selection? How did your history with this topic affect your selection?
- Was it difficult to categorize the terminology? How do you account for this difficulty?
- How did your peers' familiarity, or lack thereof, with the topic influence your explanation of the terms?
- Did this exercise change how you think about technological tools in the research process?
- Will this experience affect how you encounter a new or unfamiliar research area?

Evaluation

This game has been evaluated through individual conferences with students and self-assessment, end-of-semester essays. Students often describe the interpretive layers of the research process as "overwhelming." Through individual conferences with students, the instructor tries to understand what they find to be the most daunting element of this endeavor. Repeatedly, students report that they don't feel as if they have anything to contribute, that they are uninspired by their topics, or that they don't know how to determine a worthwhile source. This game gives students an opportunity to share their knowledge on topics that they care about and reminds them what it feels like to be invested in a topic. Students thus begin to see that they are capable of learning about a new field, for they were undoubtedly once novices of their areas. Moreover, students realize that they evaluate sources every day, making decisions about which websites to read, which YouTube videos to view. The criteria that they use in their day-to-day decisions can in fact be adapted for their academic research. Finally, by sharing their expertise with their peers, and by debating how well their peers are defining their terms, students recognize that the research process itself can be a form of inquiry. They are creating knowledge not just when they sit down to draft the paper, but even as they work through the process of what they want to communicate.

At the same time, this game is a means of fostering the writing community of our classroom. Students are invited to share their areas of expertise with their peers and in many cases this area of expertise is a topic that they care deeply about. It can help to assume the role of an amateur, giving students the chance to witness the ways in which the instructor's expertise is also limited. For students who can sometimes feel disconnected from a writing teacher who is constantly critiquing and evaluating their ideas and communication skills, this role shift can enhanced the openness of the writing community. In their self-assessment essays at the end of the semester, students often reflect that they felt their opinions were valued. Pedagogically,

such an atmosphere reaps numerous rewards, but as teachers of research writing, we know that it is crucial that students feel that they have something valuable to contribute to the conversations of their academic and social communities and that they have the information literacy tools with which to do so. This faith gives their research explorations and writing value that far exceeds the first-year writing classroom.

Tips for Introducing Subject Faculty to the Game

To introduce this game to faculty from all disciplines, focus on the importance of recognizing topic- and area-specific language and discourse and ask them if they have noticed students' seemingly indiscriminant acceptance of Internet sources as reliable. Explain that this exercise is a way to honor these differences and concerns without allowing them to alienate us from one another. Moreover, it is valuable to note that within Composition Studies, research in the subfield of Literacy Studies supports the value in asking students to identify their own fields of literacy.

Quality Counts: Evaluating Internet Sources

Maura A. Smale

Introduction

This low-tech, single-session classroom game engages undergraduate students in learning how to evaluate Internet sources by inviting them to critically examine websites and rewarding them for meeting evaluation criteria.

Objectives

After playing *Quality Counts*, students will be able to:

- understand the importance of critically evaluating information used in their coursework;
- identify appropriate criteria (such as relevance, accuracy, expertise, currency, and objectivity) for evaluating information sources;
- evaluate Internet information sources using appropriate criteria; and
- recognize that reference librarians can provide assistance with evaluating information and other research questions.

Information Literacy Competency Standards Addressed

This game addresses this ACRL Information Literacy Competency Standard: #3.

Game Background

The ability to successfully evaluate information for use in college coursework is a core information literacy competency. Evaluating sources, especially Internet sources, is crucial for student success in college and their careers and is important for lifelong learning. Students have uneven exposure to media and information literacy instruction in their K–12 educational experiences and enter college with a wide range of knowledge about the quality of Internet sources. Because many students prefer to start their research on the Internet, evaluating Internet sources is a key aspect of information literacy instruction.

Participation in the CUNY Games Network, a group of faculty and staff across the City University of New York who are interested in the pedagogical applications of games and game mechanics, inspired this game. Much current research has shown that both digital and nondigital games can be successfully incorporated into educational contexts to increase student learning. Using games for instruction is an active learning strategy that acknowledges multiple learning styles and encourages student engagement. Playing a game in the classroom is fun, too, for both students and instructors.

Quality Counts is designed to teach college students how to evaluate Internet sources by encouraging them to critically examine websites and rewarding them for meeting evaluation criteria. *Quality Counts* has a modular, flexible game play structure that can easily be adapted to different instructional contexts. The game can be used by librarians teaching sessions that range from the traditional one-shot to credit-bearing courses. *Quality Counts* may also be of interest to faculty in other departments across campus who seek to sharpen their students' competencies in thinking critically about information sources.

Audience

Quality Counts can accommodate classes with different numbers of students by varying the size of student groups. A maximum of 5 groups of students per 75-minute class session is best.

This game was designed for first- and second-year undergraduates but can also be useful in classes for upper-level undergraduates and possibly high school students. Because the information sources examined in the game are freely accessible on the Internet, variation in students' ability to evaluate sources can be accommodated in the selection of a the search topic. Use topics of lesser complexity for first- and second-year undergraduates and topics of increasing sophistication for more advanced students.

Time Required

Depending on the size of the student group, *Quality Counts* can be played in as little as 50 minutes. For one complete game to be played with a class of 20 students divided into 5 groups of 4 students each, 75 minutes is recommended.

Materials and Equipment

The game requires:

- a whiteboard/blackboard (with markers/chalk);
- assorted small candies, stickers, or other prizes for the winners;
- a computer with Internet access for each group (preferably in a computer lab or computer-equipped classroom); and
- ideally an instructor computer with Internet access and projector so that the sources gathered by students can be displayed to the entire class.

Preparation

Before the session, decide on the topic that students will use to search for information sources. If the game is played in a one-shot course session, it is best to use a topic relevant to course content. If the game is played in a more general setting, for example, a library orientation or research workshop, a current topic may be of greatest interest to the students. To provide the best chance for a wide variety of websites to be returned in search engine results, select a topic that is both newsworthy and a subject of scholarly research.

Playing the Game

Introduce the game play in the first 15 minutes. Begin by announcing to students that today they will play a game about finding quality sources of information on the Internet. Be certain to stress that it is important to evaluate *all* of the sources that they use in their research projects and papers. Remind students that different information sources are used for different purposes. For this game, students should assume that they are searching for sources for an assignment that requires only Internet resources.

Tell the students that they will be divided into groups and assigned a research topic and that each group will need to find two quality Internet sources on the topic. Write the research topic on the board for students to see during the game play.

Determine the criteria for quality through active discussion with the students. Ask them: "What is quality? What do you look for to determine whether you've found a quality source?" Encourage discussion, prompting with questions when necessary, until all students and the instructor agree on three criteria for evaluation to use in the game (e.g., expertise, accuracy, objectivity, currency, etc.). Write these three criteria on the board for students to refer to during game play.

Divide the students into groups, and explain the rules. Each group will search the Internet to find two quality sources that satisfy as many of the three criteria as possible. Each criterion is worth one point, and the group with the highest score wins. Explain the criteria thoroughly; for example, students will not be awarded a point simply for finding the author or group responsible for the source but must determine whether the author/group is an expert on the research topic. It can be helpful to write the game rules on the board or display them on a slide so students can refer to them while searching.

Allow students 15 minutes to search for and evaluate sources. Circulate throughout the room to answer their questions. Also spend some time searching the topic using a variety of search engines (e.g., Google, Yahoo!, Bing, and Ask.com) so you are familiar with the sources they may select.

After 15 minutes, ask students to stop searching. Have each group in turn share the websites they selected and their self-scores. Use the instructor computer to display the websites that students selected, and ask each group to justify their self-score for each source. Discuss the scores with the rest of the class— do all students agree with each group's scores? Why or why not?

When each group's score has been agreed on and discussed, write the scores on the board. Then move on to the next group until all students have had a chance to present their scores. Tally up the winners, and distribute the prizes.

In closing, remind students about the importance of evaluating all information sources, and ask them if they have any questions. If students ran short on time, use this as an opportunity to discuss quality versus quantity. That is, are fewer sources of better quality worth more than a larger number of dubious quality sources? Before they leave, remind students to stop by the reference desk or ask a librarian whenever they have research questions, including questions about evaluating Internet or library sources.

Evaluation

Assessment methods can range from informal to formal and vary in the amount of class time required. For an informal assessment, record observations of student reactions to the game play right after the class is over. Include the websites found to serve as a record of topics and websites discussed in each class.

A more formal assessment method that does not require extensive time in class is the One Minute Paper. Ask students to take one minute to write their answers to two open-ended questions. For example:

- What is the most valuable thing you learned in today's class?
- What one question about evaluating Internet sources do you still have that was not answered today?

Student answers to these questions can guide revisions in game play.

Students can also be asked to fill out a short evaluation form to gather some of their impressions about the game. From past experience, a majority responded that they enjoyed playing *Quality Counts* and that they had gained skill in evaluating Internet informa-

tion by playing it. When asked whether they preferred traditional classroom instruction or using a game in class, the results were more mixed and suggest that a combination of traditional and game-based instruction is an effective teaching strategy. Based on these results, a single-session classroom game like *Quality Counts* can be an appropriate way to integrate games into a research-based course.

Tips for Introducing Subject Faculty to the Game

Quality Counts is a game with broad utility across disciplines and can be used in any class in which students are expected to use the Internet to research sources for their projects and papers. Some faculty may be reluctant to use a game in class, especially those who do not play games themselves. However, this nondigital game requires only a few minutes to learn and is easy to incorporate into classes. It may be helpful to offer to play a round of *Quality Counts* with faculty to introduce to them the game.

For librarians and faculty who are interested in games in education, *Quality Counts* is a good starting point. It requires no special equipment, and it is short enough to play in one class period. Students participate enthusiastically and leave with a greater understanding of the need and criteria for evaluating sources.

Truth or Consequences: An Internet Site Evaluation Game

Susan Drummond

Introduction

Truth or Consequences is a game for undergraduates that dramatically demonstrates the varying quality of information on the Internet. In this game, groups of students use six criteria to evaluate Internet sites and then present their findings to the class.

Objectives

Students will be able to:

- apply six criteria to evaluate websites;
- determine the validity of information retrieved by comparing it to other sources, both print and electronic, on the same topic; and
- demonstrate their knowledge of a website through an oral presentation to the class.

Information Literacy Competency Standards Addressed

This game addresses this ACRL Information Literacy Competency Standard: #3.

Game Background

University students at all levels are likely to hold erroneous notions concerning the reliability and authority of information found on the Internet. Though they are often warned by librarians and subject faculty to carefully evaluate the information they find there, too often they treat all information located through Internet searching as essentially equal in authority and include information from questionable sites in their research projects. *Truth or Consequences* was developed to provide students with practice using six criteria (authorship, accuracy, purpose, currency, design, and intended audience) to evaluate a collection of legitimate and hoax websites. It demonstrates the consequences of accepting information they find

through an Internet search.

Audience

Truth or Consequences has been used successfully with classes of 20 to 30 undergraduate students. It has been particularly beneficial for first- and second-year students, who are less likely to have been exposed to methods of website evaluation than juniors and seniors. It can be used for larger classes by forming groups and asking groups to do the evaluation and presentation as a team.

Time Required

Each student or team gives a five-minute presentation. A typical class of 20 to 25 students will take 2 hours. Larger numbers of students will take longer, but grouping students will reduce the time.

Materials and Equipment

The game requires:

- an overhead LED screen connected to a classroom computer for group viewing;
- slips of paper with the names of hoax and reliable websites;
- a basket or some other container from which students select their website;
- a blackboard, whiteboard, flip chart, or other device to record team names and scores; and
- certificates of excellence in Internet evaluation.

Preparation

Print one name of a reliable or a hoax website on slips of paper and place them in a basket (see Figure 32.1 for example websites). In the session prior to playing the game, discuss Internet evaluation methods, such as the six criteria mentioned earlier. After this

Figure 32.1.
Websites for *Truth or Consequences*

- Homestar Runner:
  http://www.homestarrunner.com/toons.html

- Peep Research:
  http://www.millikin.edu/staley/peeps/

- Study of Phrenology:
  http://www.phrenology.org/index.html

- PRINCIPALITY OF SEALAND:
  http://www.sealandgov.org/index.html

- Lip Balm Anonymous:
  http://kevdo.com/lipbalm/home.html

- Pacific Northwest Tree Octopus:
  http://zapatopi.net/treeoctopus.html

- Physicians for Social Responsibility:
  http://www.psr.org

- Clones-R-Us:
  http://www.d-b.net/dti/

- Dihydrogen Monoxide:
  http://www.dhmo.org/

- Washington International University:
  http://www.washint.edu/pages/

- Mankato, MN, Homepage:
  http://descy.50megs.com/mankato/mankato.html

- History of Halloween:
  http://www.jeremiahproject.com/halloween.html

- The First Male Pregnancy:
  http://www.malepregnancy.com/

- Ova Prima Foundation:
  http://www.ovaprima.org/

- "Institute for Historical Review":
  http://www.ihr.org/

- Beef Nutrition:
  http://www.beefnutrition.org

- AIDS Website:
  http://www.virusmyth.net/aids/

- Aspartame Toxicity Information Center:
  http://www.holisticmed.com/aspartame/

- Californians for Ferret Legalization:
  http://www.legalizeferrets.org/

- The Flat-Out Truth:
  http://www.lhup.edu/~dsimanek/fe-scidi.htm

- Aluminum Foil Deflector:
  http://zapatopi.net/afdb.html

- The Plastic Hydrogen Bomb:
  http://www.scitoys.com/scitoys/scitoys/echem/echem.html#bomb

- Trebuchet:
  http://trebuchet.com/

- The Institute of Druidic Technology:
  http://www.jbum.com/idt/

- Women of Afghanistan:
  http://www.rawa.org/

- The Onion:
  http://www.onion.com/

- Gun Violence:
  http://www.csgv.org/

- 1900th Century Robot:
  http://www.bigredhair.com/boilerplate/

- Scientific Exploration:
  http://www.scientificexploration.org/

- Dissociation Help:
  http://www.dissociation.com/2007/about.asp

- Earth Liberation:
  http://www.originalelf.com/

- Dog Island:
  http://thedogisland.com

- World Trade Organization:
  http://www.gatt.org/

- Primate Programming, Inc.:
  http://www.newtechusa.com/PPI/main.asp

- Accoutrements:
  http://www.accoutrements.com/top25.html

- Havidol:
  http://www.havidol.com/

discussion, students take turns choosing a slip of paper from the basket. Record the students' names and the names of the sites they chose. Give them the homework assignment to evaluate the Internet site they chose based on the criteria you discussed (see Figure 32.2 for a sample assignment).

Playing the Game

When class begins, tell the students that they are going to play an Internet version of the *Truth or Consequences* game to challenge their Internet evaluation skills. All players will describe their site and state their opinion of why their site is reliable or likely to be a hoax. Audience members can vote as to whether or not they believe the site to contain truth or if it is a site to fool people, sell something, or provide erroneous information. Points can be awarded to the student presenters or the team based on their ability to determine the validity of the site and their reasoning in coming to the conclusion that they did, or their ability to fool their audience, if the model of the actual game is to be followed.

After each presentation, reveal whether the site reported on was reliable or a hoax, and praise the reporter for some aspect of the presentation. After all students have presented, give certificates of excellence in Internet evaluation to all those who were correct in their evaluations. Bonus points are also appreciated.

Evaluation

Truth or Consequences has not been formally evaluated. It is clear, though, that students seem to enjoy it, and it helps them to become more aware of the need to evaluate information found on Internet sites before it is considered reliable.

Tips for Introducing Subject Faculty to the Game

Subject faculty weary of student papers whose quality is marred by reliance on questionable Internet-based information and seeking a novel way of teaching and practicing Internet evaluation are likely to be interested in this game. Explain that the game has been used successfully for a number of years and that it engages students and dramatically demonstrates to them the poor quality of some of the information found on the Internet and hence the need to evaluate what they find there.

Figure 32.2.
***Truth or Consequences* Pregame Homework Assignment: Evaluating a Specific Website**

Congratulations on picking a wonderful website!!!

1. Read carefully the full page that appears when you get to your site. This means read and scroll down to the bottom. Often the best information is found in small print at the bottom.

2. Check **all** links from your page to other pages contained on the site. Sometimes the navigation buttons are on the top, the left or right sides, or at the bottoms of the main page.

3. Especially read pages titled "Introduction," "Overview," and "FAQs." Don't forget to scroll down. Check the information presented by searching other sites, databases, or the online catalog.

4. Learn as much as you can from and about the site, including author, accuracy, purpose, design, currency, and intended audience.

5. Evaluate your site on how well it makes its point. What is the strongest argument? Is there a bibliography of sources cited? What did you learn from the bibliography?

6. What did you learn from the webpage and this exercise?

Write a report of no more than **two** pages typed, double spaced, with your answers from above. Make a printout of the first page of your site and attach it to your paper. Title your paper, and be sure your name is on it.

Pick a Periodical

Tracey Johnson

Introduction

In *Pick a Periodical*, each team of two or three students chooses from an assortment of print periodicals to assemble a set that includes one each of a scholarly, a trade, and a popular publication. Each team then justifies its choices, demonstrating that students understand how to evaluate the scholarly level of a print periodical. Each team is judged by the others, who agree or disagree with the presenting team's choices. Through this game, students can apply criteria for evaluating periodicals to items that they hold in their hands.

Objectives

This game is a culminating activity after lessons on types of periodicals. Participants will be able to:

- apply the criteria for determining scholarly versus popular material to print periodicals and
- justify their choices by indicating the key features of their magazines or journals.

Information Literacy Competency Standards Addressed

This game addresses this ACRL Information Literacy Competency Standard: #3.

Game Background

This hands-on activity follows lecture or tutorial lessons about evaluating periodical articles. Students who have played this game in the library skills class at a small community college enjoyed looking through magazines and choosing examples of scholarly, popular, and trade publications; part of the fun is hunting through each magazine for the features that characterize each type of periodical and debating choices with teammates.

Audience

Any number of students, high school or college level, can play. Students should already have had instruction in distinguishing between scholarly, popular, and trade publications.

Time Required

Allow 15 to 20 minutes to play, including selection and explanations.

Materials and Equipment

The game requires:

- an assortment of periodicals,
- a list of criteria with which to determine type of periodical (optional), and
- small prizes, such as candies or pencils.

Preparation

Students should already have had a lesson on evaluating periodicals. The instructor, ahead of time, gathers enough print periodicals for every team to choose one scholarly, one trade, and one popular magazine, plus several extras of each type. This allows for choices—both correct and incorrect choices! Small prizes are gathered. No other preparation is necessary.

Playing the Game

Divide students into teams and have them sit around a table; two or three students per team works well. Scatter the selected magazines across the table. At the word "Go," all teams reach into the magazine "pot" and choose one each of a scholarly, trade, and popular magazine. They evaluate factors such as tables of contents, cover, presence and type of illustrations and advertisements, references in articles, publication frequency, and indications of a review board.

Evaluation

After about 10 minutes, or when all teams have selected their periodicals, ask each team to show what titles it chose and explain the reasoning. All other teams listen and ask questions. If the other teams agree with the presenting team, each team member gets a small prize. If one periodical seems to be an incorrect choice, it is discussed and the team gets to choose a different one; as soon as their set is judged to be correct, they get their prizes.

Tips for Introducing Subject Faculty to the Game

Instructors who require scholarly journal articles will appreciate this the most. Those who simply want students to think about the appropriateness of print periodical sources will also appreciate it. The librarian leading the instruction can point out that students who participate in the lesson and the game will be better able to choose appropriate resources for their homework and better prepared for lifelong learning.

Beat the House: Finding and Evaluating Sources

Julie A.S. Cassidy

Introduction

This activity on finding sources in a library or resource center is primarily based on the casino game *Blackjack* (also known as *Twenty-One*). For this activity, students ("players") are required to navigate the library's physical and online spaces while evaluating sources.

Objectives

Students will:

- learn the differences among specific types of resources (e.g., peer-reviewed articles versus a blog versus a newspaper article),
- practice honing their evaluative skills by having to limit the number of resources they can use, and
- become familiar with the locations of resources in their library.

Information Literacy Competency Standards Addressed

This game addresses these ACRL Information Literacy Competency Standards: #1; #2.

Game Background

Beat the House can easily be modified to fit any situation where students must go out and find information. An early version of this game was used at the University of Florida as a way for college freshmen to learn more about the campus and their individual majors. In order to gather resources and conduct interviews, the students had to visit places around campus like the counselor's office, the library, the transfer office, and different departments. Then, for upper-class students working on research projects in children's literature, the rules were modified and

the searchable space confined to the campus library at Queens College, CUNY. The game is currently used with freshmen and sophomores at the Borough of Manhattan Community College (BMCC) who are learning to evaluate sources for use in short research-based writing assignments in an English class.

Audience

Beat the House is primarily designed for undergraduates or people who are learning to evaluate sources. If the class is small, each student can be on her or his own. If the class is larger or the students share topics, then students can be paired or grouped as necessary.

Time Required

Allotting a minimum of 45 to 60 minutes is best, but the game can be modified for time constraints.

Materials and Equipment

The game requires:

- a full deck of playing cards (jokers removed),
- access to a library or resource center, and
- prizes (if desired).

Prizes are optional and can range from stickers to extra credit on a larger project. Even though stickers might seem elementary, if the instructor presents them with gusto, students will respond to the enthusiasm. For the student who wins the most hands overall, the instructor can give a larger prize like extra credit or a chance to turn in one writing assignment a week late.

Preparation

Each type of source will be worth a specific amount of points. Determine the amount of points each type of source is worth based on the type of research the students are conducting. An article in a peer-reviewed journal might be the "ace" that is either 1 or 11 points. An article in a peer-reviewed book might be worth 10 points. A newspaper article could be 8 points. A web blog might be worth 5 points. An unauthored website might be worth only 2 points. For example, research about Frances Hodgson Burnett's *The Secret Garden* could be broken down in the following manner:

- 1 or 11 point(s)—a peer-reviewed article published within the past 8 years
- 10 points—a peer-reviewed article published more than 8 years ago
- 9 points—newspaper review of *The Secret Garden* within 10 years of the book's publication
- 8 points—a newspaper article about Burnett published within 10 years of the book's publication
- 7 points—a letter or letters between Burnett and her family or friends
- 6 points—an illustration or illustrations of Burnett or *The Secret Garden* published prior to the 1920s
- 5 points—an article or review of the manuscript of *The Secret Garden*
- 4 points—an academic, educational blog
- 3 points—a nonacademic, noneducational blog or website
- 2 points—a Wikipedia entry

Before playing the game, students will need to know the basics of evaluating and identifying sources of information (popular versus scholarly, newspaper article versus blog, etc.).

Playing the Game

Beat the House is based on *Blackjack*, and the basic rules of *Blackjack* are simple—the player and dealer amass a series of playing cards in order to reach, but not exceed, 21 points. Number cards are worth the value on the card, face cards (king, queen, jack) are worth 10 points, and aces are worth either 1 or 11 points (player's choice). These basic rules apply to all three variations of *Beat the House*.

In all the variations of *Beat the House*, the first step is to distribute the list of points. The second step is to shuffle the deck of cards while the students look over the point sheet.

Variation #1—Dealer Only

The dealer deals herself or himself two cards, one faceup and one facedown. The students then disperse throughout the library or resource center in order to find sources that add up as closely as possible to 21 points.

After a preset amount of time, the students return to the dealer with their sources and add up their points. Then the dealer reveals the card that was facedown. If the dealer's cards add up to less than 16, the dealer must take additional cards, one at a time, until she or he holds at least 17 points. The dealer must hold at 17. Each student who has more points than the dealer, but does not exceed 21, earns a small prize.

Variation #2—One Card

Starting with the first player, the dealer gives everyone (including herself or himself) one card faceup. The dealer then receives a second card facedown. The students then disperse throughout the library or resource center in order to find a source (or more than one source) that, in addition to the card in hand, adds up as closely as possible to 21.

After a preset amount of time, the students return to the dealer with their sources and add up their points. Then the dealer reveals the card that was facedown. If the dealer's cards add up to less than 16, then the dealer must take additional cards, one at a time, until she or he holds at least 17 points. The dealer must hold at 17. Each student who has more points than the dealer, but does not exceed 21, earns a small prize.

Variation #3—Two Cards

Starting with the first player, the dealer gives everyone (including herself or himself) one card faceup and then a second card faceup. The dealer then receives a second card facedown. The students then disperse throughout the library or resource center in order to find sources that match the number of points on each card. If desired and time allows, students can look for additional sources to add up as closely as possible to 21.

After a preset amount of time, the students return to the dealer with their sources and add up their points. Then the dealer reveals the card that was facedown. If the dealer's cards add up to less than 16, then the dealer must take additional cards, one at a time, until she or he holds at least 17 points. The dealer must hold at 17. Each student who has more points than the dealer, but does not exceed 21, earns a small prize.

Additional Information

The student who wins the most hands overall can be given a larger prize, such as an excused tardy or extra credit. Whether or not the students use all, some, or none of the texts they find, they will have taken the time to locate and evaluate sources. They will know where to go and who to talk to for more information. Remember, though, that the student needs to be able to tell the dealer or show the dealer what she or he found. The student should know how many points he or she has in hand, while the dealer simply confirms the amount (like the dealer in a casino).

Evaluation

The success or failure of *Beat the House* is immediately evident as students return with their sources. The immediacy of the results also means that the instructor can help individual students before the next round starts.

Not only does *Beat the House* teach students to identify and evaluate sources, but it also sets a limitation on the number of sources a student can use in her or his writing. Students throughout every level of college rely too heavily on direct and indirect quotations. By placing a limit on the number of sources (similar to reaching 21 in *Blackjack* with a limited number of cards), students practice controlling the information and keep their own voices on the forefront of their writing.

After several rounds of game play, it's often useful to have the students write anonymous comments about the game that can be used for discussion. Students like the freedom of walking around during class time. More importantly, though, many students have commented that they appreciate the point sheet because it helps direct them when they are looking for sources.

Tips for Introducing Subject Faculty to the Game

The variations for *Beat the House* were developed through discussion and game play with the CUNY Games Network. *Beat the House* was also introduced to other BMCC faculty during a departmental workshop on conducting research in English 201.

The World of Information: A Socratic Method for Millennials

Bo Baker

Introduction

The World of Information is a clicker game in which students are asked to respond to a series of multiple choice questions concerning the multitude of information resources available through the library and online. Questions involve hypothetical situations designed to have no one correct answer but to promote a Socratic-style dialogue between the instructor and students and among groups of students. Student responses are presented as aggregate totals. A question may be asked multiple times to gauge how classroom opinion changes as discussion and arguments progress.

Objectives

In this session the nuances of different types of information are presented so that students will:

- be equipped with strategies to evaluate a resource's usefulness and trustworthiness regardless of its origin and
- be encouraged to effectively use a wider array of resources.

Information Literacy Competency Standards Addressed

This game addresses these ACRL Information Literacy Competency Standards: #1; #2; #4.

Game Background

The World of Information clicker game is part of a mandatory information literacy instruction session for all freshman composition students. This session, typically delivered to second-semester freshmen, addresses the differences and similarities between peer-reviewed scholarly resources and popular/trade/government resources and proposes strategies for determining the value of a source. Students watch a library-created video on the topic, and then participate in a clicker activity that asks students to think critically about the spectrum of information. These elements preclude demonstration of subject-specific databases and a free time to search for sources pertinent to the students' course assignment: an annotated bibliography.

Audience

Instruction sessions are scheduled throughout the term, and each session includes from 15 to 25 students. Students are generally second-semester freshmen, and in the past few years these sessions involved an average of 1,000 to 1,200 students per semester.

Time Required

Typically, 15 to 20 minutes is devoted to the clicker game.

Materials and Equipment

The game requires:

- a computer and projector,
- clicker devices and Turning Point software, and
- Microsoft PowerPoint software.

Preparation

The Reference and Instruction Department developed a pool of possible questions for the activity. An individual instructor then chooses the questions he or she will use for each session and prepares talking points, hypothetical situations, and arguments for the discussion.

Playing the Game

Describe the game as an activity that reinforces what students have just watched in a video. Present a question to the entire class, and ask students to respond.

When they are finished, share the classroom totals and then discuss the positive and negative aspects of each answer. Sample questions and answers include the following:

1. Your assignment is to write a scholarly paper about a local issue. You want to write about recycling on the UTC campus. You can't find any scholarly journal articles about recycling at UTC. What would you do?

   a. Instead of articles, look for books about recycling at UTC
   b. Look for articles and books about recycling on college campuses in general and relate that information to what's happening at UTC
   c. Change topics
   d. Interview UTC administration

2. Volkswagen is building a manufacturing plant that will open soon in Chattanooga. To find more information about this new plant quickly, where would you look *first*?

   a. The *Chattanooga Times Free Press* online
   b. An encyclopedia about Chattanooga
   c. An automotive trade magazine
   d. Volkswagen's homepage

3. Your professor has assigned a research paper and she wants you to use a mix of popular and scholarly sources. Which of the following popular sources are you *least* likely to choose for a college-level research paper?

   a. *New York Times*
   b. *Scientific American*
   c. *Esquire*
   d. *Newsweek*

Moderate class discussion based on what trends you observe, and ask students for arguments in favor of or against specific answers to encourage dialogue. You will also moderate the game's progress by choosing when to move on to a new question.

Evaluation

Instructors deploy a pre-quiz at the beginning of the session and a post-quiz at the end of the session. These quizzes evaluate the students' knowledge of different types of resources and library services in general. Results for both quizzes are compared to indicate changes in score and are compiled for each semester.

Tips for Introducing Subject Faculty to the Game

The Reference and Instruction Department enjoys a close relationship with freshman composition instructors and works with them to optimize classroom assignments. This extends to pre-library session work. Librarians also review each specific course section's assignment to better tailor the experience for each section.

PART VII

Bibliographic Citation Games

This section includes Games 36–43. These games challenge students to compete individually or in groups in contests that vary from correctly citing materials to using citations to understand how information sources are linked together in scholarly communications.

Database Diving: Understanding "Why We Cite" in an Online Course

Jenna Kammer

Introduction

In *Database Diving*, small groups of students compete online to trace an article to as many of its primary sources as possible. This learning activity gives students a competitive opportunity to use database searching skills while also learning about the value of scholarly communication.

Objectives

Upon completing this game, students will be able to:

- understand how resources are networked together in scholarly communication,
- find a given article in the library databases,
- use the different parts of a citation to locate specific information,
- trace a tertiary source to its primary source, and
- extract main ideas.

Information Literacy Competency Standards Addressed

This game addresses these ACRL Information Literacy Competency Standards: #2; #3; #5.

Game Background

In an online information literacy course at a community college, students work through the big six (task definition, information-seeking strategies, location and access, use of information, synthesis. and evaluation; Eisenberg and Berkowitz, 1996) by participating weekly in discussions and assignments. The Citation Unit has always included a discussion of "why" we cite so that students are able to understand that there is a reason for including all of the details of a citation in the correct order and style. The discussion was never very dynamic, and most students stated the reasons for citing in a few sentences describing plagiarism and referencing. To liven up the discussion and show students why we cite, *Database Diving* was created to give them a hands-on example about how researchers can use citations to trace accuracy and evaluate facts.

In *Database Diving*, students compete in small groups to trace an article to as many of its primary sources as they can. The teams are given an article and are asked to use the databases to find a primary source that influenced the current article. Students create a timeline that visually shows how other articles are connected to this article. Teams earn points by being the first done, tracing the most resources, and finding the oldest resource. *Database Diving* gives students an opportunity to work with citations and to apply search strategies and evaluation skills when working with online databases.

Audience

Database Diving is designed for classes of about 24 students that can be divided into 4 groups of 6. *Database Diving* has been successfully played by freshman-level community college students but can also be adapted for any level of college student, depending on the choice of article.

Time Required

For an online course, one week of discussion should be reserved for students to play *Database Diving*. Because students are working in groups, they will need this time to coordinate schedules and work out any arrangements necessary for completing the task.

Materials and Equipment

The game requires:

- an online discussion forum;
- word-processing software (Google Docs works well for the timeline; http://docs.google.com);

- access to online databases;
- one complete citation for a full-text article, preferably from a newspaper or magazine;
- an article that references other research;
- written game directions and a sample timeline (see Figures 36.1 and 36.2); and
- extra credit points for prizes: 10 points for the oldest citation, 5 points for the most references, and 3 points for being the first group to complete the task.

Figure 36.1.
Database Diving Game Directions

Hello class!

This week you will be participating in groups (your groups were assigned last week) to compete for extra credit points as well as fulfilling your weekly discussion requirement. Your task is to find the following article in the databases, read it, and then write a reference list for the different resources mentioned in the article. As you can see, it is a secondary source (a magazine) that refers to many primary sources (newspaper articles, websites). Your job is to track down the primary sources referred to in the article, write references for them, and then place them in a timeline (ordered by date published).

You may work in your private discussion thread to collect this information or work in a collaborative software program like Google Docs.

Extra credit points will be awarded to each group member based on:

10 points	For the group that finds the oldest citation (primary source)
5 points	For the group that finds the most references
3 points	For the first that completes the task

The citation you will use is:

Miller, Lisa. 2010, August. "War Over Ground Zero: A Proposed Mosque Tests the Limits of American Tolerance." *Newsweek* 156, no. 7, 26–33.

Best of luck and get ready, set, GO!

Preparation

Choose a citation for the game. It is best if the citation is from a news source that does not directly list references or citations but refers to other articles or facts from previous sources. The article should be available in full text in a database that students can easily access.

Divide the class into small groups of about six students. Then prepare a discussion thread for each group to privately discuss their searches, and create a discussion topic for students to post their final results.

Warn students a week in advance about the upcoming game and how it works. Tell them that the winning group will receive extra credit points for their entire

---

Figure 36.2.
Sample Timeline

Summer 2010

Goldsmith, S. 2010, July 14. "Cordoba House Mosque Near Ground Zero Slaps New Name on Itself with Park51." *New York Daily News.* Retrieved from http://www.nydailynews.com/ny_local/2010/07/14/2010-07-14_new_name_doesnt_mosque_their_ire_tense_hearing_on_park51_near_ground_zero.html.

Quinnipiac University. 2010, July 21. "Obama Approval Drops to Lowest Point Ever, Quinnipiac University National Poll Finds." Retrieved from http://www.quinnipiac.edu/x1295.xml?ReleaseID=1478.

Gingrich, N. 2010, July 28. "No Mosque at Ground Zero." Retrieved from http://www.newt.org/newt-direct/no-mosque-ground-zero.

Hook, J., and T. Hamburger. 2010, August 17. "New York Mosque Debate Splits GOP." *LA Times.* Retrieved from http://articles.latimes.com/2010/aug/17/nation/la-na-mosque-politics-20100818/3.

Miller, Lisa. 2010, August. "War Over Ground Zero: A Proposed Mosque Tests the Limits of American Tolerance." *Newsweek* 156, no. 7, 26–33.

team. Announce the groups, and open their private discussion threads so that teams can make plans for distributing the workload and develop a strategy. Encourage students to ask any questions they may have about the task. This activity is most successful if students have experience in database searching and evaluating information.

Playing the Game

On the first day of the game, provide written directions that include the citation the students will work with for the week. Post it to a discussion thread that the entire class can see.

In teams, students find the article in a database and determine which resources the author used when writing the article. Students research to find the original sources referred to in the article. To dig even deeper, students can find the original sources of the secondary articles as well. Students then construct a timeline of all of the sources they find. Credit will be given only for events with a complete citation.

After the teams have completed their research, they post a visual display of the citations they found to the discussion board in a timeline format. Wrap up the game by closing the discussion board and announcing the point awards in a discussion post. You can also wrap up the game by writing an analysis about what each team found.

Evaluation

While the teams can earn extra credit points for being the fastest, deepest, or most successful divers, all teams are evaluated on their final timeline using a grading rubric that includes criteria for accuracy, relevance, and thoroughness. Students also complete a self-assessment on their participation as a team member. The two assessment measures are combined to give the students their total score for the weekly discussion.

Tips for Introducing Subject Faculty to the Game

This game can easily be adapted to fit an article on any subject. For example, political science professors can choose a current political article and ask students to trace the policies or laws through the news. English teachers can ask students to find the original source for an article they are using in a persuasive essay to determine any bias or objectivity. Introducing subject faculty to the game with examples of how the game will fit into their subject is recommended.

References

Eisenberg, M., and Berkowitz, R. 1996. *Information Problem Solving: The Big Six Skills Approach to Library and Information Skills Instruction*. Norwood, NJ: Ablex.

MLA Obstacle Course

Jennifer M. Woolston

Introduction

This game of Modern Language Association (MLA) citation skills is a hands-on chance to work through a simple question and answer "obstacle course," with students using their notes, teammates, and textbook to discover the correct answers. This game is traditional in nature and is targeted at undergraduate college students.

Objectives

After playing *MLA Obstacle Course*, students will be able to:

- identify key components of both in-text and Works Cited MLA citations,
- use problem-solving skills in a team environment,
- effectively identify and name correct MLA formatting and style elements,
- employ critical thinking to correctly finish the assigned questions and worksheet, and
- identify areas of course content that need further review or clarification.

Information Literacy Competency Standards Addressed

This game addresses these ACRL Information Literacy Competency Standards: #2; #5.

Game Background

In the fall of 2009, when teaching research writing to students at Indiana University of Pennsylvania (IUP), it became evident that students could benefit from a game toward the end of the semester that displayed the skills they spent the term accumulating. Additionally, the game functions as a review of seminal points from the course while allowing pupils to engage directly with the class content.

The inspiration for this game grew out of a special IUP Reflective Practice session in which various instructors spoke to the audience about using fun activities and icebreakers in their undergraduate courses. Because students seem enthralled with game play outside of the classroom (video games, online games, etc.), it seemed like a great way to grab (and hold) their attention during an end-of-term class session.

Audience

This game is designed for groups of up to 29 undergraduate or graduate students. Working in small groups of two to three students, the teams will work together to complete the *MLA Obstacle Course*.

Time Required

Setup takes under five minutes, the time required to give each student a worksheet and explain the objectives of the game and its rules. The game takes 30 to 40 minutes, depending on the length and complexity of the worksheet. Instructors will want to save at least 10 minutes to review the worksheets with the larger class at the end of the session. This will ensure that everyone is aware of the correct answers and allows students time to ask any questions about MLA that may persist.

Materials and Equipment

The game requires:

- one instructor-designed worksheet for each student (see Figure 37.1),
- access to students' semester-long notes and textbooks, and
- prizes. (Items such as pens, pencils, erasers, and sticky notes work well as they are used in writing and research courses. Awarding prizes is also a great way to end a productive semester, because they leave students feeling positive about their course and their accumulation of knowledge!)

Figure 37.1.
MLA Obstacle Course **Worksheet**

Name: _____

You can use class notes and texts to answer the following questions. When you finish, give your worksheet to the instructor. The first student to finish completely and correctly will win!

1. In MLA formatting, a block quote (a quote of four or more lines of text) is formatted differently than a regular quote in the body of a paper. List the three ways a block quote is different from a regular quote:

   _____

   _____

   _____

2. Name three types of sources that are italicized in MLA:

   _____

   _____

   _____

3. In MLA, book chapters are noted in text this way:

   _____

4. In MLA, Works Cited lists are organized in this manner:

   _____

5. Name two online (library) databases that a researcher may use to find journal articles:

   _____

   _____

6. True or False: In MLA, a Works Cited page generally counts toward the page length of an assignment. _____

7. True or False: In MLA, authors usually include their last names in the headers of essays (next to the page number). _____

8. True or False: In MLA, when an author is citing a source that is citing another source, the in-text citation will include "qtd in." _____

9. True or False: In MLA, an author will find the publication information for books in the "front matter" (or first few pages) of a text. _____

10. In MLA, there are two general formats for citing sources in text. Using the information below, write out correct sample entries for these two methods.

Author: Jane Dough. Quote found on page 33.

According to _____, "Werewolves are friendly" _____.

"Werewolves are friendly" _____. Done.

Preparation

Create an "obstacle course" worksheet. This can be as basic or as complex as desired and should include key components of the course. For example, ask students to correctly cite their course textbook, describe the difference between a primary and a secondary source, define plagiarism, and correctly format a block quote. Other questions about elements of MLA formatting include when to employ italics, how to correctly use abbreviations in text, and how to cite a poem in text.

The questions should reflect seminal class lessons. Of course, instructors can also include some "difficult" questions that require the use of reference materials (such as class notes or the textbook) if they desire. Worksheets should include enough space for students to write correct answers.

Playing the Game

A class session highlighting key semester lessons is a fun way to jog students' memories about all of the things they have learned. Students can demonstrate what they have mastered throughout the class and have the opportunity to ask last-minute questions (if issues arise or confusion persists). They can also have a great time problem-solving with their classmates (because they are working in teams).

Students will need to bring their class notes and textbook to the session. Once the students are told that this is a review session, they can feel a sense of empowerment about displaying the information they have learned during the term. Students might also be informed that there is a prize for participating (if this is true).

Explain the rules of the game. It is a timed "obstacle course" for which they will be filling out a worksheet in small groups. The students who correctly fill out the worksheet first are the winners. Talking is allowed, but students will want to keep their voices low so that opposing teams cannot overhear their discussion. Students cannot help others in opposing groups.

The game begins when students begin filling out their worksheets. They can use their memories or consult course notes and textbooks to uncover correct answers. Students are permitted to ask questions, but if they involve MLA materials, students must save these until the end of the session.

During game play, roam the room and ensure that student discussion is kept on point and focused and suggest places for students to locate answers. For example, if a student asks a question about a given topic, remind him or her which class session dealt with that material. Do not, however, give them any of the answers.

The game ends when the allotted time is up. When a group feels that they have correctly (and completely) filled out a worksheet, they must alert the instructor. If their answers are correct, they are the winners of the obstacle course.

At this point, praise every student for trying the game and for using their stored knowledge. This is a good time to ask the class if any additional questions about the worksheets persist. Hand out prizes if you use them.

Evaluation

Student response to this activity has been positive. Many students enjoy the opportunity to work with others and to compete with their peers in a timed game. This game also allows students a chance to feel good about the vast research knowledge and MLA protocol that they have accumulated throughout the course.

This game is a refreshing way to end a research writing course because it moves beyond the traditional "question and answer" review session. This lesson is much more interactive (as every student must engage with the material) and overwhelmingly positive (as it allows for group communication) in a relaxed setting. Students have worked on the obstacle course enthusiastically, and the game is often met with a sense of eagerness.

Tips for Introducing Subject Faculty to the Game

Instructors are encouraged to examine their personal course objectives prior to adopting this game. If the instructor values review sessions, this game is an ideal way to incorporate a review into the syllabus. It will appeal to instructors of all levels, because it is easy to construct and implement.

Chasing Citations
Ryan L. Sittler

Introduction

Chasing Citations is a collaborative, kinesthetic, critical-thinking game that allows teams of students to run around the classroom while trying to assemble an APA (American Psychological Association) citation. It is meant to be a follow-up to other lessons on proper citing. The first team to successfully complete the citation wins. This game is meant for undergraduate students but could easily be adopted for middle and high school settings, as well as for use with graduate students.

Objectives

After playing *Chasing Citations*, students will be able to:

- explain why citations are used in academic and professional writing,
- define APA citation and how it differs from another citation style (e.g., Modern Language Association style),
- identify the parts of an APA citation, and
- construct a properly ordered APA citation.

Although these objectives focus on APA (as does this game), everything is easily adaptable to any citation style.

Information Literacy Competency Standards Addressed

This game addresses this ACRL Information Literacy Competency Standard: #2.

Game Background

This game was developed in response to a request for library instruction in an education class that included a discussion of APA formatting for citations in the references pages of student papers. It was intended to provide an engaging experience for the students and worked out nicely and, in fact, received some great applause from the students and the faculty member.

The game designer remembered his undergraduate days when he had scoffed at the notion of going to the library for any reason, especially instruction, an experience he found to be boring and frustrating particularly because of his dislike of lectures. A fan of active learning, he wanted to go beyond "hands on" and move into something more entertaining . . . and more kinesthetic. Hence, the *Chasing Citations* game was born.

Audience

This game is designed for groups of up to 30 undergraduate or graduate students, which are divided into at least 2 teams, but it can easily be adapted for as few as 2 students and, literally, up to 100 or more at once. You just keep creating more teams (and the level of competition). Much younger students (elementary through high school) may enjoy it, as well.

Time Required

Setup may take up to 60 minutes (depending on how fast you can write!). The session itself takes anywhere from 10 to 50 minutes, depending on how in-depth you choose to make the discussion on citation styles, how many examples you wish to show, how many times you wish to play the game, etc.

Materials and Equipment

This game requires:

- one instructor's station with a projector,
- 30 sheets of paper (or 30 small dry-erase boards),
- two medium-sized tables, and
- room for students to run around (yes, run around).

Prizes are optional. I used chocolate candy, but some healthy and/or organic options may be appropriate for your campus. I can tell you that I received no complaints!

Preparation

Preparation is relatively simple. To start, find an article in a database that would be appropriate for the session. After finding the article (or book if you so desire), create a properly formatted citation. Then print out two copies (or transcribe to the whiteboards) in pieces. The following is a book example:

> Page 1: Sittler, R. L.,
>
> Page 2: & Cook, D. L.
>
> Page 3: (Eds.).
>
> Page 4: (2009).
>
> Page 5: *The library instruction cookbook.*
>
> Page 6: Chicago:
>
> Page 7: ACRL.

You will need two copies of each "piece" so that you have enough for two teams to each create a full citation. You can customize this to the number of students who will be involved; for example, you can put one word, one piece of punctuation, or a whole phrase on a sheet of paper. The choice is yours. Take each whole citation and place its pages upside down, mixed up, on a table. Place your prizes at the front of the room and wait for the students.

Playing the Game

Introducing a discussion about citing references is not easy as it, frankly, does not sound very exciting. Alleviating the problem is simple—inform the students that following an introduction to citing references they will play a game that reinforces their knowledge. And the winners of the game will get a prize. (At this point, you can actually throw the bag of candy out onto the middle of the floor.) You can also mention that the game will involve some running around the room. The combination of food bribery and the notion of running in the classroom or library is generally enough to pique interest.

Then discuss citations. This can be custom-tailored to your personal needs in the class. The game is a lot of fun but would be baseless without a little lively discussion to inform it. Likewise, the infor-

mation may be a little dry without the game to liven it up.

The discussion can include some or all of the following (and, you will notice, these suggestions make up a portion of the learning objectives for the game as both the discussion and the game depend on each other for success):

- an explanation of why citations are used in academic and professional writing,
- a definition for what an APA citation is and what makes it unique (such as gender neutrality), and
- the parts of an APA citation.

There are many engaging active learning techniques that you may employ to cover these topics, which goes beyond the scope of this chapter. However, they also add spice to the overall experience. You can cover very little—such as only discussing the parts that make up an APA citation—or you can have a more in-depth discussion that uses this game as a culminating activity. The choice is yours.

When the students play the game, they actually get to practice constructing an APA citation. However, instead of doing it completely from scratch, they will be using the pre-created citation pieces.

Be certain that a sample article, with all necessary citation information, is displayed at the front of the room. This is the same article used to create your pre-fabricated citation pieces.

Break the class into two teams. Gather each group near one of the tables, and pick one person to act as a "leader" for each team. The team leader will ultimately be responsible for declaring a citation complete.

Inform students that they will be racing to see which group can properly create an APA style citation, based on the displayed article, first. The team leader will yell "Done!" when it is completed, and, if it is correct, that team wins.

Hold a sheet of paper, with text on it, in front of you (with the text facing the audience). Inform the students that when you say "Go!" team members are to run up to their respective tables and select a piece of paper. These sheets of paper each contain one piece of the citation and need to be arranged in order to properly display the APA citation.

The leader may stay standing/seated while the others do this (this is especially beneficial for a student who may not be able to run for medical reasons, etc.). After running to the table and selecting a piece of paper, each student should stand with the text facing out (as you are demonstrating). Students then, with the direction of their leader, need to stand side by side in the correct order to properly display the citation.

At this point, remind the students that they are playing for the prize (in this example, an entire bag of candy). Ask if they have any questions or need to have a detail clarified. When you are sure they are ready, declare "On your mark . . . get set . . . cite!" Controlled chaos ensues—and a lot of laughing.

After a group leader exclaims "Done!" I pause the groups and ask everyone to judge the correctness of the citation. This is a great opportunity for a little extra review and encourages the students to think a little more about the topic. If the citation is correct, the game is over. If it is not, yell "Go!" and encourage each group to keep working. This can continue until a group correctly finishes the citation.

Once a team has won round one, you may elect to repeat the game with other items (in a best two out of three scenario) or use other citation formats (such as MLA) to test other citation skills.

At this point, declare that the winners get the candy. However, as all students are "a little more information literate," they are "all winners" and they all deserve candy. You can deliver this revelation in the cheesiest way possible. The students laugh and

groan at the bad joke, but it just adds to the good spirit of the activity.

Evaluation

This game has never been formally assessed. However, as the students must correctly construct the citation in order to win, they do receive immediate feedback regarding their performance. This is an advantage of using games in any learning situation. Student reception of the activity is always positive. It is a break from the norm (for most students) and is met with smiles, laughter, and applause.

Tips for Introducing Subject Faculty to the Game

Because of the unusual nature of this game, it might not be appropriate for all student constituencies or with just "any" faculty member when you first try it. People who appreciate these kinds of activities will feel a natural gravitation to the game. People who do not will view it as wasteful use of time.

Education faculty and students are likely to be particularly open to this game. This tends to be a self-selecting group of individuals, and they may be more interested in seeing what it is all about. After you have tried the game a few times and have the mechanics in place, you should be in a good position to start venturing out to other faculty.

Citation Races
Gretchen Trkay

Introduction

Citation Races is a game that uses collaboration and competition to teach the mechanics of citation. This game is best suited for classes of 20 to 25 students.

Objectives

Students will be able to:

- identify, locate, and arrange necessary publication information in order to accurately cite a source using the expected citation style.

Information Literacy Competency Standards Addressed

This game addresses this ACRL Information Literacy Competency Standard: #5.

Game Background

Students often struggle not only with the mechanics of citation but also with identifying the type of source they are citing. The purpose of this session is to provide students with tips to help them identify source type, time to practice finding the information on a document necessary for citation, and encourage them to learn how to read the citation guides.

The learning activity was developed after a failed attempt at teaching citation using a citation puzzle. The challenge was to allow students to practice citation with an activity that reflected what they would need to do when completing an assignment while keeping them engaged in the process of learning. Learning outcomes assessment of the curriculum indicates that *Citation Races* has had a positive impact on student learning.

Audience

This game is best suited for classes of 16 to 25 students. Although it could be adapted for use with upper-level students (or high school students), the game has primarily been used with college freshmen and sophomores.

Time Required

Citation Races requires a 50-minute class period. The curriculum can be adapted for longer class sessions.

Materials and Equipment

The game requires the following material grouped in source packets for each group:

- one journal article retrieved from a database,
- one magazine article retrieved from a database (no author),
- one web-exclusive magazine article,
- one print book,
- one pad of sticky notes, and
- one pen.

The game requires the following material for each student:

- one condensed guide covering the citation style addressed by the curriculum and
- prizes, such as candy, pens, highlighters, pencils, etc.

Equipment needed includes:

- a computer with projector for the instructor and
- a computer with word processing software for each group or a whiteboard with dry-erase markers for each group.

Preparation

Along with preparing the source packets, the session instructor should prepare a document containing the proper source citations. They should also create an inaccurately formatted Works Cited/References page.

Playing the Game

Introduce yourself and indicate what the students will be doing. Explain the ground rules of *Citation Races*, how their groups can win, and what the prizes are. Competition alone is a successful student motivator, but extrinsic motivation provided by the potential of winning candy never fails.

To begin the game, break the class into groups of no more than four students. Hand each group of students a source packet.

Challenge One

For the first challenge, ask groups to correctly identify the types of sources in the packet. They use the source types identified in the citation guide and write down on a sticky note the source type and stick it to the source. The first group that correctly identifies the source types, and can justify their designations, wins. Ask students to explain how they determined the source types.

Challenge Two

For the second challenge, ask groups to correctly cite the journal article retrieved from a database. Using either whiteboards or Microsoft Word, students work in groups to cite the article. The first group that correctly cites the article wins. Project the correct citation, and go over the specific mechanics for how the source should be cited, making note of common mistakes. Common errors in Works Cited/References include not using the correct title ("Works Cited" or "References," depending on citation style) and not correctly alphabetizing, double spacing, or using a hanging indent.

Challenge Three

Ask groups to correctly cite the magazine article retrieved from a database. Using either whiteboards or Microsoft Word, students work in groups to cite the article. The first group that correctly cites the article wins. Project the correct citation, and go over the specific mechanics for how the source should be cited, making note of common mistakes.

Challenge Four

Ask groups to correctly cite a web-exclusive article. Using either whiteboards or Microsoft Word, students work in groups to cite the article. The first group that correctly cites the article wins. Project the correct citation, and go over the specific mechanics for how the source should be cited, making note of common mistakes.

Challenge Five

Ask groups to correctly cite the print book. Using either whiteboards or Microsoft Word, students work in groups to cite the book. The first group that correctly cites the book wins. Project the correct citation, and go over the specific mechanics for how the source should be cited, making note of common mistakes.

Wrap Up

When the challenges have been completed, ask students if they have any questions. If you have time, pass out an in-text citation worksheet and ask the students to indicate which in-text citation is correct. Again, take the opportunity to review the exercise and the answers given by students when it is completed.

Evaluation

Students learning or mastery of citation styles is clearly indicated when applying a rubric in playing the game. Students' completion of a one-minute paper will provide feedback on instruction.

Tips for Introducing Subject Faculty to the Game

Teaching citation is a common problem for subject faculty. The *Citation Races* curriculum is offered as part of a suite of instruction opportunities to which subject faculty can bring their class. It is one of the more popular classes in University of Texas Arlington's information literacy program.

New instructors in the first-year English program also attend the same session at which they participate in the same curriculum as their students. They often learn something they did not know and have fun in the process.

Speed Citation: A Race to Research Efficiency

Andrew P. Thompson

Introduction

This game for undergraduates tests their mastery of citation styles. It challenges teams of students to write citations correctly as quickly as possible and then evaluate the resources they have cited.

Objectives

Students will be able to:

- cite and evaluate sources more efficiently by competing in this game.

Information Literacy Competency Standards Addressed

This game addresses these ACRL Information Literacy Competency Standards: #3; #4; #5.

Game Background

Speed Citation was inspired by an experience of playing a game in an undergraduate language class designed to teach citation styles. Citing sources correctly is basic to any kind of scholarly writing, but it can inspire fear and frustration in those who do not master the styles, particularly in beginning students. Research goes much more smoothly when sources are cited correctly. *Speed Citation* was created to motivate students to learn citation styles by heart so that when writing papers they could focus more on the content rather than the format.

By combining the game from language courses with citation styles, this game becomes a useful tool for teaching efficiency in research writing. Students will spend less time thinking about how to cite their sources and have more time to think about the source information itself. After the elements of the citation are correctly assembled in the game, the discussion can move to evaluating these elements. These are important skills for all students, from the first research papers to the dissertation rewrite.

Audience

Speed Citation is quite flexible and can be used with many different age groups and educational levels. For first-year students, loose scoring and rules should be used. For upper-level students, the bar can be higher, with stricter scoring rules, thus creating a higher level of competition. Also more challenging questions can be incorporated about the viability of the source or why a source should be treated with skepticism.

Time Required

Speed Citation can be done in many different ways to fit time constraints. The game itself can be stretched or shortened to fit varying class times. Longer games could be used as a supplement to a lesson on citation. Short games can be used as filler after a test or quiz. A more interesting way to implement the game would be to have a round at the beginning of class every day for a semester, thus giving students more time to see progress in their abilities.

Materials and Equipment

Speed Citation requires:

- packets of source material for the students to evaluate,
- dry-erase boards or chalkboards (or computer with an overhead projection or pen and paper), and
- prizes or certificates for the winners.

Preparation

Speed Citation should follow some type of introduction to styles of citation. It is a good idea to also have allowed for some type of practice writing citations, either in class or for homework, and to have warned the students that the challenge was coming, particularly for first-year students. In higher-level courses the students have probably already had plenty of practice, so it can be done with little or no preparation on the students' part.

Faculty preparation consists of gathering packets containing the essential sections of books and periodical articles and Internet sites of various levels and types. A good mix of sources should be supplied so that there is something to base a discussion on after the game.

The faculty member should also determine an appropriate prize to give the winners and supply it. Examples of prizes are a pencil with a laudatory saying on it or bonus point or printed certificate.

Playing the Game

Step 1: Divide the class into teams. The size of teams depends on class size. In upper-division courses, class size could be pairs or even individuals. Teams should all have an easily viewable writing surface.

Step 2: Explain the rules to the students. Explain that the first team to write out a given source correctly will win that round. Give the students whatever amount of time you feel necessary to complete the task. When all citations are completed, total up points for all groups and give the *Speed Citation* prizes to the group with the most points.

Step 3: Discuss the results. Talk with the teams about some of the issues they had while trying to cite a source. If everyone had trouble with the citation, discuss why a specific source is more difficult. Finally, discuss what sort of information about the credibility of a source can be gathered by simply looking at citation information.

Step 4: Inform the students that the game will be repeated in the future. This is also a great way to motivate all the students to work on their citation skills.

Evaluation

To win the game, students must cite sources correctly, so it includes an element of evaluation. One-minute essays given at the end of the session show that students are motivated by the competitive nature of the activity and enjoy working in groups to meet the challenge.

Tips for Introducing Subject Faculty to the Game

At any point that a complaint or grumbling appears about the quality, or more often the lack thereof, of students' citations or knowledge of citation styles, you can introduce this game. Be sure to explain flexible options so that faculty can find a place for *Speed Citation* in their classroom.

Getting It Right: A Team Approach to Documenting Sources Using the MLA Style Sheet

Debra Holmes Matthews

Introduction

This game is designed to allow students to practice documenting a variety of sources (books, articles, interviews, nonprint sources, and others) in the Modern Language Association (MLA) format. The team or group with the most points at the end of the class period wins the game and the most bonus points on the next quiz.

Objectives

Students will:

- learn the correct MLA styles for a variety of sources and
- practice creating correct citations for both a Works Cited page and a parenthetical citation.

Information Literacy Competency Standards Addressed

This game addresses these ACRL Information Literacy Competency Standards: #4; #5.

Game Background

This game was designed to have students actively engage in the writing process. They are not expected to memorize a style sheet, but they are expected to be able to take the information about their source and place it in the correct format, both within the paper and on the Works Cited page, using the MLA style sheet.

In this game, which was adapted from a homework exercise, students work together. Using their handbooks, handouts for online resources, and copies of the MLA, students place a variety of sources (articles, books, interviews, recordings, artwork, and others) into their correct formats. By having students work together to create the entries, documenting sources

seems less threatening to them, and they work with their peers to achieve a common goal while having fun in the process. This group approach has been used with both freshmen and seniors, and it has been a positive experience.

Audience

Having students work within small groups to document sources correctly is an activity that can be used with undergraduate students at all levels. To make it more challenging, add to the complexity of the sources. For example, students could be given electronic sources, a government publication, a published interview, a multivolume work, or republished works.

Time Required

The game can be played in a 50- to 65-minute class period or easily extended to cover 2 class periods by adding additional source cards.

Materials and Equipment

This game requires:

- several copies of the *MLA Handbook for Writers of Research Papers* and/or handouts of the MLA style sheet (most college handbooks have a section on different style sheets, which may be adequate depending on the types of sources students are given);
- a separate handout with the format for documenting electronic sources or certain databases; and
- a whiteboard or its equivalent, several markers of various colors, index cards (any size will work, but I like the larger ones, five by eight) or cardstock, and a stopwatch or timer.

Preparation

Before playing *Getting It Right*, we will have reviewed the basic format for documenting in MLA and students have selected their topics from a list of approved topics we developed together. They have started to research their topics for an argumentative essay both online and in the library. The activity is an opportunity for them to practice documenting sources correctly before submitting the final paper.

A few days before class, I prepare 10 to 15 source cards by typing *Getting It Right* on one side and a description of one type of source on the other side of each card. Each source card will contain all of the necessary information for the students to write two entries: one for the Works Cited page and a parenthetical citation, if appropriate. For example, a source card for a personal interview contains the following: "On January 15, 2010, you completed a personal interview with Ms. Sarah Hightower at the Atlanta Hilton." I will both create sources as well as use actual sources. Depending on how challenging I want the activity to be, I will include additional information that should not be included in the entry, and the students will have to determine what is needed and what is not. I also create two or three cards that will allow a group to pass a source to another group, as well as a card that may be worth extra points, and I prepare five or six sets of materials (additional handbooks, handouts, printed guidelines for the game, and markers) for each group.

On the day of class, I arrive before students and section off the board into four or five sections and place a different marker at each location. While students will be aware that we will have some type of activity to practice documentation, I do not give them the details until the day of class.

Playing the Game

Introduce the game, explain the rules, and allow the class to make suggestions as well. Each group will designate a writer, preferably the person with the best handwriting. Only one person from each group is allowed at the board at a time. Other members of the group are encouraged to pay careful attention as the writer from the group puts the two entries for the source on the board. Once the writer sits down, he or she may not return to the board. Every mark of punctuation should be in the correct place, and points will be deducted for spelling errors or erroneous citations. The group could start with 100 points and lose 5 or less points for each error. The group with the most points at the end of the class period receives 10 points on a quiz. The group with the next highest score receives 8, 6, 4, and so forth. I have found that the competition is enough to motivate students and the points are just an added incentive.

The class forms groups of preferably no more than five students each. They have their handbooks describing MLA documentation, and I provide each group with the same set of additional handbooks and handouts for citing electronic sources and certain databases. On a table at the front of the room are the previously prepared source cards. Each group is allowed to pull one source card at a time from the stack and will have to prepare entries for whatever is selected.

Each group has 5 to 10 minutes to create the entries on the board in the space designated for that group. I keep track of the time and occasionally penalize groups a point or two if they are late in going to the board or spend too much time at the board. By a certain point, I will say that everyone should be represented at the board or start to lose points for being late.

Once each group has written its entries on the board for the first set of source cards, we stop and discuss one at a time. For example, the writer or someone else within the group will read the description of the source to the class, and I will evaluate it for accuracy by basically grading it on the board. The class will also make comments. The process is repeated for each group, and groups are allowed to select again.

Evaluation

As a result of working on documentation within groups, students seem more self-confident about using the MLA style sheet. They understand that the goal is accurate application, not necessarily memorizing the format. I try to model that behavior in the classroom as well by referring to the handbook and handouts, especially for sources that are unusual. I have observed that students who feel prepared and confident about what they are doing in the classroom are more likely to take the process seriously and complete it accurately. On the other hand, students or groups that are experiencing difficulty will be provided with additional instruction, which could take the form of homework assignments. I want to provide students with as many opportunities as possible to improve every aspect of their writing, and *Getting It Right* becomes one way of achieving that goal. One could also choose to have students self-assess the experience by writing in a directed free writing format about whether or not they found the experience of playing the game helpful and in what way. Are there changes that they would like to see in it? Over the years, I have found that some of my best suggestions for improving instruction have come from the students either directly or through observations.

Tips for Introducing Subject Faculty to the Game

Conversations about documentation and avoiding plagiarism are fairly common in an academic setting, and it is difficult to imagine an instructor who has not had to address the issue in some way. Students frequently submit papers that are not documented appropriately, and I would go so far as to guess that most instructors are looking for new ways of presenting documentation to students. *Getting It Right* uses MLA documentation, but the game could easily be adapted for American Psychological Association (APA), Chicago, Council of Science Editors (CSE), or some other format. I would stress to my colleagues that practice with documentation does not have to be a handout, done individually, or be boring. *Getting It Right* is a way to get students excited about documenting sources while creating a small community of learners within the classroom.

Name That Citation!

Holly Heller-Ross and Elin O'Hara-Gonya

Introduction

This short classroom game is focused on identifying types of bibliographic citations based on standard cues taught earlier in the lesson (http://faculty.plattsburgh.edu/holly.hellerross/Name%20That%20Citation!.ppt). It's designed to help reinforce and promote fluency (subject mastery plus speed!) in student identification skills for commonly seen types of citations (popular article, government document, book chapter, scholarly journal article, encyclopedia entry, etc.). The game provides an opportunity for students to test their fluency in a low-level competition that is fast and fun. Even though some students don't remember the popular *Name That Tune* television show this game is based on, they respond very well to the idea, the challenges, and the pace of the game.

Objectives

Students will:

- increase fluency with identification of material types in online catalogs and in database result lists.

Information Literacy Competency Standards Addressed

This game addresses this ACRL Information Literacy Competency Standard: #1.

Game Background

Research databases, book catalogs, and web search engines all blend material types in integrated ways that make research easier on some levels and harder on others. Long gone are the days of specialized book catalogs and citation indexes that only include one material type. Students are increasingly unaware of whether what they are finding in a search is a book, journal article, or film. Instructors must assist students in developing skills that allow them to more quickly identify the material type of an item in a results list based on the bibliographic citation in an online access tool results list so they can work quickly and efficiently with their search results. An effort to provide such instruction produced accurate but dry instructional content. An interest in experimenting with games and reaching students through affective domains, and creativity and play in the classroom, led the instructor to create this game to assist students with retaining the information from lectures, introduce some fun and friendly competition, and promote a class sense of teamwork.

The game has been used by two librarians at SUNY Plattsburgh's Feinberg Library, and in both cases the game is part of a half-semester one-credit information and technology literacy course. Both techniques of playing the game are included here.

Audience (Technique A)

High school through all college levels, with class sizes from 25 to 30, have successfully played the game.

Time Required (Technique A)

The game can be completed in 35 to 40 minutes.

Materials and Equipment (Technique A)

The game requires:

- presentation software and 12 citation slides or printed posters for the game,
- answer sheets for the student teams, and
- a prize (such as bonus points toward a class grade).

Preparation (Technique A)

Prepare students by following a lesson plan that includes explaining **why** students need to care about citations as readers, as students learning about a topic, and as beginning scholars. Next discuss **when** citations are needed (direct quotation, paraphrase, or use of the central idea or conclusions) and when they are not needed (sources consulted for general background and general common knowledge etc.). Then talk about **how** citations are formed. List the important citation elements for different formats, review different citation styles, and introduce some regularly used signal phrases they might be familiar with for in-text citations and other basics. Finally, students work in teams of two and practice citing a print book, an academic journal article, and a webpage using a fill-in-the-blank worksheet (see Heller-Ross, 2010, for an electronic version of the worksheet).

Playing the Game (Technique A)

First, explain the game and hand each group an answer sheet. This is a sheet with space for the group member names and fill-in answer spots numbered 1 through 12 for each of the 12 slides displaying a bibliographic citation (sample slides can be found at http://faculty.plattsburgh.edu/holly.hellerross/Name%20That%20Citation!.ppt). Then display each slide in order, allowing two minutes for teams to quietly confer, make their decisions, and write their answers on the answer sheet. Then teams trade answer sheets for the scoring. Finally, as a class, review each slide, provide the right answer as students score the team answer sheets, and respond to any questions or comments. Identify the top team (or top two teams) based on number of correct answers, and award the prize or prizes.

Remind students at the end of the game that there are common clues they can use to quickly identify material types and that this is a skill they can improve with practice!

Audience (Technique B)

The game is appropriate for high school through all college levels. Class sizes between 15 and 30 have successfully played the game.

Time Required (Technique B)

This game can be completed in 25 to 30 minutes.

Materials and Equipment (Technique B)

The game requires:

- presentation software and 12 citation slides,
- a score sheet for the scorekeeper, and
- prizes (suggestions include candy or bonus points on class grades).

Preparation (Technique B)

Prepare students by using a lesson plan that spans three class meetings. Begin the first class by facilitating a class discussion about plagiarism, placing particular emphasis on identifying student perspectives on the causes of plagiarism. In small groups the students compile lists of difficulties they routinely encounter in the citing process that contribute to plagiarism. Discuss and subsequently refute these common misconceptions. During the second meeting, ask students to pair up and examine a research paper that has been altered to contain multiple citation errors. The students identify sections of the paper missing in-text citations and incorrect citations in the References list, which is corrected as a class. During the third class, the students pair up and practice citing a print book, an online newspaper article, and a journal article from a library database.

Playing the Game (Technique B)

First, explain the game and ask for a volunteer to keep score. Divide the class into three teams, and ask them to arrange their chairs into clusters conducive to team conferring. Ask the teams to choose captains who will provide the teams' answers. Display each of the 12 citation slides. After each slide allow the teams to quietly confer for 15 to 20 seconds, and then call out "Answers?" while watching to see which team captain raises his or her hand first. Make a mental note which team captain raises his or her hand second. (If you prefer not to watch for the order in which the team captains raise their hands, ask the team captains to record the teams' answers on sheets of paper and display them to you when you call "Answers?" Award points to each team with a correct answer.) Ask the team captain to identify the citation type and the citation clues that led the team to that answer. If the team is correct, award five points. You can allow the "losing" teams to earn points by identifying an additional clue to the citation type, naming a database appropriate for locating the source, or specifying whether the source is primary or secondary. You may choose to award one or two points for those answers, and then move to the next slide.

If the team is incorrect, allow the team captain who raised his or her hand second to identify the citation type and citation clues. Continue to the third team if the second team is incorrect. After the correct answer is found, continue to the next slide. At the end of the 12 slides, ask the scorekeeper to tally the points and announce the winner. Award prizes to the top team(s). At the end of the game it is useful to remind students that citation identification is a skill that develops with practice.

Evaluation

Student assessment of the game as played in Technique A was conducted formally in 2006 and 2007, using a question about all the class learning games as part of the final student assessment survey. In 2006, 84 percent of the 24 students in one class strongly agreed or agreed that the learning games made it easier for them to learn and remember the concepts. In another class, 69 percent of the 22 students strongly agreed or agreed that the learning games made it easier for them to learn and remember the concepts. In 2007, 96 percent of the 22 students in one section and 80 percent of the 20 students in another section strongly agreed or agreed that that the learning games made it easier for them to learn and remember the concepts.

Since the fall of 2007, a librarywide course evaluation has been used that did not include that question, so the game has been assessed informally by the instructors immediately after playing. In addition, the instructor using Technique A has used the informal polling feature in the university's online course management system, with results as shown in Figure 42.1.

Tips for Introducing Subject Faculty to the Game

This game has not yet been shared with subject faculty, although it could work very well in any class where students conduct independent research and are expected to use specific types of materials.

References

Heller-Ross, H. 2010. LIB10510 Week Five September 29: Why's, When's, and How's of Citing Your Sources." SUNY Plattsburgh. http://faculty.plattsburgh.edu/holly.hellerross/LIB10510/Lib10510five.htm. This website contains links to background tutorials for use prior to this game and related worksheets.

Figure 42.1.
Evaluation Results

Fall 2010 (16 responses from a class of 28)		
10	63%	Helped me learn and was fun
2	13%	Helped me learn but wasn't fun
1	6%	Was fun, but didn't help me learn
3	19%	Wasn't fun or a good learning experience

The Bibliography Tournament

H. David "Giz" Womack

Introduction

Teams compete against each other to write the most accurate bibliographic entry for a book or journal article in the least amount of time using a standard citation style (usually Modern Language Association [MLA] or American Psychological Association [APA]). The instructor posts the necessary information about a book or journal article on a screen, and the students write the correct entry for the bibliography on a whiteboard at the front of the room.

Objectives

Students will:

- learn the skills required to write an accurate bibliography that includes books, scholarly journal articles, and websites.

Information Literacy Competency Standards Addressed

This game addresses these ACRL Information Literacy Competency Standards: #2; #3; #4.

Game Background

Part of the one-credit hour information literacy course at Wake Forest University is learning how to write a bibliography. Numerous attempts to teach students how to write a bibliography by showing them a book or scholarly journal article and walking through the steps to wire the entry had not worked; students still could not write an accurate entry on their first assignment. *The Bibliography Tournament* was designed to be a more engaging way to teach the MLA and APA styles. After initially having students shout out what came next in the bibliography, making it into a competition and allowing students to work in groups proved to be a more effective approach.

Audience

The game is for 16 (ideally, but can be more or less) high school or college students. This allows for four teams of four students, which creates three rounds of play to get a winner. The first two teams of four compete against each other. The second two teams of four compete against each other, and the winners of each of the first two rounds compete to determine the winning team.

Time Required

Based on a group of 16 students in 4 groups of 4, the required 3 rounds can be completed in 30 minutes, 10 minutes per round. In a 50-minute class, this allows for 20 minutes to hand out style guides or show style guide websites, review the basics of citation, and explain the rules of the tournament.

Materials and Equipment

The game requires:

- a whiteboard for students to write their bibliographic entry;
- a computer with projection (not required but is helpful to show the book, scholarly journal article, or website to be cited); and
- prize candy for the winning team.

Preparation

It takes 30 minutes prior to play to select the 3 items that will be cited—a book, a journal, and a website (or any combination of 3 sources)—and write an accurate citation. Allow 30 minutes in the class to play 3 rounds, with 10 minutes per round.

Playing the Game

After the information literacy class has covered finding books in the library, we discuss citing sources. After a discussion of why it's necessary to cite sources and a discussion of the basics of writing a citation, students play *The Bibliography Tournament* to put into practice the skills that were discussed in class. This game gets the students up and moving around the room, working together and using the skills they have just learned.

Establish the four teams, and give two teams a book, scholarly journal article, or website (usually projected on the screen in the classroom). Each team works together to write the citation simultaneously on the whiteboard at the front of the room using the information from the database or catalog projected on the screen and the style guide they have been given. The team with the most accurate citation wins! (Teams often suddenly start finding the errors in each other's work at this point!) From the four teams, the two winning teams compete and the members of the winning team get a prize, usually candy. Upon completion of the game, the first assignment is distributed in which students must find a book on their research topic, explain why it is a good source on their topic, and cite the source.

Evaluation

Evaluation has been informal. The improvements in the accuracy of the bibliographic entries submitted in assignment one seem to indicate this hands-on approach is more effective than traditional lecture at teaching citation styles.

Tips for Introducing Subject Faculty to the Game

Lib100 instructors at Wake Forest University meet every semester to discuss new approaches to teaching the course. Included in last year's discussion was *The Bibliography Tournament*. No marketing of the game has been implemented.

PART **VIII**

Plagiarism Awareness and Prevention Games

This part includes Games 44–48. There are two traditional games, a clicker game, and two award-winning digital games that allow students to learn about, and practice their knowledge of, what constitutes plagiarism.

Goblin Threat

Mary J. Snyder Broussard

Introduction

Goblin Threat is an online, point-and-click game (http://www.lycoming.edu/library/instruction/plagiarismgame.html) where students learn about the dreaded complexities of plagiarism in an entertaining and engaging format. The game can be played in a computer lab during class or assigned as homework. It ends in a certificate that students can print and turn in as proof of completion.

Objectives

After playing *Goblin Threat*, students will be able to:

- recognize when information sources must be cited;
- identify the many ways plagiarism can be committed, including self-plagiarism and omitting or falsifying citations;
- identify the consequences of plagiarism;
- define paraphrasing;
- list the benefits of citation beyond avoiding the consequences of plagiarism; and
- know where to go for help avoiding plagiarism.

Information Literacy Competency Standards Addressed

This game addresses this ACRL Information Literacy Competency Standard: #5.

Game Background

The amount of professional literature on plagiarism in colleges and universities proves that plagiarism is a universal problem that has no easy solution. Effective efforts to combat plagiarism involve a multifaceted approach that combines a lot of prevention with some detection. The Lycoming Library had already created a traditional online tutorial on plagiarism with a review quiz, but librarians wanted to create something new that was more engaging.

Goblin Threat was designed to be an instructional tool that softens the dreaded, but necessary, task of plagiarism education by wrapping the "medicine" in a game and allows students to actively participate with the material. The game is entirely online and can be assigned by professors as homework.

This game took four months (approximately 350–400 hours) to develop in Macromedia Flash. The programming skills were obtained through the book *Beginning Flash Game Programming for Dummies* (Harris, 2005). The librarian was aided in writing the questions by a library science intern with experience teaching high school English.

Audience

This game is most appropriate for undergraduates but could be played by any students.

Time Required

The game takes approximately 15 to 25 minutes.

Materials and Equipment

Each student requires:

- a computer with Internet access and
- the ability to print the final screen, which serves as proof of completion.

Preparation

No preparation is needed for this game. It is available at http://www.lycoming.edu/library/instruction/plagiarismgame.html.

Playing the Game

In the story of *Goblin Threat*, the campus has been taken over by plagiarism goblins. Players progress through a series of rooms where they must find hidden goblins and eliminate them by correctly answering questions about plagiarism. Quiz activities come in the form of multiple choice, true or false, matching, and hot-spot questions. Players are permitted an unlimited amount of attempts to answer each question correctly and are provided constructive feedback for incorrect answers. Once each room is cleared of goblins, a door unlocks and allows the player to pass into the next room. The last room is a dungeon that reviews the material covered in previous questions and ends in a landslide that blocks the goblins' entryway to the college. The final screen is a certificate of completion, which can be printed and turned in to the professor. Students cannot get to this page without successfully completing the game.

This game was designed to be completed as homework. It is entirely self-contained and hosted on the Internet; it is accessed by going to http://www.lycoming.edu/library/instruction/plagiarismgame.html. While it can stand alone, teaching faculty are strongly encouraged to have a brief, in-class follow-up discussion on the day it is due. A librarian is available to lead this discussion if desired by the faculty member.

Evaluation

Feedback from students and other librarians was sought constantly throughout the development of this game. This was done through two focus groups with students, e-mail discussions, and in-person interviews. During the first two months following *Goblin Threat*'s unveiling, a link to a brief survey appeared on the final screen of the game. Feedback from local students and faculty was collected through this survey and minor improvements made based on the feedback. Feedback from faculty and librarians was overwhelmingly positive, with some requests for improvement.

Requests from faculty included asking the student to submit their name at the beginning of the game and including that name on the certificate of completion as a deterrent for any student who might be tempted to make copies for their friends. They also found several minor technical glitches, grammatical errors, and places where students may become confused.

Feedback from students was also very positive. Most enjoyed the new format for learning a tedious subject. Many cited particular facts they learned through the game. Criticism from students included the juvenile nature of the game, the ability for students to keep guessing at the right answer without processing the information, and the time it took to find particularly well-hidden goblins, which they felt was a waste of time. However, these negative comments comprised a small minority of the total comments received.

Tips for Introducing Subject Faculty to the Game

Creating a game that suits a need on campus is the best way to ensure it will be used. Develop games that work for faculty, and ask for their feedback. When possible, incorporate that feedback into the game. This game has been quite popular among our faculty. It creates an avenue for discussion on the important topic of plagiarism while taking away very little class time.

References

Harris, Andy. 2005. *Beginning Flash Game Programming for Dummies*. New York: John Wiley/For Dummies.

A Planet in Peril: Plagiarism: Using Digital Games to Teach Information Literacy Skills

Ryan L. Sittler, Chad Sherman, David P. Keppel, Christine E. Schaeffer, Dana C. Hackley, and Laurie A. Grosik

Introduction

A Planet in Peril: Plagiarism is an adventure-style digital game that teaches students (or teams of students) about plagiarism—and how to avoid it—in a fun, nonthreatening environment (http://www.coe.iup.edu/thinkingworldsgame/; http://www.facebook.com/pages/A-Planet-in-Peril-Plagiarism/122897281080677). It can be used as either an introduction or a follow-up to a larger lesson on the topic. Although developed for undergraduate students, the game would likely work with middle and high school students as well as some graduate students.

Objectives

After playing *A Planet in Peril: Plagiarism*, students will be able to:

- define plagiarism;
- identify forms of obvious plagiarism (such as submitting a paper a classmate submitted in another class, using information without giving proper acknowledgment, and copying and pasting text from the Internet into a paper without an appropriate citation);
- describe what does and does not need to be cited within a paper;
- state the purpose of in-text citations;
- describe the differences between summaries, paraphrased material, and direct quotations; and
- construct proper American Psychological Association (APA) citations.

Information Literacy Competency Standards Addressed

This game addresses these ACRL Information Literacy Competency Standards: #2; #3; #5.

Game Background

Plagiarism is a common problem on college and university campuses. Librarians and other faculty are often called on to provide plagiarism awareness and prevention instruction. This game was developed by a librarian and five other Communications Media and Instructional Technology doctoral students to address this issue in a positive and engaging manner. During development, the game was also entered into—and won—the 2010 Caspian Learning Serious Games Challenge.

A Planet in Peril: Plagiarism was created using the following software packages and Internet resources. (It is important to note that while some of this software would be costly to obtain in a commercial setting, the educational licenses for the commercial products are quite reasonable. Freeware alternatives also exist. Additionally, an entire game can be created with Thinking Worlds alone; all of the extra software was not needed to make a fully functioning game.)

- Thinking Worlds development software (http://www.thinkingworlds.com/). This is the backbone on which the game was created—all elements are arranged and manipulated within this environment. Many of the 3D objects used in this game were included "stock" with the Thinking Worlds software (including the aliens!)
- Maxon CINEMA 4D modeling and animation software (http://www.maxon.net/products/cinema-4d.html). The campus environment as well as a portion of the objects were created using this package. The choice to use this program was based largely on our modeler's familiarity with the program, which allowed him to quickly produce usable objects.
- Autodesk 3ds MAX modeling and animation software with the CaspianTools utility plug-in

(http://usa.autodesk.com/adsk/servlet/pc/index?siteID=123112&id=13567410). Thinking Worlds would not directly accept 3D files output by CINEMA 4D—these files were imported into 3ds MAX and then processed by the CaspianTools plug-in, which exported the file to a format supported by Thinking Worlds.

- Adobe Photoshop CS4 image editing software (http://www.adobe.com/products/photoshop/photoshop/). This was used to create the opening credits graphics, the message text boxes, and the textures for the environment and objects produced for the game.
- NVIDIA DDS plug-in (http://developer.nvidia.com/object/photoshop_dds_plugins.html). Thinking Worlds would not directly accept image files produced by Photoshop. This plug-in needed to be installed in order for Photoshop to export them in a format that Thinking Worlds could use.
- Audacity audio editing software (http://audacity.sourceforge.net/). This was used to create the alien voices and sound FX and manipulate other sound files as needed.
- Incompetech Royalty-Free Music (http://incompetech.com/m/c/royalty-free/). The song *Chanter* by Kevin MacLeod was used during the introduction (and other compositions by this artist were used throughout the game).
- Stock.xchng (http://www.sxc.hu). Free stock photos were used to create various items within the game (such as carpets).

Figure 45.1.
The Landing Site for
A Planet in Peril: Plagiarism

Audience

This game is designed to be played by a single player either online or locally if the game is downloaded, and it is targeted at traditional-age undergraduate students early within their academic career (such as first-year students enrolled in a core writing course). It is not uncommon for individuals to play a game as part of a larger group. Therefore, it would not be difficult for a small group of students to share in the experience together. Additionally, much of the content is relevant to high school students. Graduate students and non-traditional undergraduate students may also find the game valuable and enjoyable.

Time Required

Completion of this game should take 20 to 60 minutes, depending on how quickly the student chooses to move through the game.

Materials and Equipment

This game requires:

- a computer for each student player, on which the game has been downloaded or with access to the Internet, and
- a web browser with Shockwave installed.

Preparation

This game is available on the Internet (http://www.coe.iup.edu/thinkingworldsgame/), or it can also be downloaded (see Figure 45.1). If it is downloaded, players are likely to find game play is a bit faster.

Playing the Game

Though educators would love if students were motivated to play out of interest in learning about plagiarism, they realize this is unlikely. Instead, the motivation for a student to play needs to come from an interesting story line and strong game mechanics. Narrative is important for adventure-style games, and this game is no exception.

A Planet in Peril: Plagiarism was developed to be both sarcastic and satirical. Aliens, posing as academics, try to save the world from one student's lapse in judgment (plagiarism). The story is just "the hook" to entertain and gain the attention of the students. Once they begin playing, the intent is that they will

**Figure 45.2.
Players Might Find the
Environment Semifamiliar**

**Figure 45.3.
Narrative Drives the Storyline
and Maintains Player Interest**

submerge themselves into the fantasy world, forgetting it is a somewhat dry and tedious topic they are learning and finding it a challenge to save the world from destruction by avoiding plagiarism (see Figures 45.2 and 45.3).

The game presents a lighthearted and whimsical spirit while conquering a serious subject that impacts many college campuses. It is meant to be amusing and informative without favoring either approach. Although the game is surely not hard-core enough for hard-core gamers, the developers endeavored to create something that would appeal primarily to casual gamers; the game can be played quickly with a low possibility of failure.

The game teaches students how to play by using a "just in time" teaching strategy. As new skills and game play techniques emerge, the player is presented with an explanation of what to do, how to do it, and the opportunity to try it out. Therefore, there is no need for formal instructions to be read ahead of time. Extraneous skills and game play mechanics do not "emerge" until the first time they are required. This approach has much in common with situated learning theory—information is presented in an environment, and situation, in which the player needs to utilize it. This allows them to more easily integrate the skill into their game play repertoire.

As play progresses, players are given tasks to complete that create additional challenges and reveal more

of the storyline while subtly revealing small details about plagiarism. This is a common aspect of adventure-style games and encourages players to keep moving forward. Special care was given to all challenges to ensure that they did not become too difficult for casual gamers to complete. Because the developers believe that the topic of plagiarism and information literacy is important, it is then very important that the players are able, and want, to finish the game! The game would not be a success if players quit because of frustration.

Near the end of the game, players are presented with a challenge that requires them to utilize their newly acquired knowledge about plagiarism. If they do not successfully complete the challenge, they are provided infinite opportunities to retry until they get it right. (Giving away details about this now would give away too much about the game; you will need to play in order to find out what happens!) If players "fail" at this step they are shown a negative ending to the game before they can retry. They are then provided with an opportunity to do things correctly. Upon successful completion, the player is rewarded with the "end" of the story—the final piece of the narrative.

Evaluation

At the time of this writing, *A Planet in Peril: Plagiarism* offers in-game assessment, but nothing has been done formally outside of the game. Larger student assessment opportunities are being explored but have not yet been developed.

Tips for Introducing Subject Faculty to the Game

Using digital games, starring aliens, to teach students about plagiarism may raise an eyebrow or two from some faculty members. Faculty who believe games have educational value (and do not mind the ludicrous storyline) will surely be more open to testing this approach to teaching and learning. Others may not see the value and may balk or bristle at the idea (regardless of how much literature you cite that supports this method).

The developers recommend starting with like-minded faculty and students. Then, if you have already made a game (or wish to use ours), you might be able to persuade faculty by convincing them to just try it out for a few minutes. Testimonials from these individuals may prove valuable in getting others to follow suit. Likewise, inviting a faculty member to sit down with a student while they play the game, and seeing how the student reacts, may be useful.

Special Thanks

This game would not have been possible without the encouragement of Dr. Allen Partridge and Dr. Kelly Heider.

Plagiarism Busters
Jennifer M. Woolston

Introduction

This traditional game assists undergraduates in developing a better understanding of academic dishonesty while forming the skills needed to rectify the errors and learning how to combat instances of plagiarism in their own writing.

Objectives

After playing *Plagiarism Busters* students will be able to:

- articulate a basic definition of plagiarism and potential consequences in academia,
- correctly identify when plagiarism occurs in research papers,
- work as a team to problem solve (and/or critically think) effectively, and
- construct appropriate in-text and Works Cited citations through hands-on use of the most recent Modern Language Association (MLA) style manual. (Other citation methods can be substituted for MLA.)

Information Literacy Competency Standards Addressed

This game addresses this ACRL Information Literacy Competency Standard: #2.

Game Background

This game was designed to help students learn how to avoid the pitfalls of plagiarism, one of the most important lessons students can learn within writing and research-intensive courses and one that often inspires fear and anxiety in students. The game was intended to engage students, improve their learning potential, and limit the fear and anxiety that might otherwise occur.

Audience

This game is designed for classes of up to 29 undergraduate or graduate students. The class is divided into several small groups of four to five students, the number of groups depending on the size of the class.

Time Required

Setup takes under five minutes. The actual game takes 20 to 30 minutes, depending on how many citations will need to be added or corrected on the worksheets. Most instructors will want to walk the class through the corrections made to the worksheet. Allot an additional 10 to 20 minutes for this large-group discussion.

Materials and Equipment

The game requires:

- one worksheet per student containing sample written text and omitted/incorrect in-text and/or Works Cited citations (pre-created by the instructor) and
- prizes.

Prizes are optional. I did not use any the first few times I implemented this activity, but they may be welcome additions to the game! I recommend pencils, erasers, or candy. I am sure each student in the room would enjoy "winning" something small as an acknowledgment of their efforts during the game play.

Preparation

Discuss the concept of plagiarism with the class, and identify possible sanctions for committing this academic offense. This lesson can occur during the same class session the game is played in or during a previous one. Instructors may wish to either dialogue with students to brainstorm this information as a group or present the information to the class via a video presentation. I have successfully used a 22-minute video titled *Plagiarism: It's a Crime* to illustrate these concepts in class prior to game play.

Instructors must create a worksheet containing a sample piece of writing. This sample can be limited to a few paragraphs and should include citation errors and clear examples of plagiarism. For example, quote sources without the proper parenthetical in-text citation, omit a page number, erase an author's last name, or incorrectly format a Works Cited entry. The worksheet should also ask questions after each example so that students can identify issues of plagiarism, discuss the ideas within their small group, and make suggestions for revision. Some instructors may want to include other elements of MLA formatting that students are already familiar with (e.g., omitting italics or incorrectly formatting block quotations). Example worksheets are available on the Cleveland State University Writing Center's Plagiarism Quiz website at http://www.csuohio.edu/writingcenter/WAC/Plagiarism%20Quiz.doc.

Playing the Game

Begin the session with a discussion about plagiarism and its consequences within the academy. This might initially intimidate students who are unfamiliar with proper citation methods and unsure of whether they may have unwittingly committed the offense via unintentional error. This is a great entry into a discussion of the complexities of the subject matter—and this game is a way to "wet the whistles" of novice students. It is also a safe "practice space" for students to work on textual revisions and in-text citations without worrying about penalties for mistakes.

Explain that students will work with their group members to identify instances of plagiarism and to devise strategies for revision. They may also consult their course notes and/or class textbook in order to firmly conclude the proper citation(s) necessary. Students may also be told that there is a prize for participating (if this is true). Once students learn that they will be building essential hands-on research skills and dialoguing with their peers (and perhaps making new friends in class), they are usually interested in giving the game a whirl.

Then briefly discuss the rules of the game, divide the students into small groups, and pass out the worksheets. Every student should receive his or her own worksheet. Students should talk among themselves as they tackle each example on the worksheet, ensuring that they can identify when/why plagiarism occurred, potential consequences for committing plagiarism in the academy, and ways in which they could revise the example according to MLA's citation guidelines.

Remind students to keep their voices low so that other groups cannot overhear what they are saying.

When the groups believe that they have correctly revised each example on the worksheet and answered all relevant questions, they should elect a delegate to come to the front of the room. The instructor will quickly check the delegate's worksheet—if errors persist, the student will be sent back to the group for further work. The first group to send a delegate to the front of the room with a correct worksheet is the "official" winner. (Of course, each student partaking in the activity should feel a sense of winning accomplishment once they have completed the game.)

After a winner is declared, review the worksheets with the class as a whole. Each group may be called on to suggest corrections for the worksheet content. Students should be encouraged to correct any mistakes on their personal worksheets, as these can be good study aids to refer to in the future. Once the class as a whole addresses each item on the worksheet, the game is finished. Instructors may hand out prizes at this point if they choose to include them.

Evaluation

Because students must work to figure out worksheet examples and questions together, they are actively engaged in the game (and with each other) from start to finish, and their reactions to the game have been quite positive. This activity often relieves student anxiety surrounding the issue of plagiarism and allows for some fun discussion about the rules of MLA citation. It is generally met with energy, smiles, and enthusiasm. Once students become invested in "busting" instances of plagiarism in a safe environment, they tend to become passionate about finding answers and solutions.

Tips for Introducing Subject Faculty to the Game

This game may appeal to instructors of all levels. Because it is easy to construct and implement, it may appeal to anyone interested in meeting the game's proposed objectives. Explain that it should be used during the beginning of a course focusing on research and academic writing as a hands-on follow-up to the initial introduction of the subject matter. Using this game further along in a course may be viewed as a waste of time, because students will already be somewhat versed in proper MLA citation methods.

Fun with Plagiarism: Using Clickers to Discuss Academic Honesty

Theresa Westbrock

Introduction

The New Mexico State University Library's instruction program receives a fair amount of requests for instruction covering plagiarism. Additionally, the instruction program has a longstanding relationship with the UNIV 150 program. Historically, students enrolled in the three-credit UNIV 150 class spend two class sessions in the library. The first session is a librarian-led discussion of plagiarism, and the second is a more traditional introduction-to-library-resources instruction session. Discussing plagiarism with freshmen, completely out of context of a writing assignment, has presented quite a challenge. By incorporating clickers (remote personal response systems), we were able to transform the often one-sided plagiarism discussion into one that incorporates polls, guessing games, and debate-provoking questions that actively engage the students.

Objectives

After completing *Fun with Plagiarism*, students will know:

- what constitutes instances of plagiarism,
- what to do when faced with ethical dilemmas later in their academic careers, and
- the potential severity of plagiarism and other forms of academic dishonesty.

Information Literacy Competency Standards Addressed

This game addresses this ACRL Information Literacy Competency Standard: #5.

Game Background

Routine plagiarism discussions with each section of UNIV 150 Introduction to the University semes-ter after semester were beginning to feel more like redundant lectures that no one was interested in, students or librarians. Students weren't engaged, librarians were discouraged, and the situation begged attention. So, how does a librarian entice a group of freshmen into discussing plagiarism without sounding accusatory or, worse, boring? In a word, clickers.

The incorporation of clickers into the plagiarism discussion added an active learning component via competition, keeping the students involved, engaging them anonymously, and allowing them to offer personal information and to guess at answers without risking embarrassment. The activity invites true discussion by priming students with leading questions before the actual discussion.

Audience

This game works in all size classes. It has primarily been used with lower-division undergraduates in the UNIV Introduction to the University class, but it's also been successfully used with focused groups of graduate students.

Time Required

This game generally takes from 50 to 70 minutes, but it is relatively easy to scale to time constraints.

Materials and Equipment

This game requires:

- clickers and
- a clicker-ready PowerPoint presentation (sample slides are described in "Playing the Game").

If students have access to the Internet and individual workstations, then the Scavenger Hunt (step three in the Playing the Game section) can be included.

Generally prizes are not given. When they are, library-branded highlighters and bookmarks are used.

Preparation

A small amount of practice is necessary, because the questions (and the students' answers to the questions) lead the discussion. However, after one or two presentations, it becomes quite simple to lead the game in an entertaining and effective manner.

Playing the Game

In this game, students use personal response devices, commonly known as clickers. Clickers are handheld devices that use infrared or radio frequency technology to allow students to send answers in response to the instructor's questions. The answers are recorded and then tallied and displayed in PowerPoint slides. Answers can be associated with individual students or can be anonymous. In this game, the facilitator provides information and then asks students to answer questions anonymously. The use of clickers allows the instructor to gather aggregate data on students' opinions and understanding and stimulates actual classroom discussion. Note: All questions are verbal in order to give the presenter as much freedom as possible to adapt the session.

1. Warm-Up: Slides One and Two

The purpose of the Warm-Up slide is to familiarize students with using the clickers while creating a fun and comfortable environment. One of the challenges of a one-shot session is trying to establish rapport with a group of strangers. Slide One should ask students to guess the correct percentage when given a statistic dealing with academic honesty and plagiarism among high school and college students. Keep a list of statistics, gathered from articles about plagiarism, to use with this slide. This list needs to be updated with new articles that report student plagiarism statistics (e.g., Casey, 2008; Kleiner and Lord, 1999; Morris and Kilian, 2007). The following are example questions:

- What percentage of high-achieving high school students admit to cheating at least once? (The answer is 80 percent.)
- What percentage of high school students who admit to cheating report having been caught? (The answer is 5 percent.)

These questions can be followed by a short discussion about the perceived necessity of deterrents to dishonesty in an academic setting: Are students less likely to cheat if they think they'll be caught? Is it okay to cheat if no one will ever know?

Usually, students stay engaged for about three of these "guessing game" questions. Presenters use whichever of the statistics work best with their individual styles and discussions points.

Now move to Slide Two, which shifts the focus from general statistics to the students' individual and personal experiences. Timed properly, this slide greatly increases the energy level in the classroom. Students seem to enjoy being polled, especially about their high school experiences (which are now part of their individual, unique pasts). Each of these questions can be followed by a meaningful discussion about academic ethics and students' roles in their own and others' academic experiences.

Slide Two is a yes or no slide that asks the student if they have ever (1) cheated, (2) witnessed someone cheating, and (3) turned someone in. After Slides One and Two, students are generally awake, engaged, and primed for the following discussion about plagiarism.

2. Discussing Plagiarism: Slides Three to Six

Slides Three to Six begin the discussion of plagiarism (defining, understanding, awareness of consequences) and do not include clicker activity. Whereas this discussion can be tedious on its own, students seem much more likely to participate in the discussion after the warm-up.

Slide Three includes the definition of plagiarism provided in the student code of conduct of the institution where the session is being offered. Include a source citation at the bottom of the slide.

Slides Four through Six present a more detailed definition of plagiarism, point out why it occurs, and explains the consequences of plagiarism at the institution where the session is being offered. Again, cite any information taken from the code of student conduct.

3. Scavenger Hunt

The scavenger hunt is optional and requires that students have access to the Internet. This activity provides a break during the plagiarism discussion and enlightens students about the fates of a few real-life plagiarists.

Put students in small groups, and assign them each a name of a real-life plagiarist (possibilities include Doris Kearns Goodwin, Jayson Blair, Michael Hand [NMSU], Kaavya Viswanathan, and Park Yung). Give them five minutes to hunt around the Internet and find out (1) who the person is, (2) what the person was accused of (regarding plagiarism), and (3) what the consequences were. Then have each group give a short report on what they found. Use each example as appropriate to initiate short discussions about the nature of plagiarism in the "real world." The scavenger hunt serves as a segue to the next discussion.

4. Discussion of Avoiding Plagiarism

The next discussion provides tips on avoiding plagiarism and information on other types of academic dishonesty that are also prohibited. Citing the student code of conduct or other local academic integrity document is recommended and gives authority to the points you make.

5. Wrap-Up Quiz: Slide 7

The Wrap-Up Quiz reinforces some basic rules regarding plagiarism and academic honesty and is also a way to spark debate among the students. As with the Warm-Up exercise, we keep a collection of sample questions/situations for Slide Seven. Different presenters like to use different examples based on their individual discussion style. Some questions do not have a right or a wrong answer, and those allow excellent opportunities for students to debate. This helps to show students that there is a lot of gray area when debating ethical situations.

The point of the Wrap-Up Quiz is to engage students one last time, drawing on their individual ethics and what they have learned from the overall discussion. The following example situations have sparked many well-thought debates among students:

- A student lists sources in his bibliography that he has not read.
- After making only a few changes, a student turns in a paper she had written and turned in to another class.

- "John, Betty, and Tom were assigned a group project that culminated with a term paper. Tom only attended one group meeting and did not participate in writing any of the paper. Tom told Betty and John he was having a very busy semester. Thus, Betty and John wrote the paper without his help. However, they did include his name on the paper as a co-author. All three received a B on the project" (Morris and Kilian, 2007).
- Joe includes a definition from Wikipedia in his paper but does not cite it because there is no author to cite in a Wikipedia entry.

Evaluation

Evaluation is done on the fly, after each question. Many of the questions do not have a correct answer; rather, their purpose is to get students debating situations. After using a version of this presentation for three years, instructors have found students to be continually engaged during the game. They team up, state their views, listen to each other, and change their minds. It is rewarding to witness students learning through discovery.

Tips for Introducing Subject Faculty to the Game

Present the game at a department meeting, use the game in a workshop setting, or incorporate the game into existing, regularly occurring instruction sessions.

References

Casey, M. 2008. "Digging Out Roots of Cheating in High School." *New York Times*, October 13: A28.

Kleiner, C., and M. Lord. 1999. "The Cheating Game." *U.S. News & World Report*, 127 no. 20: 54.

Morris, D.E., and C.M. Kilian. 2007. "Do Accounting Students Cheat? A Study Examining Undergraduate Accounting Students' Honesty and Perceptions of Dishonest Behavior." *Social Science Review Network*. August. http://ssrn.com/abstract=1010277.

Using Scenarios to "Get Real" with Students about Copyright and Plagiarism

Susan Ariew

Introduction

Scenarios can be entertaining, active learning games to reach and teach students about information ethics. By discussing and analyzing scenarios, students can better understand ethical issues in real-world settings.

Objectives

Students will be able to:

- determine, via group discussion of scenarios, if a copyright or plagiarism "offense" (i.e., ethical violation) has been committed.

Information Literacy Competency Standards Addressed

This game addresses this ACRL Information Literacy Competency Standard: #5.

Game Background

The context for this game was a unit in a three-credit, undergraduate course on library and Internet research skills (LIS 2005) at the University of South Florida. The course was part of the curriculum of the School of Library and Information Sciences. The unit on information ethics included instruction about copyright, plagiarism, and fair use. Instructors wanted to avoid the usual boring lecture. The scenario approach that asked students to analyze whether an ethics violation had occurred allowed for engaging students in debate and discussion. Once a class became invested in the scenarios and reported on their work, instructors stepped into the "teachable moment" with useful information to fill in gaps in student knowledge.

Audience

Questions about information ethics cut across all disciplines, so using scenarios to "make it real" can work in a variety of instructional settings, whether it is in teaching library and information science, English, rhetoric, communication, journalism, or an applied ethics class for philosophy. The optimal group for this game is a high school or undergraduate class of 10 to 25 students. Because the game requires putting students into small groups or in pairs to analyze scenarios, this number of students is desirable so that as many students as possible are engaged in the process of discussion and analysis.

Time Required

The time required for this game is variable, depending on the size of the group and the number of scenarios instructors choose to cover. If there are seven scenarios discussed by groups or pairs of students in the class, minimally one would need at least five minutes for analysis and then two to five minutes per group to report back their ideas and receive teacher feedback with supplemental information for students. Minimally this means 40 to 45 minutes for the entire activity if the instructor uses 7 scenarios.

Materials and Equipment

The game requires:

- handouts or note cards describing each scenario,
- supplemental material and scenarios to display using PowerPoint during the feedback portion of the activity (if desired), and
- optionally, Internet connections to show any useful websites (such as the Creative Commons site) that might be relevant to the discussion.

Preparation

Instructors need to have their own information/answers to all scenarios in order to fill in gaps and correct any misconceptions students may have during their discussion and analysis, along with authoritative resources to support those answers.

Playing the Game

Distribute a handout with the scenarios and the instructions. Assign each group or pair of students a scenario to work on. Read the instructions. These are the instructions used in the LIS 2005 class:

> You have five minutes. Read each scenario. Act as the judge and give the type of offense (plagiarism, copyright infringement, or other ethical dilemma), and give your verdict—guilty or not guilty. Then explain your verdict. Use what you learned in class readings to justify your verdict. Your verdict will be shared with the class. If you are not sure about a verdict, do some more research on the computers to try to verify the answer.

It is helpful for the entire class to see all the scenarios so that later on they can weigh in on the analyses of others assigned to the scenario. After five minutes, ask each group to report their "verdict" and justify it. Be prepared to offer supplemental sources and information.

Scenario 1

Source: Davidson, R. 1973. *Genesis 1-11*. Cambridge: Cambridge UP.

Original Wording: "Such 'story myths' are not told for their entertainment value. They provide answers to questions people ask about life, about society and about the world in which they live" (p. 10).

Mary's Paper: Specifically, story myths are not for entertainment purposes rather they serve as answers to questions people ask about life, about society and about the world in which they live. Has Mary plagiarized or not?

Scenario 2

George has a presentation tomorrow for his public relations class. While searching the Internet, he found the perfect graphic to illustrate one of his key points. Even though he's pretty sure the graphic is copyrighted, he decides to cut and paste it into his PowerPoint presentation anyway. He decides to list the website and date he visited the site below the graphic. Did George do anything wrong?

Scenario 3

Last week, someone stole Linda's car. Although the police were able to recover the car, the thief had taken all her CDs from the car. Adam, Linda's chemistry lab partner who has had a crush on her since the first day of classes, decides this is the perfect opportunity for him to tell Linda how he feels. They have similar tastes in music, so he decides to burn some of his CDs for her. He doesn't want to do anything illegal, so he only burns the CDs she already had, figuring it's not a problem because she had already bought the CDs herself. Has Adam done anything wrong?

Scenario 4

Stan has to write a paper on *Othello* for his Literature class. The following is a source Stan used in his paper. Did Stan do anything wrong?

Original Wording:

> The main image in *Othello* is that of animals in action, preying upon one another, mischievous, lascivious, cruel or suffering, and through these, the general sense of pain and unpleasantness is much increased and kept constantly before us. More than half the animal images in the play are Iago's, and all these are contemptuous or repellent: a plague of flies, a quarrelsome dog, the recurrent image of bird-snaring, leading asses by the nose, a spider catching a fly, beating an offenceless dog, wild cats, wolves, goats and monkeys. (Spurgeon, 1952: 335)

Stan's Paper: The majority of the animal images in the play are Iago's, and all of these are contemptuous or repellent. He refers to a plague of flies, a quarrelsome dog, bird-snaring, leading asses by the nose, a spider catching a fly, beating an offenseless dog, wild cats, goats and monkeys. Through these images the general sense of pain and unpleasantness is increased and kept constantly before us (Spurgeon, 1935: 335).

Scenario 5

Jane has a final economics paper due on Monday. One of her sources, a journal article, uses a quote from a book. Jane likes the quote and wants to use it in her paper but can't find the book in the library. Because it's already Sunday and her paper is due the next day, she doesn't have time to get the book through interlibrary loan. Even though she doesn't have the original book, she has the quote from the journal article, so she decides to use the quote and cite the book. Has Jane done anything wrong?

Scenario 6

Rob just got a DVD burner for his birthday. He decides it would be a great idea to burn the DVDs he rents from NetFlix. He figures it's not a big deal because the DVDs will be for his own use and he won't be giving them out to his friends. Has Rob done anything wrong?

Scenario 7

David heard that *Lost* is a great TV show, but he missed the first season. He decides to go to his favorite file-sharing site on the web and download the first season episodes to watch them. He figures ABC won't mind because he can catch up and continue watching season two, which is good for them commercially. Has he done anything wrong?

Evaluation

Because this was a game included in the context of a course, students were given lab quizzes based on the content in the unit that they took for a grade. Later, some concepts presented in the game were included in the end-of-term exam. If this is done in collaboration with academic faculty, librarians can still create short quizzes or assessments to determine student learning outcomes.

Tips for Introducing Subject Faculty to the Game

Occasionally faculty request plagiarism workshops for students. This is a good format for such a workshop. Because this game takes up quite a bit of class time, it works best in the context of a one- to three-credit class on information literacy or research methods.

References

Spurgeon, C.F.E. 1952. *Shakespeare's Imagery and What It Tells Us*. Cambridge, England: The University Press.

PART IX

Finding, Identifying, and Discovering the Significance of Primary Sources Games

This part includes Games 49–51. In two games students use the Internet to find primary sources. In one of the games they use secondary sources to identify and explain historical artifacts.

Ellie Jones and the Raiders of the Lost Archives

Kimberly A. Jones, Melissa Langridge, and Jeff Miller

Introduction

This game is best suited for a standard introductory history course at the college level or an advanced history course at the high school level. It teaches primary resource research in a narrative style where students are required to find information to present to the president (or another figure) about a certain topic.

Objectives

Students will be able to:

- effectively search the web,
- find credible information,
- evaluate if a source is primary or secondary, and
- organize and reflect on information discovered.

Information Literacy Competency Standards Addressed

This game addresses these ACRL Information Literacy Competency Standards: #2; #3.

Game Background

In this game, the main character, Ellie Jones, granddaughter of the infamous Indiana, has assigned a mission to the class. She has sent the library instructor orders to test their field agents and send her the best ones for an important assignment. This game offers an informative way to solve a problem in any field by using primary resources in research. The basic lesson plan can be modified for use in other disciplines such as psychology and sociology.

In this example scenario, Ellie Jones needs information to brief the president on the history of containment policy. The game has been played with college freshmen with success. The outline has been modified for various courses (e.g., we changed the report to one on pop culture and urbanization for a sociology class). An easy way to reformat the game is to work with a professor on the topic of the paper and use the major umbrella term (containment, urbanization, adolescent psychology) as the overarching theme. We've used Google to research topics under that umbrella (Red Scare, Vietnam War, etc.) and had students research those topics as teams and then tie them back to containment. It teaches students how to use a search engine to access valuable resources, how to use primary resources, and how to present research in a library classroom.

Audience

The game is suitable for college freshmen and high school seniors.

Time Required

The game can be played in one 50-minute instruction session.

Materials and Equipment

The game requires:

- computers with Internet access,
- note paper and writing utensils,
- a game worksheet (see Figure 49.1 for an example),
- name tags, and
- red licorice whips or Smarties upon completion of assignment.

Preparation

Preparation takes about 15 to 20 minutes. Make photocopies of the worksheet, review keyword searches to see if links are still active, and set up a room if teaching at an institution where laptops are available.

Playing the Game

Begin by asking the students the following questions: "How would you describe a primary resource? A secondary resource? And, more importantly, what's the

> **Figure 49.1.**
> **Sample Worksheet**
>
> **Project Red Scare**
>
> *For each of these questions, work with your partner to find the answer. One person will be the secretary, the other the historian (researcher). You will be asked to present your findings to the class. Make sure to indicate where you found the information (web address) and the search strategy you created to find it.*
>
> **Team Vietnam**
>
> 1. How long was the war in Vietnam?
>
> 2. How many casualties did Vietnam produce?
>
> 3. What is Agent Orange? How did it aid in the war effort?
>
> 4. How did Vietnam relate to containment?
>
> *Write down all of your answers to the following questions:*
>
> Do you think this moment in history was worth it? What would you have done differently?
>
> **Team Red Scare**
>
> 1. What does the term "Red Scare" mean?
>
> 2. When was the first Red Scare? How was it defined?
>
> 3. When was the second Red Scare? How was it defined?
>
> 4. How did the Red Scare relate to containment?
>
> *Write down all of your answers to the following questions:*
>
> Do you think this moment in history was worth it? What would you have done differently?

difference and why does it matter? What are a few examples of each in your own life? Where do you think you would find U.S. historical primary resources?"

Then demonstrate some places where primary sources might readily be found. For example, demonstrate how to search ProQuest Historical Newspapers' version of the *New York Times* or search Google for online archives.

With the *New York Times*, you might demonstrate a basic search and then ask the students to search for articles on the Monroe Doctrine. When the students have completed their searchers, you might ask: "What search strategy did you use? What is the Monroe Doctrine? How did it affect U.S. foreign policy? Is this a primary resource? How would you use it?"

For Google searching, introduce the idea of using Google to find online archives, and then point out some institutes that might have primary resources online (universities and colleges, government resources, specialized companies). The goal is to show students *how* to find the archives. Walk through the search, calling on students to help come up with ideas to create a search strategy. Then walk them through how to evaluate useful results and how to create an awesome search strategy.

Then have students search for the actual Monroe Doctrine and ask: "When was it written? What search strategy did you use to find it? From which resource did you find it?"

After this introduction to searching, explain the game scenario. Ellie Jones, the granddaughter of the infamous Indiana, will be briefing the U.S. president on the history of containment. She needs her research team to look at historical examples to come up with information for the presentation; the group that does the best job goes with her to Washington, DC. Their mission, should they decide to accept it, is to find historical examples of containment, especially during the Cold War, and evaluate how successful they were.

Divide students into four groups of five. Give each student in the team a specific question to answer that relates to the entire group topic. The students will do research on their question, asking for help if needed. Then, they come together as one team to synthesize a debate. Ultimately, students will come up with a cost-benefit analysis of the controversial time period in U.S. history that was assigned to them. Each question is designed to have students find primary resource(s) on the subject and use them to analyze the term "containment" (see examples of topics and worksheet in Figure 49.1).

When the students have completed their research, the teams present their information to the class. The class will vote on the best information based on criteria laid out. The team that won would get the chance to present with Dr. Jones (or, in this case, a prize such as Smarties or licorice whips).

Evaluation

This exercise has been evaluated through direct observation and by students completing a 1-2-3 assessment: (1) What did you want to learn? (2) Did you learn it? (3) What did you already know? We discovered that students respond to the idea that the information they are learning has outside implications and that they enjoy exploring online archives through Google. Students respond well to the framework of the narrative and the competition that presenting embeds into the program. However, we have also encountered students using sites such as Wikipedia rather than a site with primary resources, so this is something to keep an eye on.

Tips for Introducing Subject Faculty to the Game

This game is particularly valuable for instructors who wish their students to learn how to evaluate web resources. When approaching subject faculty, it is useful to emphasize the positive educational benefits of active learning and the effective manner in which this game provides practice in identifying the difference between primary and secondary sources and evaluating websites.

Where in the World: Using the World Digital Library to Enhance Information Literacy and Global Learning to Gather, Analyze, Evaluate, and Use Information

Helen Bond

Introduction

This game challenges students to find primary sources and cultural heritage items on the Internet and assess and evaluate the accuracy of the sources. It has been used successfully with undergraduates and graduate students.

Objectives

Students will be able to:

- locate, retrieve, and evaluate artifacts from the World Digital Library relevant to their needs and the item's purpose and
- correctly cite the bibliographic information.

Information Literacy Competency Standards Addressed

This game addresses this ACRL Information Literacy Competency Standard: #3.

Game Background

Effectively using the wealth of information available to solve problems and find solutions is critical to the success of college students. Students often have access to multiple information resources on the Internet, but few recognize the potential of using digital repositories, such as online archives and primary sources, to add depth, legitimacy, and cultural understanding to their assignments. Students can enrich their work with artifacts such as letters, maps, drawings, legal documents, transcripts, photographs, sound recordings, and even motion pictures. Using primary sources and cultural heritage items in the classroom encourages critical thinking and enables students to assess and evaluate the accuracy of sources and to consider other perspectives (Frazier, 2008).

This introductory game challenges students to locate resources such as items or artifacts in the collections of the World Digital Library that are relevant to their assignment or topic. For example, teams of students with access to the Internet and a computer try to locate five items about colonization in Africa in five minutes or less. Then they rank the items in order of usefulness to the topic, with one being the most useful and five the least. The game can also be played with individual students with computers competing against each other. The *Where in the World* game can be made more challenging by asking students to locate artifacts in only certain areas of the world, during certain time periods, in a specific language, or to limit their search to certain types of artifacts such as maps or photographs.

Students will soon discover that to find items that originate in a certain part of the world, they can click on that region of the world and then use other functions of the World Digital Library to further refine the search. This makes it more challenging to find the required number of items and encourages students to think critically about the worth of each when it is time to rank the item's usefulness. This helps students to recognize that search information can be combined with other indicators in a variety of formats to produce newer and more relevant sources of information.

Audience

Because the World Digital Library collections are so diverse and geographically widespread across multiple regions, formats, and time periods (8000 BC to present), the game is useful in many different disciplines with undergraduate and graduate students.

Time Required

The game takes approximately 20 to 40 minutes, depending on the number of searches, topics, and descriptors. You may need to allow 7 or 10 minutes for each search round if this is the first time students have played the game or used the World Digital Library.

Materials and Equipment

Where in the World requires:

- access to a computer and the Internet, with each team having at least one computer or the same number of computers per team (perhaps in a computer lab); and
- small prizes (if desired), such as inflatable globes, maps, pencils, and pens.

Preparation

Preparation for *Where in the World* is minimal. The instructor must become familiar with the World Digital Library to better align the content of the library and the game to the assignment or course goals. This can be done by logging on to the World Digital Library website and browsing the collections and reading the background of the World Digital Library. Particularly helpful is browsing the Frequently Asked Questions section that explains how the content can be used and any copyright restrictions.

Playing the Game

To begin, review the project, assignment, or research topic that is going to be the focus of the *Where in the World* game. Explain that their assignment must include resource materials from the World Digital Library. Ask who has ever heard of or used the World Digital Library. Explain that to help them use the World Digital Library, you are going to play a game that will introduce them to the library's collections and how to navigate them to find what they need for their assignment.

Students can play in teams or as individuals. The instructions are similar for team and individual competitions. Put students in groups of threes, with a computer for at least two of the members. It is preferable to have a computer for all three members, but if this is not possible, members can rotate computer use. Next direct students to the website of the *World Digital Library* at http://www.wdl.org/en/. No registration or access fees are required. Once everyone has logged on tell students they will use paper and pencils to record the search criteria for each *Where in the World* round.

Search criteria can be combined in many different ways to produce a variety of searches with different levels of complexity. For example, the initial *Where in the World* search should be a very basic one, such as asking students to locate five items or artifacts about their topic in general. These items can be from any time period and from any region of the world and can be in any format, such as maps, manuscripts, photographs, and motion pictures. This basic search serves as an orientation to the World Digital Library.

Now increase the challenge. For example, ask students to locate five items about a topic, such as transatlantic slavery. Two of the items must be from the Americas, two must be from Africa, and one must be from Europe. In addition, one item must be a map and the other item must be a photograph from the period of 1600–1800. The format of the other three items is up to them. They must provide bibliographic data for each item that indicates where the item originated, the time period, and other information about the item.

Instruct teams that the first group to find all five items that satisfy the search criteria in five minutes or less and rank them according to how useful and relevant they are to the search topic will receive a reward! The reward might be bonus points or small inflatable globes, maps, pencils, or pens. The ranking of items can also be done during the debriefing session, especially if your focus is on navigating the collections. Items can be ranked with one being the most useful and five the least useful. Students use the bibliographic information provided about the item that describes the item to evaluate its worth. Students can raise their hand indicating they are the first person to make the find. To verify that they have met the search criteria, a team member or members must state what the items are and verify time, place, region, and other search criteria. They can also indicate how they ranked the items and why. Again, this can be saved for the debriefing session. If a computer and LCD screen is available, students can reproduce the items on the overhead screen for all to enjoy.

I suggest including a debriefing session at the end of the game to help students process and reflect on what they have experienced and learned. I typically ask them if they liked the game, what they learned, and what unique strategies or useful tips or tricks they used to discover their artifacts. The ranking and justification of items can also be done during the debriefing session.

Evaluation

The debriefing session is an excellent starting point for evaluating the game's success. Toward the end of the debriefing session, ask the teams of students to come up with at least two things they liked about the game and at least two ways that it might be improved. Students are instructed to write this information down on an anonymous note card that is left at a designated location in the classroom. Students are often very insightful and have offered excellent suggestions, such as needing more or less time, and devised very inventive and creative search criteria.

Tips for Introducing Subject Faculty to the Game

Faculty are always looking for ways to engage their students in thoughtful, collaborative, and competitive activities. Monthly department meetings are an excellent venue to share new ideas and new practices.

References

Frazier, Emily. 2008. "Teacher Spotlight." *Teaching with Primary Sources Newsletter* (Summer). http://www.loc.gov/teachers/tps/newsletter/pdf/TPSNewsSummer08.pdf.

What Am I?: Understanding Primary Sources Challenge

Theresa McDevitt

Introduction

This is a traditional game for undergraduate or graduate students to demonstrate the value of primary sources and the techniques helpful in locating information to interpret them.

Objectives

Students will:

- be able to distinguish between primary and secondary sources,
- recognize that understanding the past is based on interpretation of primary sources and that the significance of primary sources is not always immediately evident, and
- learn to use search techniques to locate background information for the interpretation of primary sources.

Information Literacy Competency Standards Addressed

This game addresses this ACRL Information Literacy Competency Standard: #4.

Game Background

Special collections and archives librarians are often asked to provide an introduction to their collections to undergraduate and graduate students in disciplines where primary sources are of interest. While students are often bored with abstract discussions of archival practice, the distinction between secondary and primary sources evade them, and the rows of manuscript boxes in archives stacks leave them cold, they love to look at historic artifacts and like to compete with one another to determine their true purpose. This game was designed to provide an engaging introduction to the difference between primary and secondary sources, the need to find background information to

fully understand artifacts and other primary sources, and the value of the special collections and archives department in an academic library.

Audience

This game has been used successfully with groups of 20 to 30 students in both graduate and undergraduate classes in a variety of disciplines.

Time Required

This game can easily be played in 60 minutes with a group of less than 30. Classes with more students (and therefore more groups) would require more time.

Materials and Equipment

The game requires:

- historic artifacts that will not be destroyed by being handled (if none are available you can adapt this game for use with historic photographs, which are readily available on the web);
- *What Am I?* game worksheets (easily adapted from the *Artifact Analysis* worksheet available from the National Archives at http://www.archives.gov/education/lessons/worksheets/artifact.html);
- reference sources that provide descriptions of historic artifacts or a list of Internet sites that discuss techniques on interpreting historic artifacts and access to computers with Internet access; and
- certificates for winners.

Preparation

Choose historic artifacts from your collection, or borrow some from a local historical society. Particularly useful are artifacts or photographs that relate to the manuscript collections available in your archives. One artifact is needed for each group of students. Prepare *What Am I?* worksheets.

Playing the Game

Introduce students to the difference between primary and secondary sources. Stress the importance of primary sources to understanding history but that one often needs contextual information to correctly interpret a source.

Then inform students that they will be playing a game of *What Am I?* where the object is to answer questions about a historic artifact. Divide students into teams (four to a team is best). Each team is given an artifact, the game worksheet, and 10 minutes to answer the questions.

When the 10 minutes is up, ask each group to pick a reporter to present the group's findings. Rate them from 1 to 10 on the correctness of their deductions. The team with the highest points get bonus points or a *What Am I?* winner's certificate.

Then ask: "How did you answer the questions?" After they have given their answers, ask: "What else might you do to be sure you are right?" Answers might be "Look on the Internet under any words that appear on the artifact, ask an elderly person," etc. End the discussion by informing them that they could look the artifacts up in reference works that describe such artifacts, or look them up on the Internet, where there are many sites such as *The History Detectives* (http://www.pbs.org/opb/historydetectives/techniques/index.html) that offer tips on how to identify artifacts. It is also a good time to tell them that related manuscript collections from your archives would offer more clues on the significance of the artifacts.

Evaluation

Students enjoy this exercise, and it does seem to illustrate the difference between primary and secondary sources and the importance of using other sources to help interpret primary sources.

Tips for Introducing Subject Faculty to the Game

It is useful for any class where an understanding of the difference between primary and secondary sources and the need to do research to interpret them is taught.

PART X

Games to Assess and Wrap Up Information Literacy Instruction Sessions

This section includes Games 52–54. These games can finish off semester-long information literacy or other classes by asking students to demonstrate their grasp of library fundamentals and information literacy concepts by using an Internet toy that generates "word clouds" from text, or to create presentations demonstrating their understanding of information literacy topics, or play a game that allows them to uncover the underbelly of research as they answer a series of questions.

Winning Wordles
Rhonda Huisman and Kathleen A. Hanna

Introduction

While the one-minute paper and other "quick and dirty" assessment tools have their place in library instruction, often they result in vague responses from students that leave the librarian in doubt of the students' understanding of the material. By creating word clouds (sometimes called "tag clouds"), students can demonstrate their grasp of library fundamentals and information literacy concepts in less than 10 minutes. Wordle (http://www.wordle.net) is a free, user-friendly online tool that can be used as a scalable assessment activity in which students create a visual representation of their learning and librarians rapidly evaluate their comprehension of library jargon, key concepts, and more. Wordle is suitable as both a pre- and a post-test tool.

Objectives

Students will:

- demonstrate their retention, understanding, and application of key concepts related to library skills and information literacy;
- participate in collaborative working groups, quickly establishing an appropriate level of cooperation, and conduct peer revision of their final product;
- demonstrate their ability to follow instructions in a timely manner; and
- seek follow-up assistance as needed.

Information Literacy Competency Standards Addressed

This game addresses this ACRL Information Literacy Competency Standard: #3.

Game Background

According to Angelo and Cross (1993), the one-minute paper is often modified to meet the needs of discipline-specific assessment, goals, or circumstances.

Winning Wordles repurposes this widely used technique by incorporating a visual imagery tool that is freely available on the Internet and has seen some success in K–12 teaching. Wordle (http://www.wordle.net) offers a promising interactive and entertaining method of assessing what students learned during library instruction sessions by creating word clouds, either as a group or individually.

Audience

Winning Wordles is suitable for first-year seminar/freshmen learning community courses and upper-level undergraduate college students in classes of all sizes. The activity can be modified depending on room size and access to computers.

Time Required

The game takes 10 to 15 minutes, depending on the version played.

Materials and Equipment

The game requires:

- a computer with Internet access, preferably with an LCD projector connected to demonstrate the Wordle images on a wall or screen;
- note cards and pens or pencils; and
- accompanying reading materials, if desired, such as
  - information literacy standards,
  - library mission statement,
  - other related information or resources used for comparison, and
  - a subject- or topic-specific article (students may require a printed copy).

Preparation

Familiarize yourself with the Wordle website (http://www.wordle.net), and practice creating, modifying, and publishing word clouds using different features and options. Note which features will be most useful to students based on their anticipated level of engagement and time constraints. The Wordle forum is very active and offers help in further customizations, formatting issues, etc.

Determine the learning outcomes or objectives for the instruction session and which information literacy standards will be addressed. Collaborate with faculty to establish which topics should be covered during the session. Terminology used during the instruction should be consistent among librarians, faculty, and students.

Conduct a library instruction session based on a particular topic, such as database searching, determining authority of websites, plagiarism/citation management, general library skills, or another topic created around the ACRL Information Literacy Competency Standards. Game play may be used for the entire instructional session or it can be a wrap-up activity to the library instruction, but it should follow instruction.

Playing the Game

To introduce the game, explain what Wordle is and that Wordle(s) will be published on a website or in an online course management system. Students are motivated to work together to create a Wordle cloud based on information covered during instruction. If used as pre- or post-test, allow an additional 5 to 10 minutes for students to develop and create the pre-test Wordle.

Prior to instruction hand out note cards to small groups or individuals. Give them instructions on a particular area that they are to become "experts" in during the session, or they can create a top-10 list of library information.

After instruction, students have one minute to record their answers on the note cards, relevant to their given topic or overall library information. Their answers do not need to be in proper sentence or grammar format, and no punctuation is necessary (but it is nice).

At the end of the minute, students will record their answers in Wordle (either on their own computers in a lab setting or at the front of room on the instructor computer). In the case of a small class, the deadline can be extended to allow students to post on the course management system or website, and voting by

other students could take place in a short period of time on the best Wordle (based on colors, font, language, and layout).

You can also use one of these alternative games:

- Database searching/synonyms: Pick a topic for the class to search (individual or group) and see how many words they can come up with that are related to that topic.
- Database searching/general: When doing database instruction, cover multiple aspects of database searching skills (e.g., keywords, Boolean, wildcards, subject, topic, dates, peer/scholarly, types of articles, results list, abstract, references, etc.), and then have students create a Wordle and compare the words in their Wordle to your previously prepared Wordle. Students who match the most words in your Wordle receive a prize that you deem appropriate.
- Words missing? Create a Wordle on a particular topic but intentionally omit several words. The first student(s) to figure out which words are missing win a prize. You may need to give hints, such as the first letter of a word. If desired, re-create a new Wordle in the classroom with the missing words included.

The game can continue for multiple instruction sessions based on different competencies or topics, and Wordles can be posted on a website or printed as a handout, bookmark, or other tangible item during this recursive process. The goal is to use the Wordle cloud as a "check for understanding" snapshot, similar to the one-minute paper (Angelo and Cross, 1993), increase interaction among students, and provide opportunities for students to ask questions of the librarian. Prizes are not required, but the winning Wordle(s) can be printed on a T-shirt or other tangible item, such as a sign, or posted on a website.

Evaluation

The game serves as the student assessment, although a follow-up survey about the exercise can also be used if desired. The librarian may also wish to do a comparative analysis of multiple Wordles done over time by the same students on different topics, such as website evaluation versus database searching or scholarly versus popular articles.

Students might also be asked to reflect on whether the words that were most prominent in their Wordles were truly representative of the important points of the instruction. What words were missing? What words could be taken out? Does the design, color, or font, make a difference in the effectiveness of the Wordle? Librarians can also use these Wordles as a check on their instructional methods and verbiage. Did students use library terminology/jargon, or create their own words, with modified language?

Tips for Introducing Subject Faculty to the Game

Demonstrate Wordle to the faculty member, using information literacy standards, their course syllabus, or discipline-specific standards as your sample words.

Indicate how the website can be used as an assessment tool, similar to a one-minute paper or short reflection essay, and that there is increasing professional literature in which word clouds have been used successfully in multiple settings and disciplines. Explain how you envision it being used in their course (e.g., compare and contrast two pieces of literature written in the same time period, two speeches from historical figures on similar topics, two opposing topics in their discipline, etc.).

References

Angelo, T.A., and K.P. Cross. 1993. *Classroom Assessment Techniques: A Handbook for College Teachers*. San Francisco: Jossey-Bass.

Three Cs: Competition, Comprehension, Creativity

Carrie Donovan and Rachel Slough

Introduction

Students have deeper learning experiences when actively engaged in the material and encouraged to think creatively. *Three Cs* can be applied in a variety of instructional settings to support these types of learning experiences.

Objectives

Students will be able to:

- demonstrate an understanding of library resources and/or services (specific topics will vary by class).

Information Literacy Competency Standards Addressed

This game addresses this ACRL Information Literacy Competency Standard: #4.

Game Background

This game grew from library instruction for an introductory speech class where the course instructor requested opportunities for the students to present material to each other. With variations, we have used it successfully for classes across disciplines and skill levels.

Audience

This game works well with any student group in both instruction sessions and orientation activities.

Time Required

Ten to 15 minutes of search time plus 3 to 8 minutes per group for presentations should be sufficient.

Materials and Equipment

The game requires:

- at least one computer per group if students are to use databases/catalog,
- printed directions (optional but helpful to save on explanation time), and
- prizes (optional but helpful).

Preparation

Clarify learning objectives and plan. Print out directions if you wish.

Playing the Game

Divide students into teams of two to eight students per team, as determined by class size and goals. Explain that class will be staged as a competition and points (and possibly prizes) will be awarded. Students must work together within their teams. The activity can take several forms, depending on your objectives and time. After material is presented, students will summarize/rephrase the content or explore the library/resources and teach each other. The game focuses on a final presentation given by each group of students. Award points based on the *Three Cs* of content, clarity, and creativity, with prizes for the highest scores. Each category (each of the Cs) can have up to three points. If possible, encourage the classroom instructors to score with you or by themselves, particularly on the creative section. You can assist students throughout the activity and fill in any information they may not have mentioned at the end of each group presentation. Possible variations include the following:

- Divide the number of databases you would teach, assigning one to each group. Ask each group to find out and teach their classmates the most useful features of this resource, the contents, and when/why they would use it. Give them 10 to 15 minutes to explore and 3 to 8 minutes to present with the *Three Cs*.
- Divide the library into different areas, and assign one team to each area. Have the team find out as much as they can about said area/department/

resource in 10 minutes, then have them present to their class with the *Three Cs*.

- Explain the *Three Cs* game at the beginning of class, present the material or do other activities, and end the class with the *Three Cs* as a way of checking student knowledge and filling in learning gaps.

Evaluation

This technique has been used with introductory and advanced courses as well as with student athletes and first-year outreach programs. Students have been very involved, performing dances, raps, and skits about the library and library resources. This game also allows the librarian to check student understanding throughout the class and to adjust teaching to student needs. At the same time, it provides flexibility and a student-driven lesson that is fun and engaging.

Tips for Introducing Subject Faculty to the Game

This game has been presented to faculty who teach speech or communication courses and want more opportunities for students to practice as well as an option for outreach activities.

Team Challenge: Exposing the Underbelly of Research through Small Group Work

Laurel Johnson Black

Introduction

Team Challenge helps students in a college-level research writing course find answers to basic research questions in a team-based environment. In playing the game, they will gather, critique, and revise information in ways that build community with their peers.

Objectives

Students will:

- demonstrate less apprehension about college-level research because they will understand how to access information through their university as well as on the Internet,
- practice interviewing skills,
- familiarize themselves with some of the campus resources,
- practice evaluating the credibility and appropriate uses of resource material,
- understand the collaborative nature of research, and
- analyze effective presentation of research.

  As a result of working in teams, students will:

- better understand the subjective nature of research and the frequent need for collaboration to locate "correct" answers.

Information Literacy Competency Standards Addressed

This game addresses these ACRL Information Literacy Competency Standards: #1; #2; #3; #4; #5.

Game Background

Team Challenge is a game designed to help address the fears and simmering frustration of students facing a semester of research writing by using the power of the small group (team) to take the sting out of making mistakes. It allows teams to get information citation right (or wrong), complete (or incomplete), cited fully (or not). It does this by allowing students to collaborate in finding answers to questions and to challenge each other as a team.

Specifically, the game creates teams that compete to answer questions connected to an individual instructor's course goals and concerns. The example included here is designed for a research writing course in which each team is encouraged to self-select its own research topic.

Completion of the game helps individual students realize that researching and writing is complex but still learnable and that working together is acceptable at the university level. In the process, student teams will use a variety of research methods to find the answers, meet a number of outcomes for information literacy education that will enable them to use their university's library resources, and learn from each other some strategies for finding, evaluating, integrating, documenting, and presenting information sources. They also find that they have a voice that they can use for the actual process of research writing in college, which then builds their general confidence.

Audience

The basic format—to form a team, to look for "treasure," to share treasures/findings—can be adapted to multiple audiences based on the level of difficulty of the questions and requirements for sharing. Because most incoming college students are unsure about the ethics of working as a team, this allows them to see how teams can be useful in college-level courses.

Time Required

Typically, one class period will be needed to set up the game, another one will be needed for final presentations by the teams and to provide points, and the research time in between will vary according to the instructor's goals for the game itself. Each instructor can decide the simplicity or the complexity of each game and structure questions according to class goals.

Materials and Equipment

The game requires:

- a simple, instructor-designed checklist of requirements to help students structure their work and respond to the work of others (optional but helpful) and
- a community web space for posting comments, challenges, and responses.

Preparation

Typically, preparation takes place within the first two weeks of class. To prepare, the instructor will have shown students how to use their course handbook or any research handbook with extensive examples of documentation for citation formats and tips on using databases, doing interviews and gathering qualitative data, generating a thesis or central question, and organizing and presenting information. Students will have visited online the library resources, and they will have completed a course background survey designed to help them reflect on their knowledge and skills relative to researching and writing and to provide the instructor with a good sense of the level of knowledge and range of attitudes of the students in the class. Small and large group discussion about backgrounds, knowledge, which citation formats have been used, what students fear, and what they know about how they will use writing in their majors or intended fields all provide the initial background to this game and can also generate some of the questions for students to answer.

Playing the Game

After telling students to read all the instructions, rules, and basic questions to be answered, have them form teams. The following format can be used to set up the game, prepare the teams, and help each team clearly understand its mission (the questions that each team must answer follow the game rules and description):

Instructions

Your job as a team is to find the answers to the questions that are listed below. Each team will earn points for correct answers and responses (where there are only one or two correct answers) and for thoroughness, selection of appropriate research methodology, careful evaluation of the credibility of the source, and ability to integrate the material you find into a brief report in which your own voices are combined with the words and information you've gained from your sources. You should refer to your course textbook and consider all the other "authorities" around you who can help you find information and evaluate it. Follow the directions below to help your team finish first:

Steps to Completion for Teams

1. Create a team that is no larger than six people.
2. Look at the list of questions titled "Questions for Each Team to Answer" (shown in Figure 54.1). As a group, figure out a way to shift those from questions to tasks. In other words, ask yourselves as a group, "How should we, as a team, answer each question, and what must be done by us to do that? What tasks are common to each question? What is unique to each? Where will the information we find be recorded? How will it be shared among team members?" Come to a consensus about what the tasks are needed to answer the questions. Divide up tasks. Complete a note to the instructor about who is in your group and which member will complete which specific task your group has decided must be done. Some helpful tips include: Remember to look at the due date and then set a timeline for each task to be completed. Remember to build in time to dig deeper—perhaps what seems like it will be easy to find will prove more difficult than you thought! Remember also to leave time to write the report, revise, and proofread.
3. Look carefully at the readings that your instructor has given you in advance (if any) that discuss the presentation of material. Questions your team will want to consider for the final presentation of your findings could be the following: "What lends itself to a more visual and less narrative presentation? What is better presented in prose?"

The Rules of Team Challenge

1. All reports and source material must be posted for everyone to see in the designated folders on the designated website. Please help readers understand

---

Figure 54.1.
***Team Challenge* Game: Questions for Each Team to Answer**

- How many citation formats can you identify? List.

- What fields of study are connected to each format?

- What do other students who have taken this course say about it in general? Why? Was it worth it? How did it help them? (Or did it help them. . . ?)

- What is the best comment you can find in a public forum about this course's teacher? What's the least favorable?

- How many sections of this course are offered this semester?

- How many databases are currently offered by the library?

- Where can the policy regarding plagiarism be found?

- How many writing courses are required by the university?

- Find two scholarly (peer-reviewed) articles about student or professional writer's block. Write out a full citation for those articles, using two different formats: one in a format used by science educators and one in a format used by business professionals. List some of the suggestions for getting over writer's block offered by the authors.

- Find two other articles that explore writer's block, plagiarism, or the rewards or difficulties of writing up research. These should come from "popular" sources. Create an abstract for each article for your classmates. Provide a citation for each, one in American Psychological Association and the other in Modern Language Association style.

- Find a court case that involved copyright violations or high school or student journalists. Explain what was at stake and how/why it was decided.

- What are the copyright rules and policy for the library's e-reserve service?

- What are the pet peeves of Indiana University of Pennsylvania library faculty when it comes to student research? What do they enjoy most?

- In what other ways is ENGL 202 being taught this semester? What do you think are the benefits and drawbacks of some of these approaches? Why?

- Based on your research and personal experience, how does your team think learning to find, evaluate, quote/paraphrase, and document information should be taught and when should it start? Why might there be some debate on this?

- Include questions devised by the class here.

---

what materials your team has used by highlighting or marking in some way the material used.

2. Each team will read the other teams' reports. Teams can challenge (and praise!) the correctness, methodology, format, credibility of sources, and thoroughness of each answer. Your instructor will tell you how to post these responses.

3. Challenges to correctness or format must be accompanied by what the challenging team believes is the correct answer or format for citation or in-text documentation. Challenges to methodology, credibility, and thoroughness must explain why the methodology is inappropriate or less appropriate,

why credibility may be different than claimed, and what additional information or explanation would be *crucial* in making an answer more thorough. (This is not about style, but content.)

4. All challenges and responses to other teams' reports must be posted to a shared site or folder by the assigned date so that teams can consider their response to the challenge.

5. Challenges and responses will be discussed in class.

6. If the challenging team is wrong, it loses two points. If the challenging team is right, it gains two points and the team in error loses two points.

7. Challenges and scores are tallied during class and points are awarded. Additional points are awarded by the instructor for writing quality. As with many sporting events (e.g., figure skating), answers that are more subjective will receive points ranging from 1 to 5 from other teams, with the top and bottom scores thrown out. The instructor will also provide scores for such questions.

What You Can Do with Your Acquired Points

Over the course of the semester, teams can choose how to use points they earn for assignments like this and for in-class team work. The instructor can make suggestions on how to use points, but teams should also be allowed to suggest other appropriate uses for points!

Evaluation

It is relatively easy to determine if students were able to find answers to straightforward questions and if they understood how to evaluate their source's reliability, as the challenge and point system provides empirical evidence. If the instructor has to answer the same question over and over, then that area of the game format needs to be adjusted for the next class in which it is used. Additionally, practice in guided reflection permits the instructor to determine whether anxiety or crippling fears have been alleviated. Thus an instructor might ask students to informally reflect on whether they feel more comfortable, what they've learned, etc.

Tips for Introducing Subject Faculty to the Game

Team Challenge is a good game to teach to other faculty by creating a miniversion of it for a faculty workshop. It may help to divide up questions in advance into those that can be challenged on correctness and those that are less clearly simple "right" or "wrong" questions. Questions can be divided and offered separately based on methodology or kind of source. Creating a chart showing where faculty/players excelled and where they need more work also helps faculty gauge where their own game might succeed or fail. Faculty can quickly learn how to adapt the basic format of *Team Challenge* to their own needs and purposes.

Part XI

LOST in the Academy: Library Orientation Session Techniques Help Students Navigate New Territory

The *LOST in the Academy* series includes Games 55–60, a series of inter-related games that help students navigate the complexities of any library's services and databases by enabling them to perform effective research. Each game can be played by itself, but playing them in sequence builds on the previous game, beginning with the construction of a map of the library and ending with a Rube Goldberg–style alternative to quick access to information.

A Treasure Map

Nancy Riecken

Introduction

This game is the first in the *LOST in the Academy* series. It introduces students to the physical environment of their library. Surprising as it may seem, many college students are unfamiliar with libraries. Many first-generation college students have had little experience with reading for entertainment, let alone finding source materials for research projects. They need to learn their way around their campus library in order both to become responsible for their own learning and to discover the satisfaction of being able to go right to the materials they need. An excellent way to introduce them to the library is through *A Treasure Map*: they seek out places in the library where needed materials and information are found, from copy machines to card catalogs, from the librarians themselves to computer services, from DVDs and popular magazines to academic journals and reference shelves, and from government documents to materials within their chosen discipline. Once students know their library's layout and the wealth of material available to them, they should become more successful in their coursework.

Objectives

Students will:

- learn the layout of their library and
- create a clear map of resource materials at their library from a list provided on the Map Key within the time limit.

Information Literacy Competency Standards Addressed

This game addresses these ACRL Information Literacy Competency Standards: #1; #2.

Game Background

Many students are familiar with the *Lost* television series in which a group of people find themselves on an island, unable to escape and having to develop survival skills. This game is the first in a series of games modeled after that program.

Like those characters, it suggests that college students must develop their own set of survival skills in order to succeed in the academic environment in which they find themselves. They are lost in the academic community of their college campus. The first task they have to perform is to learn how to use the library, which is the one place their professor keeps telling them and their classmates to go to get the information provided on a list that they are given. They enter the realm of the library and see before them rooms of shelves and cubicles and computers. They must find each item on the list, create a map and key, and bring the completed materials back to the all-knowing information librarian.

Audience

This game is devised for college students who need to become familiar with the layout of the campus library. These students may have little experience with the purpose of or resources available at a library. Because their success in all of their course work is directly related to their ability to use the library services, this game is directed at students who may have some qualms about discovering and using the treasures hidden in those mysterious stacks of books, journals, and electronic sources.

Time Required

The game can be played in about 30 minutes, but if the map is large and the list is detailed, set a longer limit or divide students and have them construct maps for separate areas in a large library.

Materials and Equipment

The game requires:

- a skeleton map of their library that includes some or all of the locations listed in Figure 55.1,
- a list of locations or items they must find in the library (such as the one shown in Figure 55.1),
- pencils or pens to fill in the map,
- a poster graph with each student's name to record scores, and
- a gold star to mark the student's name on the poster who finds all of the resource materials most quickly.

Preparation

Prior to the game, a library orientation session may include a tour of the library. A skeleton map of your own library must be sketched out for your students. Items for them to find that are not listed in this game but that are important to your library may be added to the list.

Playing the Game

Begin the game with this introduction:

Life was going along just fine until you crashed into a college campus and found yourself face to face with a totally foreign population of freaks, nerds, and apparent aliens: your college professors. There is no escape: if you don't succeed, you'll be on academic probation, which is the wide and broad path to expulsion. Dropping out is not a realistic option. You do not want to spend your life making French fries and lattes. The world you so naively left just a few weeks ago does not look kindly on returnees without jobs, goals, or any plans for their future. You must survive and succeed in your new environment.

As you traverse the campus's foreign ground, wandering from dormitory to gymnasium, from dining center to lecture hall, you are overwhelmed with the diversity of your new environment. Ideas are everywhere, and they

---

**Figure 55.1.
Library Treasure Map List**

On the accompanying treasure map to the physical features and resources of the library, match the areas or items below to the map. Write the number next to the area where it is, and circle it.

1. Circulation Desk
2. Virtual Library OPAC
3. Reserve Shelf
4. Library Computer Lab
5. Circulating Books on Economics
6. Photocopier
7. Current Periodicals Display
8. Videos and DVD Collection
9. Circulating Books on Computer Science
10. Group Study Room
11. Children's Picture Book Collection
12. Current Newspapers Display
13. DVD/Video Viewing Areas
14. Encyclopedias Collection
15. Tutoring Center
16. Periodicals Collection
17. Circulating Books on Nursing
18. Careers Collection
19. Reference Services Area
20. Fiction Collection

---

are presented in foreign lexicons of their respective disciplines. You do recognize that your future depends not in overpowering the academy but in assimilating yourself to your new world and establishing a new identity. Unfortunately, you possess no tools suitable to meet the onslaught of the academics. You feel yourself slipping over the edge into a catatonic state of oblivion. The days pass, and you move mechanically from class to class; the overwhelming armies of the disciplines strike again and again upon your feeble and untrained brain. Giant Despair is drawing you into his grasp. You have no tools either adequate or sufficient to meet the onslaught of what has become an enemy greater than any your untutored, pop culture, media-driven mind has heretofore been capable of imagining. Oblivion at this point is a welcome thought.

"Hey! You! Where's the library?" You open your eyes and squint through the glare of the sun shining through the trees above you. Of course, you've fallen asleep on the grassy knoll after your English class, once again overwhelmed by an assignment you have failed to understand. The wide world of folk pass to and fro around you, and one of them is kicking your foot and asking for directions. "Ah . . . ah . . . maybe . . . over there?" You recall having passed by the building earlier in the semester. "I'm lost. Can you show me?"

"Yeah, well, lost is pretty normal around here. But sure, I gotta get up anyway." You and your fellow lost-mate join the throng passing through the doors of the library. Suddenly a bright light shines upon your face. The cool breeze of the air-conditioning surrounds you. Friendly faces welcome you. You're directed to a sign-in sheet that reads "Library Orientation Sessions." You sign your name. Help has arrived.

After that introduction, give each student a skeleton map of their library and the list of items to find. On their own, each student finds the locations of the items and marks the locations on the map either with letters or numbers. They also develop a Map Key that lists the locations of the resource materials. Give them a time limit.

Each student looks for each item on the list and then marks the location of that item on the skeleton map, filling in the details of the map as needed to clearly identify the location of the item. The item is marked on the map as either a letter or number. A

corresponding Map Key listing the resource item is completed using the letter or number of the item's location. That key may either be the original list handed out with the skeleton map or you may require an optional Map Key to be designed and placed on the map itself.

Library personnel will judge the accuracy of the map and award first place to the most clearly and accurately drawn map (or maps of separate library areas). Copies will be made, and all students will receive a copy of the best map.

The first-place winner receives the honor of having his or her map reproduced for use in the other games by the rest of the students. Top three winners are rewarded for time and accuracy. Extra credit is given for enthusiasm and artistic flair.

Evaluation

Students demonstrate the effectiveness of the game by their improved ability to use the library after the game.

Tips for Introducing Subject Faculty to the Game

Faculty interested in using engaging hands-on activities will be interested in this game. Introduce the topic with the following discussion questions and invite discussion:

> Who hasn't been lost at some point? A new city presents new challenges, whether we travel there by car or train or plane. How do we find our way around a new environment? Where's a good place to eat, or go to a show, or get a room? What's available for kids or teens or moms or dads? Everyone needs something different, and the more familiar we are with a new environment the easier it will be to navigate through it. The story scenario (above) can be used to remind students that they're not alone in their experiences of being in unfamiliar territory. It will hopefully elicit positive comments not only for this game but for those that follow.

> Once your students complete this (and each) of the games in the *LOST* series they should be more receptive to discussion about a wide variety of library source topics. Take note

of the questions they ask during the activity. Don't just tell them the answers, but team them up with (1) other students who may have already discovered what they're still looking for or (2) library personnel who can make suggestions. There's no rule against giving hints! You want your students to succeed, but you want them to know that they are the ones who have become successful at all aspects of information literacy.

Remember, each game is a stepping stone to increased information literacy. If they succeed here, they are more likely to succeed at the next step. Each step gives them a stronger sense of their own value as students. In a very real sense, these games walk through Maslow's Hierarchy: from having their basic needs met your students attain a level of self-actualization that will serve them in their future academics, profession, and community life.

Uncovering Buried Treasure
Nancy Riecken

Introduction

This game is the second game in the *LOST in the Academy* series. In the first game, students design a library treasure map. In this game, students select a topic sheet that contains a specific research topic and the clues they need to develop a basic understanding of the topic. Working in pairs, and using the map from the first game and the list of clues, they unearth specific source materials that they will use to help guide their success in the succeeding games.

Objectives

Students will be able to:

- work as a team and support each other's efforts and
- find appropriate library resources that advance their knowledge base of the topic.

Information Literacy Competency Standards Addressed

This game addresses these ACRL Information Literacy Competency Standards: #2; #3.

Game Background

In this game, students are given the following assignment:

> You must research the topic of "treasures" your professor has given you, but you don't know anything about the topic or where in the library to find materials that will help you understand the topic. You and your class members discuss the topic from a variety of perspectives. You and a classmate work together to locate specific source materials on the aspects of the "treasures" that interest both of you.

Audience

College students often view a topic as a black/white, either/or issue or one with only one or two possible perspectives. In addition, they may generalize so broadly that when they try to communicate effectively they end up not really having much to say. This game aims to help those students see the need for specificity by using particular terms that pertain to the topic of pirates and buried treasure. It takes them back to childhood games where their imagination could run wild. Using unusual terms in creative ways, they begin to develop a focus on a topic that will be fun to research.

Time Required

This game should be completed within 30 minutes. Limiting the allotted time will force students to work closely together in pairs and to focus on the best materials for the topic.

Materials and Equipment

The game requires:

- the library map used in Game 55 and
- a clue sheet for each research topic.

Figure 56.1 provides a sample clue sheet. The directions are based on the topic of pirates. Instructors might provide multiple topics connected with the theme of treasure, based on students' brainstorming during the orientation session, such as treasure maps, legends of buried treasure, unclaimed treasures, modern pirating, pirating videos, etc. Class members may draw them from a hat or a basket and scour the library together in teams.

Preparation

As part of the library orientation session students should be introduced to the broad topic of "treasure" and asked to brainstorm words or phrases that generate

Figure 56.1.
Clue Sheet for Uncovering Buried Treasure

No treasure hunter is worth a doubloon if he or she can't follow the clues to a buried treasure! You've already accumulated a good pile of knowledge of resource locations through trudging the length and breadth of your library. You know every rock and tree and shelf and corner to look under and around to help you ferret out the treasures that have been buried right under your nose.

Following is a list of clues that will help you unearth enough basic knowledge of your topic to start you on the road to being a successful treasure hunter. Find the following information and fill in the blanks after each clue. Include the specific source and page number for each item of research information. You'll use these clues later to develop your expertise. Provide definitions for the following terms as they relate to piracy:

• Avast

_____

• Belay

_____

• Black spot

_____

• Corsair

_____

• No quarter

_____

• Poop deck

_____

• Rum

_____

• Swag

_____

Explain the difference between a treasure hunter and a pirate.

Find a general reference information article on "pirates."

Find a reference source for "Black Sam Bellamy."

Find a current periodical that would be an appropriate source of information for pirates.

Find a library book that would be an appropriate source of information for pirates.

Find a video or DVD that provides information on pirates.

multiple perspectives. Use that list of topics to develop clue sheets specific to those perspectives. Students will use the clue sheets to complete the game.

Playing the Game

Students practice teamwork to help discover appropriate resource materials for their topic. This is a timed game to be played in pairs. The team that finds appropriate materials and can provide a written explanation of that material most clearly on the topic handout will win. Option: You may use the same clue sheet from this game after conducting an electronic database orientation session. Have your students locate appropriate materials using the electronic sources.

Using the clue sheet and the map from the first game, students work in pairs to determine where the source material may be found for each clue. They will locate the material, indicate the location of each item on the map, and complete the clue sheet. This game has a 30-minute time limit and requires good teamwork. Students should determine who will search for what. Clarity is essential in this game, because the clue sheets will be used as the basis for searching for more information that will lead to their success.

First-place points will go to those students who complete the clue sheet and mark their maps most quickly and most clearly. Faculty assigning the topic will determine the clarity of the information provided.

Evaluation

The game itself tests students' ability not only to navigate and use the library but to come up with materials that can be used effectively and imaginatively for a research project. This means "good" sources—authoritative and reliable sources that open the doors to better research. Students who do more than just find dictionary definitions will be able to demonstrate strong research and thinking skills.

Tips for Introducing Subject Faculty to the Game

Faculty members were once "real" people, just like students! In fact, they often show sparks of creativity and multifaceted thinking by making connections between ideas. Explain that this game helps students see opportunities in academic research for creative thinking processes. It encourages them to connect between basic ideas about pirates and treasure, cool subjects for the playground or the movie theatre, and begin to develop ideas for a strong thesis. Any project that requires investigation of the research process will benefit by starting with this game. By having students work in pairs, they brainstorm ideas with each other and demonstrate multiple perspectives. Once the class engages in conversation after the fact, even more research ideas may be generated.

Spelunking through the Caves of Technology

Nancy Riecken

Introduction

Who isn't afraid of the dark? The unknown? The mysterious? Although our students may have grown up with a mouse in their hands (and most of us have not), we tend to be much more comfortable with the technology of the academy than they are simply because we use it repeatedly. The only thing our students really need to be afraid of, however, is "fear itself," and this game aims to move students from familiarity of the physical library environment to the slightly scary environment of the library's electronic databases. Traveling through the various trails of technology, they'll become increasingly familiar with the particularities and landmarks that will enable them to navigate the electronic research process with ease.

Objectives

Students will be able to:

- think through their research project needs and
- find appropriate research materials for a particular audience.

Information Literacy Competency Standards Addressed

This game addresses this ACRL Information Literacy Competency Standard: #3.

Game Background

In this game, students are given the following assignment:

> Who is interested in treasure? You've discovered from the last game that your fellow students see this topic from various perspectives. Your professor expects you to develop a research project on "treasures" as related to your specific topic ("pirates," as in the previous game). You find current materials from

sources your library may or may not have in its collection and determine exactly what specific material is appropriate for your research project. You know you can't drive all over creation looking for outside materials or wait two weeks for them to arrive by pack mule from some other library three hundred miles away. You need that material now, or your grade will experience a steep decline. Your friend has suggested "Why not use the electronic databases?" "The what?" you reply. Technology is not your thing, you argue, but that excuse doesn't fly. You might as well learn how to use it. With fear and trepidation you enter the "caves of technology."

The "caves" are a series of source trails within your library's homepage (articles, books, images, audios, videos, and subject resources) that lead to particular databases. Your goal is to find appropriate sources for your research project. Based on your clue sheet in the last game, you already have some general knowledge of this subject. Now you must focus on a particular topic for a particular group of readers who already have some general knowledge but want to know more about treasure (as it is related to pirates). Your search of the electronic databases will help you develop a focus.

Audience

How many of your students are surprised that they must turn in typed assignments instead of handwritten work? How many more accept the need to type their work but balk at learning how to submit various files through various electronic systems? Even those for whom such technology is navigable, the "other" technology of the electronic databases seems like a mystery too deep to fathom. These are the students to whom this game is addressed. They may be so afraid to search the library's electronic databases that they simply don't; the result is failure. By practice (good ol' trial and error), they'll become adept at keyword searching, recognition of authoritative sources, and incorporation of those sources in the research project at hand.

Time Required

Students should take 60 minutes to search the databases and find appropriate materials. Discussion will take more time, and determination of winners may be announced at the end of the discussion of sources. Students may work alone or in teams.

Materials and Equipment

This game requires:

- The *Caves of Technology* handout (see Figure 57.1) and
- a computer lab that has access to the library's electronic databases.

Preparation

A library orientation session connected to this game will provide basic information of the college's electronic database search tools and how to save the source in its link for future access. This may vary according to your library's procedures. Students must be able to access their library's databases and have a basic understanding of keyword searching and limiting the search by date, full-text articles, and peer-reviewed publications. Introduce the topic of "audience" as it relates to people who would be interested in treasure: Is there a specific age group or gender to address? Discuss the particular demographics of the audience to be addressed (children interested in "playing pirates," fans of pirate movies, devotees of Howard Pyle or Johnny Depp or Long John Silver, professional treasure hunters, private detectives, writers of spy stories, etc.). Also discuss authority of sources. Encyclopedias and dictionaries, both print and electronic, and other general reference sources (which students have already used to gain general knowledge of the topic in the previous game), as well as blogs, should not be used. Only published, authored sources are acceptable for this research project. Authors, however, may include corporate authors, such as government or professional publications.

Playing the Game

This game is played in the computer lab, using the *Caves of Technology* handout. Working alone or in teams, students will find appropriate source materials from each of the four trails that represent the library's databases. Using the subject "treasures" and specific keywords that connect to their more focused topic (i.e., pirates, modern piracy, treasure hunting in South Carolina, pirating videos in the United States, etc.), they must find one current and appropriate full-text article dealing with this subject from each trail in the cave. Once they find a good source, they should notate it by author, title, and date in the appropriate cave trail on the map. They must save the source material by saving either the document or the link. By keeping a clear record of the article and database they will be better able to organize and document their research.

To begin the game, inform the students:

> Your research topic is "treasure" (related to pirates). You must find one appropriate article from each of the library electronic databases by navigating through each of the cave trails indicated on the handout. Choose your source materials carefully! Find your sources and save them as indicated below. Whether or not you are the first to find the sources will not make you the winner in this game. *You must find appropriate, authoritative sources that you can use successfully when you develop a research paper on a particular aspect of treasure (related to pirates).* Discuss with your partner the appropriateness of the sources. Discussion often results in developing a clearer focus on specific ones.

Discussion of sources is important in the evaluation process. Students will discuss their top choices in the lab or classroom and argue why each choice is appropriate and authoritative. The final determination of authority will rest with their professor, but an important part of the evaluation process is recognizing good research: The students themselves should vote for best sources. The top students who find acceptable authoritative and appropriate sources will be given the highest number of points.

When the game is completed ask the students to retain the articles they find. They will need them for the next game.

Figure 57.1.
The Caves of Technology

The following four trails enable you to navigate the Caves of Technology that make up your library's electronic databases. You must find authored, published source materials on your topic of "pirates" from each of the bulleted databases. Be selective and discerning! Find appropriate sources that will be suitable for your research argument. Include the author, title, and date of publication next to the database from which you find the source material.

Trail #1: Articles

- EBSCO Host
- ProQuest
- Gale
- Lexis Nexis
- CQ Press

Trail #2: Books

- Library Catalog
- Books 24×7
- Credo Reference
- Ebrary
- Gale Virtual Reference

Trail #3: Images, Audios, and Videos

- EBSCO Images
- Net Anatomy
- New York Public Library Digital Gallery
- Audio Archive
- History and Politics Out Loud
- Movie Archive
- PBS Video Collection

Trail #4: References

- Access Science
- Annals of American History
- Biography Resource Center
- Britannica Encyclopedia
- Lit Finder

Evaluation

The game actively engages students in the research process and provides directly to them an assessment of their own ability to effectively search out source materials. Good, authoritative sources will enable them to develop their research. Discussion helps them see the process from multiple perspectives and enables them to further focus and develop their ideas.

Tips for Introducing Subject Faculty to the Game

The subject of this game is one that has interest for students and faculty on many levels, whether it's finding treasures on the beach, in gem fields, or in government "unclaimed" sites or just hoping to "hit the big one." Everybody loves a surprise, and everybody wants to be a winner. Explain that by becoming familiar with the technology caves of electronic databases, students will be able to see that, with a little bit of digging, they can uncover a wealth of material that will help them succeed in their research projects for all of their course work. The discovery of multiple sources from multiple databases is encouraged. Saving those sources, either in a file folder within the database, by e-mailing them, or saving on a travel drive, is similar to putting found treasures in a treasure bag. Instructors might suggest the "treasure bag" motif as a way to keep track of those sources to be used for effective research.

AARG! This Treasure Is Mine!

Nancy Riecken

Introduction

The overthrow of any despot begins with a good outline. Well, call it a plan of attack. Students who have been able to navigate the physical and electronic research environments have attained a degree of expertise in the most effective research tools. With a strong supply of source materials that focus on the particular elements of their argument, they can now organize them to their best advantage: in a play-by-play outline. Working together, students will organize and develop their outlines in a manner that will present their argument most clearly and thereby demonstrate their formidable strength to the powerful Ruler of the Treasure Trove. Fear not, Rulers! Your overthrow does not result in your subjugation but in the successful passing of the academic baton.

Objectives

Students will be able to:

- navigate the library's physical and electronic environments,
- organize research,
- develop a clear argument, and
- manage the tools of research effectively.

Information Literacy Competency Standards Addressed

This game addresses these ACRL Information Literacy Competency Standards: #3; #4; #5.

Game Background

This fourth game in the *LOST* series is based on the following scenario:

> The despotic current Ruler of the Treasure Trove, your professor, stands in the way of your possession of a valuable mound of treasure. You must overpower the Ruler by demonstrating your ability to manage the tools of

research effectively. Your team must break through each section of the research process, indicated on the handout. You already have both general knowledge of the topic and more specific knowledge on how to approach your audience. You have conducted enough research at this point to have developed specific ideas for a more focused argument. Now you must organize your research effectively to overwhelm the Ruler with your expertise.

Audience

It takes a team to develop good research techniques, organize source materials, and connect them to the issue at hand. This game aims to help college students work together on a topic they've been discussing, brainstorming, and researching for a period of time. The outline pulls their ideas together, and, as shown by the handout, different strengths are demonstrated by different sources wielded in the hands of the various team members. The audience for this game recognizes that strength lies in teamwork.

Time Required

The time required for this game will vary, and students will probably want to work through this game more than once (even by dividing the game into parts) in order to develop their outline most clearly. Teamwork is essential; together, students determine which sources to use most effectively with which points and how those sources should be used to make their points.

Materials and Equipment

The game requires:

- an Attack Planning handout for team members to develop their argument (see sample in Figure 58.1) and
- sources located in the last game.

Figure 58.1.
Attack Planning Session: It's Time to Take Down the Ruler of the Treasure Trove

---

It's time to show your hand. You've fulfilled all the requirements. You've got what it takes to create a specific argument for an excellent research paper. All that is left is to awe your professor with your use of your library resources. Don't go it alone! This takes team effort. Working with your partner, determine what you can use and what you don't need to use to overpower the current Ruler of the Treasure Trove. Don't waste your time with unnecessary forays into blind alleys or rabbit trails! Focus on each barrier before you. Take it and move on to the next.

"This is what we know . . ."
- Our basic knowledge
  - How do we organize our basic knowledge about pirates?
  - What do the general sources tell us?

"This is what our intelligence reports have brought in . . ."
- Our specific sources
  - What do our specific sources tell us about pirates?
  - What specific points do those sources make that we can combine to form an attack group against the Ruler?

"Here's our plan of attack . . ."
- Our main thesis
  - Based on the various attack groups we've organized, what is our main plan of attack (the focus of our argument)?
  - How will we introduce that argument to others?
  - Based on our interests, what we know, and what our sources tell us, what do we plan to argue?

"We place our troops here, here, and here . . ."
- Our points that support our thesis
  - We need to lay out a clear outline for our argument. What are our strongest means of making our argument attack work? These are the main supporting points of our argument.
  - What connection do those means have with each other? They should be able to stand on their own!

- We need to list those means here. They form the focal points by which we'll win.

"Because Henry's sword is sharp and Mary can take down three with one blow . . ."
- Our strong means of attack require troop support. These will come from good quotes, paraphrases, and summaries from our specific sources. Our troops are our tools, and their ammunition is in the quotes, paraphrases, and summary statements we use from their work.
  - Which sources can we best use for each supporting point? We need to list those sources here.
  - What summary points can we use from our sources to validate ourselves being able to fight this argument? We can't forget to cite them! We rely on the strength of our sources for our own strength.
  - What specific quotes and paraphrases do we have from each source to make our point strong? We need to provide them here, along with citations showing exactly where they were found. If we don't, we've dropped our ammunition and can't use it!

"I've seen them in action. They've got what it takes . . ."
- Our documentation to validate our sources
  - Strong sources deserve full credit for their support. We must provide source documentation for our argument in the form of a Works Cited or References page.
  - Ship-shape order is essential. Check the rule book for American Psychological Association or Modern Language Association documentation!

"We did it, troops. To the victors go the spoils!"
- Our explanation of how we became Rulers of the Treasure Trove in the form of an abstract of our argument
  - We'll make closing remarks to our audience in the form of a strong conclusion.
  - For the sake of posterity, we'll also create a short record summarizing our argument and main points. This is called an abstract.

Preparation

Prior to playing this game, conduct a library orientation session on in-text citations and Works Cited documentation of sources. The game is best played in the library or in a computer lab. Groups of two are retained from the previous games. You may wish to have larger groups, but four should be the limit for this game.

Playing the Game

Students continue to work in the groups formed for the previous games and work with the articles located in the previous game. They are provided with the Attack Planning handout and are instructed to use all of the research materials and notes they have retained from previous games and to complete the handout. Their success depends entirely on how well they have learned to navigate the library's physical and electronic environments and how well they are able to organize their research and develop a clear argument and pass through each of the levels of the game. When the game has been completed, the instructor (aka the current Ruler of the Treasure Trove) scores the arguments submitted. He or she must then choose the strongest argument and admit defeat by granting the highest score to the team that produces the strongest argument in the handout. An alternative could be team presentations to the rest of the class of their outline and source support. Points may be given by classmates for best presentation and then added to their instructor's evaluation.

Once this has been completed, the members of the winning team become the new Rulers of the Treasure Trove. The real motivating prize of this game is the amazing feeling of success group members feel when they overpower their professor and prove their ability to construct a clear research outline.

Evaluation

Because the goal of this game is effective organization of points and use of source support to establish and defend the points, the best evaluation will come from two sources: the Ruler of the Treasure Trove (their professor or faculty leader) and their peers who are engaged in the same struggle. Which team wins? This good, clean competition will result in the new Ruler of the Treasure Trove, so the best evaluation will be demonstrated through analysis of the outline/source support content. Let the students present their outline and support to the rest of the class. Score each presentation by points. Have a formal "vanquishing" ceremony or "passing the baton" ceremony.

Tips for Introducing Subject Faculty to the Game

It should be noted that none of us is an eternal Ruler of the Treasure Trove. Our purpose is to pass our knowledge, expertise, and effective techniques on to others. Harry Truman said, "It is amazing what you can accomplish if you do not care who gets the credit." What we do should not be done to glorify ourselves but to bring out the best in others. The best educators are willing to see their students surpass their own abilities, to strive further, to see farther, to reach heights heretofore unattainable. That may be a lot to expect from all of our students, but what a pleasure it is when we witness that in any of them! Success comes when we can provide learning activities that stretch the imagination, help students see a variety of perspectives, and develop an ability to interact with and use sources to expand their own understanding of difficult subjects.

Don't Jeopardize Your Academics

Nancy Riecken

Introduction

Once students become familiar with using library resources for their research in one area, they can easily adapt their methods to assignments in other classes as well as research they may want to conduct on their own at higher academic levels. This game demonstrates students' ability to quickly and clearly communicate their knowledge of library resources and services that they've gained through the other games. It is based on the popular *Jeopardy!* game. There are several optional methods of playing the game. One thing that can make this game competitive and challenging is the opportunity to stack up more than points for good communication: offer a Crown for the Master of Library Resources. Even better, provide real prizes (cool college stuff). A carrot gets the rabbit running.

Objective

Students will:

• demonstrate knowledge of the library resources.

Information Literacy Competency Standards Addressed

This game addresses this ACRL Information Literacy Competency Standard: #4.

Game Background

In this, the fifth game in the *LOST* series, students are presented with the following scenario:

> You have demonstrated your understanding of the library resources and how to access and use library materials. Now it's time to compete against your classmates! Let's play *Jeopardy!* Earn points, win prizes, and see if you can become a Master of the Library Resources!

Audience

The format of *Jeopardy!* is usually familiar to most students, and the focus on competing in knowledge-related topics levels the playing field for students who have already proven their ability to understand how to accomplish the goals set forth in the other games. This game works particularly well with competitive students who have successfully mastered the previous games. Some students, however, may be more successful competing in one of the timed variations of the game. Determine which type of students you have and offer variations suitable to your group.

Time Required

Depending on the version you use, this game generally takes around 30 minutes. If your students are highly competitive, speed may be a greater priority and even incentive for their successful responses. On the other hand, there may be more than one possible response to some of the clues, and discussion may be needed to determine the best of the possible responses.

Materials and Equipment

The game requires:

• *Jeopardy!* questions and answers (like the game boards shown in Figures 59.1 and 59.2).

Depending on which way you play the game, students must supply either the questions or the answers.

Preparation

Hold a library orientation Q & A review before playing this game. You may choose to create 3 × 5 cards or list the categories and number of items on a board. Alternatively, you may supply a handout that provides only the questions or the answers and have your students fill them in on their own or in response to alternatives, as indicated in "Playing the Game."

Figure 59.1.
LOST Jeopardy! **Board 1**

	LIBRARY *REVERSE* JEOPARDY						
Subject Categories	**Library Places**	**Library Services**	**Books & Catalogs**	**Print Resources**	**Online Resources**	**Research Process**	**Citing Sources**
Answer 6:							
Question 6:	Library Places— Question 6	Library Services— Question 6	Books & Catalogs— Question 6	Print Resources— Question 6	Online Resources— Question 6	Research Process— Question 6	Citing Sources— Question 6
Answer 5:							
Question 5:	Library Places— Question 5	Library Services— Question 5	Books & Catalogs— Question 5	Print Resources— Question 5	Online Resources— Question 5	Research Process— Question 5	Citing Sources— Question 5
Answer 4:							
Question 4:	Library Places— Question 4	Library Services— Question 4	Books & Catalogs— Question 4	Print Resources— Question 4	Online Resources— Question 4	Research Process— Question 4	Citing Sources— Question 4
Answer 3:							
Question 3:	Library Places— Question 3	Library Services— Question 3	Books & Catalogs— Question 3	Print Resources— Question 3	Online Resources— Question 3	Research Process— Question 3	Citing Sources— Question 3
Answer 2:							
Question 2:	Library Places— Question 2	Library Services— Question 2	Books & Catalogs— Question 2	Print Resources— Question 2	Online Resources— Question 2	Research Process— Question 2	Citing Sources— Question 2
Answer 1:							
Question 1:	Library Places— Question 1	Library Services— Question 1	Books & Catalogs— Question 1	Print Resources— Question 1	Online Resources— Question 1	Research Process— Question 1	Citing Sources— Question 1

Playing the Game

The game can be played in groups, teams, or individually. At least three players should participate. Points may be scored for correct responses. Determine the point value you want to place for each question, upping the value as the questions increase in difficulty. The complete questions and answers are given as an answer key (see Figures 59.1 and 59.2). Note that there are 7 broad subject categories, with 6 questions per category, for a total of 42 possible questions. Add or delete items that will help you be more specific to your library. Students can respond either to the questions or to the answers, depending on which way you choose to play the game. Values can be assigned to each box.

As in real *Jeopardy!*, several students compete against each other. When a student selects a box, that question is read. If you play with team members, they'll take time to discuss the possible responses. You can assign a "five-second rule" or determine your own best way for submission of responses. Points

Figure 59.2.
LOST Jeopardy! Board 2

LIBRARY *REVERSE* JEOPARDY

Subject Categories	Library Places	Library Services	Books & Catalogs	Print Resources	Online Resources	Research Process	Citing Sources
Answer 6:	*Reference Collection*	*Library Instruction*	*WorldCat*	*Specialized Dictionaries*	*Virtual Library*	*Information Literacy*	*APA Style*
Question 6:	In what collection are books located, such as statistical sources, that <u>cannot</u> be checked out?	What help provided by trained library staff teaches students how to use all kinds of library resources better?	What catalog can search for book titles or authors in other libraries' catalogs in the world, or by country or state?	What reference books have definitions and short entries in alphabetical order on specialized topics?	What is Ivy Tech's "library on the Web" called, with its online catalog, databases, selected websites, and guides?	What is the set of knowledge skills that a person needs to have to navigate the world of information effectively?	What documentation style is used most for nursing, psychological, and scientific reports?
Answer 5:	*Current Periodical Displays*	*Ask-a-Librarian*	*Bibliographies*	*Encyclopedias*	*NetLibrary*	*The Web*	*Noodle Tools*
Question 5:	Where do I find the latest issues of magazines the library has?	What is the online reference question e-mail service that connects you to a librarian?	What are lists of books and resources on a subject called, such as "Lib Guides," that aid in topic searching?	What reference books are usually in many volumes of general articles on topics arranged in A–Z format?	What is the name of one popular electronic book database?	What means of online information is known more for its massive quantity, is unfiltered, and lacks organization?	What online service helps in putting together your citations?
Answer 4:	*Computer Labs*	*Interlibrary Loan*	*Keyword Searching*	*Almanacs*	*e-Books*	*Boolean*	*Copyright Guide*
Question 4:	Where do I go to use computers to find information and to write papers?	What services do I use to request books from libraries outside my library?	What type of searching works with limitless words or synonyms—a plus for online catalogs over card catalogs?	What reference books have lots of statistics in them?	What are the electronic versions of print books called?	What are these advanced search features called—"and," "or," "not,"—that can limit or expand a topic?	What are the guidelines to follow in using large amounts of material by an author for public use?
Answer 3:	*Media Collection*	*Reserve Materials*	*IvyCat*	*Scholarly Journals*	*Opposing Viewpoints*	*Critical Thinking*	*MLA Style*
Question 3:	Where are the DVDs, videos, and other audio-visual materials kept?	What books are kept in a restricted area of the library, and often placed there by instructors?	What is the online catalog called for finding books in the Ivy Tech college libraries?	What are serials that list references cited for research at the end of each article?	What is a special online database that arranges articles by current controversial subjects?	What thinking helps in differentiating between good and poor sources and in analyzing/meeting an information need?	What style of documentation is used mostly for reports in the humanities?
Answer 2:	*Group Study Rooms*	*Reference Librarian*	*Publication Date*	*Magazines*	*EBSCOhost*	*Secondary Sources*	*Works Cited Page*
Question 2:	Where is there a quiet place to study, watch instructional DVDs, yet large enough for groups to meet?	Whom do I ask for professional help in answering reference questions and finding information?	What date identifies when the book was written and thus its currency?	What are serials that are published for the popular audience on general topics?	What big article indexing company has many thousands of online periodicals in multiple article databases?	What materials are second-hand research, rather than first-person accounts of an event?	What is the page that lists the references used to complete a research paper?
Answer 1:	*General Collection*	*Circulation Desk*	*Call Number*	*Periodicals*	*Article Database*	*Library*	*Plagiarism*
Question 1:	Where do I find books that I can <u>take out</u> of the library?	Where do I go for checking out books, or for asking general library questions?	What is a book's or library material's address or identification number?	What is the name for magazines, journals, or newspapers published on a regular series basis?	What is a periodical index of articles from many journals, searchable by subject, and most as full-text?	What place is an organized storehouse of quality information in many formats and with staff to help you?	What is an abuse of someone else's words and ideas without giving due credit to the author?

are recorded for correct responses and deducted for incorrect responses.

You might want to vary this game by making it an exercise for all students, who must complete the most boxes within an allotted time. In this case, either the answers or the questions must be blocked out. Another alternative is to transcribe the questions on one side and the answers on the other side of 3 × 5 cards. Place them face up either way, and have students solve each card by providing either the correct question or answer. Another alternative is to use the questions only, with a sheet given to students to fill in within a limited amount of time. Choose the variation most suitable to your group of students.

Evaluation

As in *Jeopardy!*, the student with the ability to communicate an understanding of library resources will receive the most points. This can get quite competitive, particularly if you offer a prize other than mere points at the end of the game. Students are more inclined to get really excited if there is a prize at the end. Book bags, mugs, posters, or other items that your college bookstore or library may be willing to donate will usually increase competitive interest. A coffee shop or bookstore gift card is also a great incentive. At this stage of the learning process it's time for students to "win a prize" other than the traditional "joy of learning" that we too often focus on. They need stuff!

Tips for Introducing Subject Faculty to the Game

Because this game can become highly competitive, faculty may want to form teams and encourage competition between various classes, with a Grand Master of Library Resources crowned at the close of competition. Students are prone to do just about anything if there's something in it for them, and even a $5 coffee card or a nice book bag can be enough of an incentive to stand up and shout out correct responses to library resource clues. Depending on interest, the game could even become a special event. Yes, this could be big!

How Not to Find It Fast in the Library

Nancy Riecken

Introduction

This final game in the *LOST* series is based on Rube Goldberg's manner of taking the long way around. Students work in teams to develop a 10-minute skit that demonstrates how close they can come to finding the right materials in the library and still miss the mark. Negative reinforcement is used to direct students to use the library most effectively. A simple procedure must go strangely awry and involve a multitude of complex processes.

Objectives

Students will:

- show their adeptness at communicating information literacy in a manner that generates understanding in others.

Information Literacy Competency Standards Addressed

This game addresses these ACRL Information Literacy Competency Standards: #1; #2; #3; #4; #5.

Game Background

This sixth game in the *LOST* series is introduced with the following scenario:

> You've caught on to the library resource systems! What was once an environment in which you found yourself completely lost, you are now able to navigate through quickly. But not everyone can! You remember your first attempts at finding information in the library, don't you? This final game gives you the opportunity to remind yourself and your classmates of many of those early attempts to get the information you needed. The wrong way always took longer, was more confusing, and had poor results. You and your team

members will brainstorm how to make a simple process difficult. Your team will demonstrate how not to effectively perform one of the following library research processes. You'll need to select your own area of concentration from a list of suggestions in order to almost, but not quite, get the material you need to meet your research objective.

Audience

This game has been played successfully with college students.

Time Required

This game takes about 30 minutes to play.

Materials and Equipment

The game requires:

- any props students feel are appropriate for their skit and
- the accolades of their fellow students as the prizes.

Preparation

This final orientation session will require students to search Rube Goldberg and review his cartoons and the variety of Rube Goldberg contests available to students. Students should discuss the wrong way to conduct research and then divide into groups to brainstorm and develop skits.

The play's the thing, and this final game displays the talents of all members of the class. Students work in teams to develop their 10-minute skit. Each group will perform the wrong way to meet a research objective. Their success will be based on creativity and imagination, number of wrong steps taken to complete the process, and their clear understanding of the "right" way in order to demonstrate the "wrong" way.

In preparation the group will brainstorm, develop, and demonstrate how to perform library research the wrong way. They should rely on everything they've learned in the library orientation sessions they've attended as well as through the games you've played thus far. The simple process they choose to demonstrate must contain at least 10 discreet steps that process information in a manner that does not contribute to the effective use of resources.

Playing the Game

To begin the game, tell the students:

> Your group will brainstorm, develop, and demonstrate how to perform library research the wrong way. You must rely on everything you've learned in the library orientation sessions you've attended as well as through the games you've played thus far. The simple process you choose to demonstrate must contain at least 10 discreet steps that process information in a manner that does not contribute to the effective use of resources. You may choose from the following scenarios or decide on your own:

- "Ask another student"
- "Google it"
- "Browse the shelves"
- "Pose a question through online library services"
- "Ask the least tech-savvy library employee"
- "Wander the electronic databases without a clue"

Evaluation

Students may gain quite an audience from their skits. Their professor, library staff, fellow students, and the crowd that gathers will provide evaluative feedback. The most obvious will be "I tried to do it that way, and sure enough, it didn't work for me either." The clearest evaluation of effective learning will be seen when other students sign up for the library orientation sessions and the opportunity to participate in these games.

Tips for Introducing Subject Faculty to the Game

When introducing subject faculty to this game, librarians should stress the educational value of active learning activities like this one.

Game On: Moving to the Next Level with Educational Games

Librarians and others who teach information literacy instruction sessions and are looking for ways to improve their instruction, engage and motivate their students, and increase their learning outcomes can use the 60 games included in this book to achieve these goals. They will be supported in their decision to do so by the research discussed here, which holds that intelligent use of digital and traditional educational games can make instruction more active and student centered and improve general and information literacy instruction. These 60 games are only the beginning. Librarians will want to move beyond these games to find other games, create their own, and use them in different ways. This final chapter is designed to provide advice from experienced, enthusiastic instructors who are comfortable using games and to suggest further reading to assist the reader in moving beyond what is contained in this book. Unless otherwise noted, the advice included in this section was offered to the editor either via e-mail or as part of the games submitted for this book.

Advice for Using Games in Instruction

1. Start Small and Jump In!

This advice comes from contributor Maura Smale, Information Literacy Librarian at New York City College of Technology, CUNY, and author of *Quality Counts*. That was how the editor got started. She discovered the transformation quality of games when she broke students into teams and substituted a *Jeopardy!*-like contest at the end of a class session in place of a worksheet meant to reinforce the main points in the instruction. With the game, students perked up and were clearly motivated to be the winning team. There weren't even any prizes! She was hooked and vowed whenever possible to include at least one game-like activity in every class she taught thereafter.

While some of the games in the book are complicated and require preparation, many are short and simple and can be easily added to a lecture-based session to increase interest and motivation, check for understanding of concepts, or provide an opportunity for feedback or practice.

2. Be Flexible!

This suggestion comes from many of the contributors in one form or another and relates to integrating games, creating games, and adapting your teaching style. Maura Smale suggested that would-be gamers consider that both games and features of games can often be easily adapted to instruction sessions from the one-shot orientation to a semester-long class in a subject area. She suggests many activities can be made into contests to engage students or that giving out small prizes can be "surprisingly effective motivators for student participation."

Tracey Johnson, of Shawnee Community College Library and author of *Pick a Periodical*, created it because she felt that students were not enjoying class, and they weren't getting the concepts either. So she relied less upon lecture and allowed the students to actually sort through a collection of a variety of periodicals and figure out the differences for themselves. The result was that the students were more engaged, and they learned!

Ryan Sittler, co-editor of two books about using active learning techniques in information literacy instruction, recalled creating his *Chasing Citations* game to "go beyond 'hands on' and move into something more entertaining . . . and more kinesthetic." He remembered that as a student he had found library instruction to be "boring and frustrating," so he designed a game where students were actively engaged and had plenty of opportunity to move around. Christina Sheldon, Instruction and Reference Librarian, California State University, Los Angeles, suggests instructors examine games of all types—online games, those in other disciplines, or those originally designed for K–12 students—and to not be afraid to adapt them to information literacy instruction. She declares that "Fun is fun, at every age level!" In fact, as Susan El-Shamy (2001) notes in her *Training Games*, many exercises can easily be developed into games by dividing the students into groups and introducing competition, time limits, and prizes.

Contributors, including Nancy Riecken, author of the *LOST in the Academy* series of games, note that using games also might require users to be more flexible in teaching style. Games and other student-centered learning techniques often involve giving up some control of the classroom, becoming more of a facilitator, and allowing students to shape their learning and teach one another.

3. Get the Right Game!

While including any game in a lecture session might be fun and improve your students' desire to attend your class, only games based on educational objectives can be considered true educational games. In fact, Karen Markey et al. (2009) suggest that students actually preferred targeted minigames that were directly related to classroom assignments and helped them to accomplish the requirements of the class.

4. Find a Friend!

Use of educational games is practiced widely across the nation. In any college or university, it is quite likely that professors in any discipline from English and German to Biology and Nursing are using some type of educational game in their classes. To get started, seek out one of these people. Ask for their help, sit in on their classes, or have lunch or coffee with them and discuss your plans. People who use games in their classes are excited about it and generally only too happy to help others get started.

5. Find a Network!

Teaching improvement groups of all types often offer sessions on active learning and educational game use and development. At Indiana University of Pennsylvania, the faculty Reflective Practice Project, which promotes effective teaching through the use of workshops, offers games in teaching sessions every year. Similar groups exist in colleges and universities across the country. You might also find local or regional groups specifically focused on game development. Maura Smale reported her involvement in the CUNY Games Network, which meets several times

per semester to discuss the practical applications of game-based learning in their courses and other instructional settings. Smale notes, "It's great to have a group of educators to bounce ideas off and brainstorm with." Nancy Riecken urges would-be gamers to: "Talk with others. See what other people are doing that works, within and outside your discipline."

6. Do Research!

Do literature reviews and search the Internet for more games that can be adapted for your instructional needs. Whether in information literacy or other more general active learning instruction books or journal articles, blogs, podcasts, and sites including descriptions of games or free digital games—all can help you to find and adapt games and many can lead you to great contacts!

7. Attend Conferences and Workshops!

In the swiftly evolving library and information technology professions, attending workshops and conferences is more important than ever before and one of the best ways to discover the newest information on improving services and teaching and networking with others. Don't just limit yourself to library and information studies workshops, but attend any on teaching and using games. Jen Jones, author of *Tinkertoy Towers*, and an experienced corporate trainer and instructor in Business and Communications at Duquesne University, suggests that instructors should sign up "for every activity workshop that comes along."

8. Ask Your Students!

Students are very much aware of the mechanics of games and what makes them fun and useful, and their input in designing activities can be quite valuable. Mary Snyder Broussard, Instructional Services Librarian at Lycoming College, improved her *Goblin Threat* game by gathering feedback from students. Laurel Black, author of *Team Challenge* and past director of Center for Teaching Excellence at Indiana University of Pennsylvania, writes that, "Students usually know way more about gaming, motivation, and structure than those of us who are not digital natives. Before simply presenting your game rules, it's really helpful to have students talk about on-line games." If games are truly to be student centered, and student learning is the ultimate goal, as Nancy Riecken suggests, when designing games consider what "students like to do, what they connect to, what their lexicon is," and "make sure that your games are understood by them."

9. Don't Panic!

If the game does not work out exactly as it did in the book, or in your plans, don't worry. Do a debriefing at the end or a one-minute paper—you will probably find that the game yielded different, but still positive results. Just as students' performance is improved through feedback, users of instructional games should use reaction to games, both positive and negative, to improve the students' instructional experience. As Sheri Gordon (2009), in "What's Your Game Plan?," notes, "Educators shouldn't be afraid to take the step. If you make a mistake, just revise and keep going."

10. Don't Settle for What Worked Last Semester!

Contributors also suggest that those using educational games should remember to continue to assess and adapt games so they maintain relevance for students. Jen Jones urges gamers to "seek out new activities or discover creative new ways for using existing ones." Evaluation of both how games are received and their educational outcomes are essential steps in a winning game plan.

The More Winners, the Better!

One of the chief motivating factors of games is challenge and the element of competition. Completion can help build community within teams, but it can also lead to stress, frustration, and disappointment for those who are not winners. Some of the contributors, most notably, Jen Jones, who has worked extensively in a corporate setting doing team-building training, urge game planners to tone down competition in team-building games. Even when completion is used, our contributors have often tried to structure the games so as many students as possible can be winners. Sheri Gordon (2010) suggests that "focusing too much attention on individual winners will leave most participants out in the cold." She suggests that the more students who can be winners, the better.

Further Reading

The 60 games included in this book will get readers started, but soon they will want more. The following is a short list of books, journal articles, and Internet sites where readers can learn more about using games in information literacy instruction and instruction in general.

Information Literacy Instruction/Activity Books and Journal Articles

Birks, Jane, and Fiona Hunt. 2003. *Hands-On Information Literacy Activities*. New York: Neal-Schuman.

This book includes over 20 ready-to-go activities, including a few games that can be used to teach a variety of subjects, from database searching to types of information. A CD-ROM with handouts is included.

Branston, C. 2006. "From Game Studies to Bibliographic Gaming: Libraries Tap into the Video Game Culture." *Bulletin of the American Society for Information Science and Technology* 32, no. 4: 24–26.

This article explores the promise of using digital games in information literacy instruction.

Broussard, M.J.S. 2010. "Secret Agents in the Library: Integrating Virtual and Physical Games in a Small Academic Library." *College and Undergraduate Libraries* 17, no. 1: 20–30.

This article by the author of two games included in this book describes a digital game that was used to replace a lecture for students in freshman composition with good results.

Burkhardt, Joanna M., and Mary C. MacDonald. 2010. *Teaching Information Literacy: 50 Standards-Based Exercises for College Students*. Chicago: American Library Association.

This useful book includes 50 varied exercises linked to ACRL Information Literacy Competency Standards.

Cook, Doug, and Ryan Sittler. 2009. *Library Instruction Cookbook*. Chicago: Association of College & Research Libraries.

This book includes 97 different activities that can be used in library instruction classes.

———. 2009. *Practical Pedagogy for Library Instructors: 17 Innovative Strategies to Improve Student Learning*. Chicago: Association of College & Research Libraries.

This book includes 17 techniques for introducing library resources to college students.

Doshi, Ameet. 2006. How Gaming Could Improve Information Literacy. *Computers in Libraries* 26, no. 5: 14–17.

This article urges librarians to consider using digital gaming as an instructional tool.

Gradowski, Gail, Loanne Snavely, and Paula Dempsey. 1998. *Designs for Active Learning: A Sourcebook of Classroom Strategies for Information Education.* Chicago: Association of College & Research Libraries.

Over 50 classroom strategies are described that have been used successfully for information literacy instruction sessions.

Grassian, Esther S., and Joan R. Kaplowitz. 2001. *Information Literacy Instruction: Theory and Practice.* New York: Neal-Schuman.

This useful text provides extensive background for information literacy instruction and learning theory that provides the foundation for developing effective instruction, including information on games and a section on active learning.

Harris, Amy, and Scott E. Rice. 2008. *Gaming in Academic Libraries: Collections, Marketing, and Information Literacy.* Chicago: Association of College & Research Libraries.

This book offers insight into how gaming is used in libraries across the country and includes chapters on how academic libraries are using games in instruction and orientation.

Jacobson, Trudi E., and Beth L. Mark. 1995. "Teaching in the Information Age: Active Learning Techniques to Empower Students." *Reference Librarian* 51/52: 105–120.

This article provides students centered activities that can be adapted for game play.

Karle, Elizabeth M. 2009. *Hosting a Library Mystery: A Programming Guide.* Chicago: ALA Editions.

This wonderful book provides background information necessary to plan a successful mystery event/game in your library.

Leach, Guy J., and Tammy S. Sugarman. 2005. "Play to Win! Using Games in Library Instruction to Enhance Student Learning." *Research Strategies* 20, no. 3: 191–203.

This excellent article includes an extensive literature review of the research on using games in college and university teaching, discusses integrating games into one-shot library instruction sessions, and the authors' development and use of a *Jeopardy!* game.

Marcus, Sandra, and Sheila Beck. 2003. "A Library Adventure: Comparing a Treasure Hunt with a Traditional Freshman Orientation Tour." *College & Research Libraries* 64, no. 1: 23–44.

This article describes the replacement of a traditional library orientation tour with a library mystery tour for freshmen community college students with positive educational results.

Markey, Karen, et al. 2009. "Will Undergraduate Students Play Games to Learn How to Conduct Library Research?" *Journal of Academic Librarianship* 35, no. 4: 303–313.

This article describes research done at the University of Michigan where a comprehensive information literacy skills building game, *Defense of Hidgeon*, was used. They found that digital games held promise for information literacy instruction but that students would prefer targeted minigames to comprehensive games.

Markey, Karen, et al. 2010. "The Benefits of Integrating an Information Literacy Skills Game into Academic Coursework: A Preliminary Evaluation." *D-Lib Magazine* 16 (July/August). http://www.dlib.org/dlib/july10/markey/07markey.html.

This article is a follow-up to Markey et al. (2009). In it, researchers tested a new game called *BiblioBouts* that included shorter, more targeted games directly related to classroom assignments that allowed collaboration with peers. The researchers found it far more successful with students, who gained confidence and competence in doing library research and found the process so entertaining that they did not realize that instruction was going on.

Smith, Felicia A. 2007. "Games for Teaching Information Literacy Skills." *Library Philosophy and Practice.* http://www.webpages.uidaho.edu/~mbolin/f-smith.htm.

This article describes how the author used crossword puzzles, word search games, and other activities into games and other active learning activities to teach information literacy concepts.

Taylor, Terry. 2007. *100% Information Literacy Success.* Clifton Park, NY: Thomson Delmar Learning.

This informative text includes hands-on activities that could easily be adapted to create games.

VanLeer, Lynn. 2006. "Interactive Gaming versus Library Tutorials for Information Literacy: A Resource Guide." *Indiana Libraries: Journal of the Indiana Library Federation & the Indiana State Library* 25, no. 4. http://hdl.handle.net/1805/1502.

This article discusses the use of online games for information literacy instruction and provides a useful list of background sources.

Whitmore, Marilyn. 1996. *Empowering Students: Hands-On Library Instruction Activities*. Active Learning Series No. 1. Pittsburgh: Library Publications Series.

This work includes lesson plans for 19 library instruction sessions, including a few games. Also see other books in this active learning series, listed at http://library-instruction-pubs.com/index.php.

Websites, Blogs, and Discussion Lists

Google searches can yield dozens of free, ready-to-use games, and both information literacy instruction and general sites like the following can offer one-step access to some of the best games out there.

Active Learning Techniques: An Online Toolbox for Librarians. McMasters University, Hamilton, Ontario, Canada. http://library.mcmaster.ca/instruction/libtoolbox.htm.

This website offers general information on instruction that promotes active learning, examples of information literacy sessions which stimulate active learning, and links to general resources.

Bibliographic Gaming: A Blog for Librarians Interested in Using Video Games to Teach. http://bibliogaming.blogspot.com/.

This blog includes posts on workshops, conferences, games, and other issues related to using games in information literacy instruction.

E-learning Online—Online Games to Teach Information Literacy. http://wiredinstructor2.blogspot.com/2007/01/50-free-online-games-teach-information.html.

This site offers links to 50 online games that can be used in information literacy instruction.

ILI-L (Information Literacy Instruction Discussion List). http://www.ala.org/ala/mgrps/divs/acrl/about/sections/is/ilil.cfm.

This list is a wonderful way to discuss game use and other instructional techniques with other interested library instructors.

MERLOT: Information Technology Portal. http://informationtechnology.merlot.org/teach.html.

This site provides access to "peer-reviewed teaching and learning materials," including games that support information literacy instruction.

PRIMO: Peer-Reviewed Instructional Materials Online Database. http://www.ala.org/apps/primo/public/search1.cfm.

The PRIMO site includes "peer-reviewed instructional materials created by librarians to teach people about discovering, accessing and evaluating information in networked environments" and some games, including one that appears in this book.

University of Arizona Librarian. 2002. *Information Literacy Outcomes with Ideas for Active Learning & Assessment*. http://www.library.arizona.edu/documents/ust/Outcomes_Activities.pdf.

This webpage offers suggestions for active learning activities related to information literacy objectives that might be adapted to create an educational game.

References

El-Shamy, Susan. 2001. *Training Games*. Sterling, VA: Stylus.

Gordon, Sheri. 2010. "What's Your Game Plan?" *THE Journal: Technological Horizons in Education—THE Journal* 37, no. 5. http://thejournal.com/articles/2010/05/01/whats-your-game-plan.aspx.

Markey, Karen, et al. 2009. "Will Undergraduate Students Play Games to Learn How to Conduct Library Research?" *Journal of Academic Librarianship* 35, no. 4: 303–313.

Information Literacy Competency Standards Addressed by Games

Standard	Related Games
1. The information literate student determines the nature and extent of the information needed.	1, 4, 6, 7, 8, 9, 11, 14, 15, 17, 18, 19, 21, 25, 26, 27, 30, 34, 35, 42
2. The information literate student accesses needed information effectively and efficiently.	1, 4, 5, 6, 7, 8, 9, 10, 11, 12, 13, 14, 15, 16, 17, 18, 19, 22, 23, 24, 25, 26, 30, 34, 35, 36, 37, 38, 43, 45, 46, 49, 54, 55, 56, 60
3. The information literate student evaluates information and its sources critically and incorporates selected information into his or her knowledge base and value system.	1, 2, 4, 6, 8, 14, 18, 19, 20, 21, 27, 28, 29, 30, 31, 32, 33, 35, 36, 40, 43, 45, 49, 50, 52, 54, 56, 57, 58, 60
4. The information literate student, individually or as a member of a group, uses information effectively to accomplish a specific purpose.	1, 3, 4, 5, 6, 19, 20, 21, 30, 35, 40, 41, 43, 51, 53, 54, 58, 59, 60
5. The information literate student understands many of the economic, legal, and social issues surrounding the use of information and accesses and uses information ethically and legally.	1, 7, 8, 18, 19, 25, 30, 36, 37, 39, 40, 41, 44, 45, 47, 48, 58, 60

Source: Standards are from the Association of College and Research Libraries. 2000. *Information Literacy Competency Standards for Higher Education*. Chicago: ACRL. http://www.ala.org/ala/mgrps/divs/acrl/standards/informationliteracycompetency.cfm.

Contributors

Cynthia Akers, Information Literacy Coordinator, University Libraries and Archives, Emporia State University, is co-contributor with Caleb Puckett of Game 28; she can be reached at cakers@emporia.edu.

Susan Ariew, Academic Services Librarian for Education, University of South Florida Tampa Library, contributed Game 48; she can be reached at sariew@usf.edu.

Susan Avery, Instructional Services Librarian, Undergraduate Library, University of Illinois at Urbana-Champaign, contributed Game 29; she can be reached at skavery@illinois.edu.

Bo Baker, Information Commons Librarian, Lupton Library, University of Tennessee at Chattanooga, is co-contributor with Caitlin Shanley and Lane Wilkinson of Game 9 and contributor of Game 35; he can be reached at bo-baker@utc.edu.

Laurel Johnson Black, PhD, Associate Professor of English, Indiana University of Pennsylvania, is contributor of Game 54; she can be reached at Laurel.Black@iup.edu.

Helen Bond, PhD, Assistant Professor of Education, Curriculum and Instruction, School of Education, Howard University, is contributor of Game 50; she can be reached at hbond@howard.edu.

Kawanna M. Bright, Head of First Year Services, University of Texas at San Antonio, is co-contributor with Hyun-Duck Chung of Game 5; she can be reached at kawanna.bright@utsa.edu.

Mary J. Snyder Broussard, Instructional Services Librarian, Snowden Library, Lycoming College, is contributor of Games 7 and 44; she can be reached at broussm@lycoming.edu.

Julie A.S. Cassidy, PhD, Assistant Professor, English, Borough of Manhattan Community College, is contributor of Game 34; she can be reached at julie.sinn@gmail.com or jcassidy@bmcc.cuny.edu.

Randy Christensen, Associate Professor of Library Media, Sherratt Library, Southern Utah University, is co-contributor with Richard Eissinger of Game 18; he can be reached at christensen@suu.edu.

Hyun-Duck Chung, Librarian for Management and Entrepreneurship, Research and Information Services, North Carolina State University Libraries, North Carolina State University, is co-contributor with Kawanna M. Bright of Game 5; she can be reached at hyun_duck_chung@ncsu.edu.

Christine Cusick, PhD, Associate Professor of English and Composition, Seton Hill University, is contributor of Game 30; she can be reached at cusick@setonhill.edu.

Carrie Donovan, Head of Teaching and Learning, Indiana University Bloomington Libraries, is co-contributor with Rachel Slough of Game 53; she can be reached at cdonovan@indiana.edu.

Susan Drummond, Instruction Librarian, Stapleton Library, Indiana University of Pennsylvania, is contributor of Game 32; she can be reached at Drummond@iup.edu.

Richard Eissinger, Associate Professor of Library Media/Instructional Services Librarian, Sherratt Library, Southern Utah University, is co-contributor with Randy Christensen of Game 18; he can be reached at eissinger@suu.edu.

Lyda F. Ellis, Instruction Librarian and Assistant Professor, James A. Michener Library, University of Northern Colorado, is co-contributor with Andrea Falcone of Game 16; she can be reached at lyda.ellis@unco.edu.

Andrea Falcone, Instruction Librarian and Assistant Professor, James A. Michener Library, University of Northern Colorado, is co-contributor with Lyda F. Ellis of Game 16; she can be reached at andrea.falcone@unco.edu.

Laurie A. Grosik, PhD Candidate, Communications Media, Indiana University of Pennsylvania, is co-contributor with Ryan L. Sittler, Chad Sherman, David P. Keppel, Christine E. Schaeffer, and Dana C. Hackley of Game 45; she can be reached at l.a.grosik@iup.edu.

Dana C. Hackley, PhD Candidate, Communications Media,, Indiana University of Pennsylvania, is co-contributor with Ryan L. Sittler, Chad Sherman, David P. Keppel, Christine E. Schaeffer, and Laurie A. Grosik of Game 45; she can be reached at d.c.hackley@iup.edu.

Kathleen A. Hanna, Associate Librarian, Liaison to the School of Physical Education and Tourism Management, Indiana University Purdue University Indianapolis (IUPUI), is co-contributor with Rhonda Huisman of Game 52; she can be reached at kgreatba@iupui.edu.

Holly Heller-Ross, Associate Dean of Library and Information Services, Feinberg Library, SUNY Plattsburgh, is co-contributor with Elin O'Hara-Gonya of Game 42; she can be reached at hellerhb@plattsburgh.edu.

Amy Harris Houk, Information Literacy Program Coordinator and Reference Librarian, University Libraries at the University of North Carolina at Greensboro, is contributor of Game 8; she can be reached at a_harri2@uncg.edu.

Rhonda Huisman, Assistant Librarian, Liaison to the School of Education/Center for Teaching and Learning, Indiana University Purdue University Indianapolis (IUPUI), is co-contributor with Kathleen A. Hanna of Game 52; she can be reached at rhuisman@iupui.edu.

Tracey Johnson, Librarian, Shawnee Community College Library, Shawnee Community College, is contributor of Games 12 and 33; she can be reached at Traceyj@shawneecc.edu.

Jen Jones, Instructor of Communication, Department of Rhetoric and Communication Studies, Duquesne University, is contributor of Game 3; she can be reached at jonesj260@duq.edu.

Kimberly A. Jones, Reference/Instruction Librarian, Medaille College Library, is co-contributor with Melissa Langridge and Jeff Miller of Game 49; she can be reached at kaj52@medaille.edu.

Jenna Kammer, Instructor of Library Science, Library Instruction Program, New Mexico State University—Dona Ana Community College, is contributor of Game 36; she can be reached at jkammer@nmsu.edu.

David P. Keppel, PhD Candidate, Communications Media, Indiana University of Pennsylvania, is co-contributor with Ryan L. Sittler, Chad Sherman, Christine E. Schaeffer, Dana C. Hackley, and Laurie A. Grosik of Game 45; he can be reached at d.p.keppel@iup.edu.

Blaine Knupp, Reference Coordinator, Stapleton Library, Indiana University of Pennsylvania, is contributor of Games 11 and 23; he can be reached at beknupp@iup.edu.

Laura Krulikowski, Music Library Assistant, Orendorff Music Library, Indiana University of Pennsylvania, is contributor of Game 17; she can be reached at L.E.Krulikowski@iup.edu.

Melissa Langridge, User Education Coordinator, Niagara University Library, is co-contributor with Kimberly A. Jones and Jeff Miller of Game 49; she can be reached at mlangridge@niagara.edu.

Tracy Lassiter, PhD Candidate and Teaching Associate, English Literature and Criticism, Indiana University of Pennsylvania, is contributor of Game 21; she can be reached at t.j.lassiter@iup.edu.

David Magolis, PhD, Assistant Professor, Andruss Library, Bloomsburg University of Pennsylvania, is co-contributor with Linda Neyer of Game 1; he can be reached at dmagolis@bloomu.edu.

Debra Holmes Matthews, PhD, Associate Professor of English and Chair of Humanities, Macon State College, is contributor of Game 41; she can be reached at debra.matthews@maconstate.edu.

Jeff Miller, Social Studies Instructor, Sweet Home Middle School, is co-contributor with Kimberly A. Jones and Melissa Langridge of Game 49; he can be reached at jmiller@shs.k12.ny.us.

Emily Missner, Information Services Librarian for Business and Economics, Drexel University Libraries, is contributor of Game 13; she can be reached at edm25@drexel.edu.

Susan Nelson, Assistant Professor, Reference and Instructional Services Librarian and Coordinator of Access Services, Snowden Library, Lycoming College, is contributor of Game 4; she can be reached at nelson@lycoming.edu.

Linda Neyer, Health Sciences/Science Librarian, Andruss Library, Bloomsburg University of Pennsylvania, is co-contributor with David Magolis of Game 1; she can be reached at lneyer@bloomu.edu.

Elin O'Hara-Gonya, Senior Assistant Librarian, Feinberg Library, SUNY Plattsburgh, is co-contributor with Holly Heller-Ross of Game 42; she can be reached at oharaea@plattsburgh.edu.

Linda L. Plevak, Reference and Instructor Librarian, Northeast Lakeview College Library, is contributor of Games 25 and 26; she can be reached at lplevak@alamo.edu.

Toccara Porter, Diversity Resident Librarian, William F. Ekstrom Library, University of Louisville Libraries, is contributor of Game 2; she can be reached at tporter23@yahoo.com.

Caleb Puckett, Reference and Instruction Librarian, University Libraries and Archives, Emporia State University, is co-contributor with Cynthia Akers of Game 28; he can be reached at cpucket1@emporia.edu.

Kimberly Ramírez, PhD, Assistant Professor of English, LaGuardia Community College, City University of New York, is contributor of Game 20; she can be reached at kramirez@lagcc.cuny.edu.

Nancy Riecken, PhD, Program Chair, English and Communications, Assistant Professor of English, Ivy Tech Community College, is contributor of Games 55, 56, 57, 58, 59, and 60; she can be reached at nriecken@ivytech.edu.

Christine E. Schaeffer, PhD Candidate, Communications Media, Indiana University of Pennsylvania, is co-contributor with Ryan L. Sittler, Chad Sherman, David P. Keppel, Dana C. Hackley, and Laurie A. Grosik of Game 45; she can be reached at c.e.schaeffer@iup.edu.

Caitlin Shanley, Instructional Design and Technology Librarian, Lupton Library, University of Tennessee at Chattanooga, is co-contributor with Bo Baker and Lane Wilkinson of Game 9; she can be reached at caitlin-shanley@utc.edu.

Christina Sheldon, Instruction and Reference Librarian, University Library, California State University, Los Angeles, is contributor of Games 10, 22, and 24; she can be reached at csheldo@calstatela.edu.

Chad Sherman, PhD Candidate, Communications Media, Indiana University of Pennsylvania, is co-contributor with Ryan L. Sittler, David P. Keppel, Christine E. Schaeffer, Dana C. Hackley, and Laurie A. Grosik of Game 45; he can be reached at c.d.sherman@iup.edu.

Ryan L. Sittler, Instructional Technology/Information Literacy Librarian, California University of Pennsylvania, is contributor of Game 38 and co-contributor with Chad Sherman, David P. Keppel, Christine E. Schaeffer, Dana C. Hackley, and Laurie A. Grosik of Game 45; he can be reached at sittler@calu.edu.

Rachel Slough, E-Learning Librarian, University of Wisconsin-La Crosse, is co-contributor with Carrie Donovan of Game 53; she can be reached at slough.rach@uwlax.edu.

Maura A. Smale, Assistant Professor, Information Literacy Librarian, Ursula C. Schwerin Library, New York City College of Technology, CUNY, is contributor of Game 31; she can be reached at msmale@citytech.cuny.edu.

Rosalee Stilwell, PhD, Associate Professor, English Department, Indiana University of Pennsylvania, is co-contributor with Theresa McDevitt of Game 6 and contributor of Game 14; she can be reached at stilwell@iup.edu.

Andrew P. Thompson, Graduate Student, Department of History, University of Cincinnati, is contributor of Game 40; he can be reached at Apthompson819@gmail.com.

Charlene Thompson, Reference/Instruction Librarian, Benjamin P. Browne Library, Judson University, is contributor of Game 27; she can be reached at cthompson@judsonu.edu.

Gretchen Trkay, Instruction and Information Literacy Librarian, University of Texas at Arlington Library, is contributor of Game 39; she can be reached at gtrkay@uta.edu.

Judith Villa, PhD, Associate Professor, English Department, Indiana University of Pennsylvania, is contributor of Game 19; she can be reached at jvilla@iup.edu.

Theresa Westbrock, Instruction Coordinator, New Mexico State University Library, is contributor of Game 47; she can be reached at twestbro@lib.nmsu.edu.

Lane Wilkinson, Reference and Instruction Librarian, Lupton Library, University of Tennessee at Chattanooga, is co-contributor with Bo Baker and Caitlin Shanley of Game 9; he can be reached at lane-wilkinson@utc.edu.

H. David "Giz" Womack, Librarian, Instruction and Outreach, Z. Smith Reynolds Library, Wake Forest University, Winston-Salem, NC, is contributor of Game 43; he can be reached at womack@wfu.edu.

Jennifer M. Woolston, PhD Candidate and Teaching Associate, English Literature, Indiana University of Pennsylvania, is contributor of Games 15, 37, and 46; she can be reached at cpfm@iup.edu and j.m.woolston@iup.edu.

Index

About the Editor

Theresa R. McDevitt, PhD, Government Documents/Reference Librarian at Stapleton Library, Indiana University of Pennsylvania, has worked in academic libraries since 1979 in a variety of roles. She has been a Public Services librarian, a Government Documents specialist, a Special Collections and Archives librarian, and acting associate dean and interim dean of libraries. With a PhD in American history from Kent State University, as well as master's degrees in library science, education of the deaf, and history, she has taught hundreds of individual bibliographic instruction sessions and many one- to three-credit semester-long information literacy courses in addition to courses in history. She is editor of two other books, *Women and the American Civil War: An Annotated Bibliography* (Greenwood Publishing Group, 2003) and *Government Publications Unmasked: Teaching Government Resources in the 21st Century* (Library Instruction Publications, 2003), and dozens of journal articles and book reviews. She can be reached at mcdevitt@iup.edu.